Created and designed by the editorial staff of Ortho Books

Edited by
Lance Walheim

Designed by
Craig Bergquist

Front cover photography by
Wolf von dem Bussche

Photography by
William Aplin
Clyde Childress
Michael Landis

Illustrations by
Ron Hildebrand

The world of TREES

Contents

Points of view

People have their own ways of looking at trees. For some they are the key that unlocks childhood memories. To a child they represent adventure. To the landscape architect, trees are a tool, and the future-wise city planner sees trees as a cure for over-urbanization. From any point of view, all agree that trees are things of beauty and importance — worth planting and worth preserving.

This book is the product of answers to questions from hundreds of people. They came from every level of expertise — from people who didn't know an oak from a maple, but loved trees, to people who had devoted their lives to the study of arboriculture, and loved trees. What this book contains — more than anything else — is a deep commitment to trees. There's a lot of hard information here, too — how to choose a tree that suits your needs, how to plant it, how to grow it, how to maintain it. As for our debt to all the people who asked the questions, provided the answers, verified the answers, and then checked them again — ladies and gentlemen, our humble thanks.

A backward glance

Of the questions that were asked about trees and those we asked ourselves, one intense concern was voiced again and again: the concern that changing land use had cost us a heritage of trees. Many people volunteered memories — of climbing trees (and falling out), of treehouse trees, of spring blossoms, summer fruit, autumn nuts, winter ice sculptures. But it's better when they speak for themselves.

A man with a wealth of rich memories remembered a childhood spent "living with the squirrels in the pecan tree," and "the giant maples, standing tall, shutting out the sky along the Cowlitz River, the hemlock that dipped its branches in the swirling eddy of the

◁

A familiar autumn chore that's often more fun than work is the stuff that memories are made of.

Snohomish." A Georgia man wrote, "Even now, I get excited every spring with the soft greens of the new foliage of the deciduous trees, and again each fall, when brilliant foliage colors the whole southeastern forest."

Another Southerner recalled, "a cluster of oaks, two of which had been bent to the ground at an early age and could be climbed and ridden like an elephant or horse. There was a treehouse built in three loblolly pines; the first floor of the house was ten or twelve feet above the ground."

An Easterner wrote, "I spent much of my childhood in trees, sometimes falling out of them. I vividly remember the sting of iodine being tenderly

dabbed on my wounds (iodine can't be dabbed tenderly!)."

A Pennsylvanian told us, "I grew up in a steel mill town in western Pennsylvania. In spite of the filth of the town and the ugly, treeless downtown, many streets were lined with great sycamores. They made the crowded neighborhoods bearable and cooled the streets, front yards, and porches. They were dirty trees, shedding leaves, bark, and fuzzy 'monkey balls' in the fall, but they added so much to the quality of that dingy town."

A California woman offered a solution to the development that altered her home town. She wrote, "On our

Public parks can be the source of a special kind of civic pride. This park is a good example, offering refuge from the city.

We talked with people who remembered a childhood spent with "the giant maples, standing tall, shutting out the sky along the Cowlitz River and the hemlock that dipped its branches in the swirling eddy of the Snohomish, in the state of Washington."

Turning the world upside down: the undisturbed reflection of summer trees seen across a lake.

Winter's on its way; the sweet gums turn red and the river turns an icy blue.

90' x 100' lot we have created our own refuge. We welcome birds and squirrels; the skunks and raccoons investigate by night. Our goal has been to be able to look out any window and never see another structure. We have almost achieved that objective. It is a good feeling, the feeling of wilderness, even though we know that the neighbors we love are almost within touch."

A natural corollary to childhood memories of trees is the sorrow people expressed that the big old trees, the kind that leave landmarks in memories, have been cut down to make room for new developments — highways, shopping centers, housing tracts.

A Northeasterner remembered, "There were still some woods in the suburbs when I grew up but bulldozers have cleared those woods for new houses. Few substantial trees have been replanted. It's a curious trait of some people — they'll clear a forest and plant dinky, trinketlike shrubs rather than shade trees. It's like collecting knickknacks instead of designing a room for comfort."

It has not only been the needs of an expanding population that have taken cherished trees; diseases and natural disasters take a toll, too. A Massachusetts woman told us, "I grew up in New England in an old Victorian home that had two circular driveways — one to the front and one to the back. Each circle had one majestic elm in its center. The Dutch elm disease slowly took both trees. We sprayed and pruned, but were unable to save either one. To me those trees were part of the character of the house and the grounds. It has been twelve years

since the elms came down, but I will never forget them." A transplanted Britisher recalled his school days in England during World War I. "The patriotic thing to do was to permit the felling of ornamental trees for use as pit props in the coal mine shafts. The loss of privacy resulted in the use of chestnut palings imported to England from America — hundreds of miles of pickets woven into wire strands, the wood derived from the trees killed by the Chestnut Blight." A Texan wrote, "There were two old hackberry trees in front of the old farmhouse where I grew up and my parents still live.

"Many hours were spent under the shade of those trees on hot summer days, playing such games as boys play. A tornado destroyed the trees in 1969 and the house looks so bare."

Big, old trees can be preserved for children and grandchildren, giving us a sense of social and personal continuity.

The first snow in October changes the landscape: the tall trees seem to protect the house in the woods.

The first cold snap of fall transforms giant maples from a quiet canopy of summer green into a tunnel of color.

Many people spoke of the link with the past that they sensed from trees, a sense of regional history. For many, the character of a place was determined by its trees. A Midwesterner reported, ''Nebraska, except for the extreme eastern portion and along the stream courses, was a dry and wind-swept prairie. To the pioneers in Nebraska the planting of trees provided a sense of immediate security. They were a link with the immigrants' home in the eastern woodlands of Europe, they broke the force of the ceaseless wind, provided fuel for heating and cooking, shade from the hot summer sun, and visual relief from miles and miles of unenclosed space. The trees that survive here are symbols of the pioneer spirit that settled the state.''

From Southern California a woman wrote, ''The California oaks around our mountain cabin were multifunctional. They provided beauty, an 'outdoor living room' shaded from the unrelenting sun, the fun of a car-tire swing that hung from a high limb, and an appreciation that we were not the first to use this place. The rock formations under the oaks contained grinding basins where the Indians prepared their acorn meal many years before.''

An Easterner told of the town his grandparents had helped settle. ''They planted seedlings from the surrounding woods. Sugar maples, red maples, Norway maples, and some oaks canopied the streets, forming cool, dark tunnels in summer. In the fall the chill of the frosty nights set the whole town ablaze with the celebration of color. The sidewalks became a great place to shuffle knee-deep through the leaves which hid such pitfalls as

chuck holes, ditches, and an occasional camouflaged skunk!''

Trees are our roots, both personal and social; trees give us our sense of place. The desire to preserve the heritage of big, old trees for children and grandchildren was voiced again and again. A California man said, ''My own kids don't have the same experiences I had. There are only a few climbable trees in the neighborhood — too many pines and eucalyptus which aren't good cilmbers. One great Valley oak used to support a long rope swing. The kids (including a few of us older ones) would play for hours swinging way out over the hillside. Now someone has bought the land and will soon build houses. People are willing to build playgrounds but don't seem to understand either the nature of Nature or the nature of play.''

Spring and fall can be equally flamboyant in the world of trees. These flowering plums have become a hallmark to locals in the Napa Valley of California. Their flowering is a sure sign that spring has arrived.

A Mississippi man reported, "My daughter and I were inspecting the trees we have planted in our yard and she said, 'I sure will be glad when they get big enough to climb.' That made me feel very sad, for she is eleven years old and the trees are only two years old. She will never climb among the branches of a fifty-year-old mulberry in her backyard as I did — despite the fact that I knew my mother would tan my hide for getting mulberry stains on my clothes. Perhaps my grandchildren will be able to enjoy the pleasures of a tree swing or a good climb or a picnic in the shade of a big oak in Grandpa's backyard."

A man from South Carolina phrased the solution succinctly when he said, "The optimum balance between cutting and conservation must be reached if my kids are to have a rich life."

Another can declared, "The only way we are going to succeed in preserving, conserving, and improving the trees we have is through teaching people about trees — or better yet, allowing them to learn."

The need to review our priorities is clear in many areas of environment and human habitat.

One Southern California woman reported, "My awareness of trees came very early and as an instantaneous revelation. One day while enjoying the beauty of Balboa Park, my parents pointed out to me the amazing fact that every tree, shrub, and flower in the park had been planted by man. I will never forget the impact of that first enlightenment: that it is possible for ordinary people to create enduring legacies of beauty through the planting of trees."

Another Southern California woman wrote, "Our boulevards were lined with huge, old eucalyptus trees. They were very tall, never still, swaying gracefully in the gentle sea breeze. One by one they gave way to commercial development. Now there are none left. That section of our city is strangely bare, and we miss the pungent, medicinal fragrance of the eucalyptus on damp, foggy mornings. Yes, we miss those trees like old friends.

"On the positive side — we have the new Wilderness Park in Redondo Beach. It was developed from a former Nike missile site and the entire park was designed to have the look of and to be a complete wilderness experience. The park is a little over eleven acres, located on one of the highest points of the city. Hundreds of trees were designed into the landscaping to identify the three separate camps. The 'pine camp' includes Arizona pine, Japanese black pine, Canary Island pine, and Aleppo pines. The 'gumwood camp' has several varieties of eucalyptus, and the 'sycamore camp' has many varieties of that beautiful tree. Natural wood and slumpstone bricks have been used in construction to keep the rustic look. There are two ponds with recirculating water to create natural-looking streams. The animals have already found this area and add to the wilderness effect."

This seems to be the result of removing the big, old landmark trees from the commercial and residential areas of our daily lives. We are compelled to create zoos where we can visit the trees that are no longer part of our environment.

Trees can create mystery: what awaits at the other end of this small bridge?

Towering palms lend architectural strength to this public walkway.

The crossroads of the seasons, autumn is a time for thoughts of a passing summer and a time to plan for the coming winter. An emotional season sparked with color and glory.

A Colorado woman had a very different experience with trees. She wrote of a scarred old pine called Old Monarch that dominated the landscape outside her grandparents' cabin in the mountains high above Denver. As a child she played in the aspen grove at its base and observed the eagles nesting in its top. She watched one day as a violent midsummer thunderstorm struck the tree with lightning, causing it to burst into flames which were quenched moments later by a cloudburst. She writes, "After the storm we went to inspect the tree. The eagles' nest had been destroyed, but the eagles were very much alive. Old Monarch just had one more deep black scar to show for the latest onslaught. Grandma turned to me and said, 'See, honey, when your roots are firm and you grow to your full height, nothing can destroy you.' I was too young to understand the full meaning of those words but old enough to remember them."

Landscape architects

The landscape architect has been concerned with the same problems as these good people. Long ago, Garrett Eckbo in his book *Landscape for Living* wrote, "Trees, rather than buildings, are the best measure of a civilized landscape. A community in which many mature trees survive and more are planted regularly demonstrates a sense of time, history, and continuity on the land. It takes ten years or longer to produce a reasonably mature tree in most parts of the country. Few urban land users anticipate tenure longer than five years.

This is not progress, growth, development, or vitality. It is insanity — a squirrel cage in which most of us chase madly round and round only to find the same old ugly city in the end.

"Trees as a primary landscape resource can do many things: establish a three-dimensional structural continuity throughout the community; establish pleasant connections and transitions between buildings, open spaces, streets, and fields; produce maximum greenery and climate control for minimum effort; provide the diffusion and filtering of light and heat which warm climates need; develop the sense of shelter and security."

Recently, Edward Holubowich wrote in the American Public Works Association Reporter, "A landscape designer is only one component of a complex team which affects ultimate density of trees and other physical environmental resources. City planner, architect, engineer, administrator, and politician must accept responsibility in evolution and preservation of urban environments, for their decisions often profoundly affect the visual and physical quality of places where we live, work, and have fun.

"Once Man procures survival essentials, he starts to create pleasant surroundings that permit him to exploit his fullest potential. He beautifies himself and his immediate environment, then turns to the broader world around him. Nearly every North American urban area has examples of this phenomenon — stately homes with charming architectural detail, streets and boulevards lined with mature trees, neatly groomed parks and open spaces. We almost

To provide a sense of security, homesteaders often surrounded their newly built homes with trees similar to the ones from the Old Country.

Junk

Trees can screen our junkyards, improving the view by hiding what is unattractive.

Industry

Trees absorb noise, filter the air, and limit the visual impact.

Skyline trees

Tall-growing trees create a skyscape and give a neighborhood character. They also put color in the sky in the fall.

always 'show off' these areas to visitors.

"With the industrial revolution's advent, our society's attitudes toward environment in general have changed. Desires for physical comfort, safety, and convenience have changed not only our economic emphasis, but have taken their toll on urban environment: paved and widened streets and highways and sidewalks claimed space; utility lines cluttered the landscape; the internal combustion engine in its myriad forms took

away clean air. Yet all this symbolized progress.

"In haste to solve economic problems we've become willing to destroy some natural environment. One of the most abused landscape elements has been our trees.

"An eminent city planner, Frederick Gutheim says: 'Planting large shade trees must become a paramount objective of all who would improve cities' appearance. And it is the main hope for any redemption of the lost character of American cities.' "

Character? Ian Nairn calls it identity. His words: "Townscape depends on two things: relationship and identity. It means making parts of the environment fit together — the supermarket, the gas stations, the car lots; identity is the recognition and enhancement of the specific needs and qualities that make one place different from another. And here, right at the start, a big warning: that no identity at all is better than a false one. The needs and qualities must be real, not artificially tickled up.

Neighborhoods

Trees give neighborhoods their own character, enhancing good architecture and hiding bad. They also modify the climate, and create a pleasanter place to live.

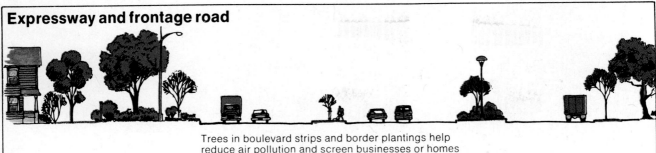

Expressway and frontage road

Trees in boulevard strips and border plantings help reduce air pollution and screen businesses or homes from noise of street traffic.

"In each distinct part of town you ought to be able to feel 'I am in it, I am near the edge of it, I am just outside it.' So that the town is a collection of distinct areas, not an amorphous gray mass."

Trees save energy, money

With the proper selection of deciduous trees planted at the west and south sides of the house you can reduce the cooling bill in summer and the heating bill in winter. Electricity usage studies have shown that shaded houses use 2 KWH per square foot and unshaded use 3.3 KWH per square foot. From California's hot interior valley, we are told that a wall shaded by trees is 15 degrees cooler.

The saving percentage may vary from 20% to 10% but in every climate the energy-saving value of the tree is being recognized.

Effectively shaded houses have less need for expensive air conditioners. Even when air conditioners have already been installed, they will perform more efficiently and be less costly if the house is shaded.

William Flemer III, of Princeton Nurseries in New Jersey, points out that in the Plains States, winter heating bills have been significantly reduced by using trees as shelter plantings or windbreaks. These states typically have high winter winds. In South Dakota, for example, the fuel consumption of identical experimental houses was 25% less in a house on the protected side of a tall windbreak than in the exposed house.

He adds that in the more sheltered Eastern states, where the fierce winter winds are not typical, savings are less dramatic but equally apparent. Fuel consumption of the same house was compared from the time of no windbreak to the time one reached the height of the house. A savings of 10% per winter was recorded. Since the Eastern states are highly populated, this savings becomes more significant.

Outdoor shade

Consider the value of trees also in terms of human comfort. Have you ever stopped to rest under a shade tree on a hot, still day and noticed a gentle and refreshing breeze? Shade trees are the original evaporative coolers. A column of warmer air goes up through the tree, causing a slight breeze at ground level by "feeding" this thermal column of ascending warm air.

Private collection

Tree collectors collect trees for the same reasons that other people collect other things — because they love them. Some tree collectors begin quite innocently. They decide, for example, that they want to grow that exquisite blue-flowering tree they saw in Mexico last year and they don't propose to let the fact that they live in upstate New York get in their way. The fact that both seeds and seedlings are nearly impossible to find only makes them more determined. They study the native habitat and reproduce it as closely as possible. They read books and ask questions — often unanswerable, because nobody's done it before. And that is the great contribution tree collectors make — they are constantly testing range, tolerance, and adaptability of exotic trees.

Tree collecting is the natural by-product of travel, from Captain Cook's botanical expeditions which brought specimens back to Kew Gardens, to the returning vacationer with seeds in his pocket. Collections begin when you see something you've never seen before and must have, or when you have something you can't give up; so you take it with you.

Business districts

Business districts can be beautiful with trees. The lines of buildings are softened. Trees give a street a sense of harmony. Shade helps cool sidewalks and pull together diverse elements.

One man's efforts: This long row of coral trees (Erythrina caffra) *in Southern California was originally started from three cuttings taken by landscape architect, Bill Evans.*

Unusual flowers, curious fruit, an odd leaf structure, or bark texture, or branching pattern, or trunk shape can all be the basis of a collection. A tree may be defined as rare because it is being grown well out of its natural range or because there are actually extremely few in the world. Trees, like animals, are constantly evolving, with some species becoming extinct or nearing extinction. The role of the collector who obtains and grows such trees is that of the curator of a living museum. Collectors frequently make use of local arboretums and botanic gardens to get ideas or information or to share their own growing experiences. Arboretums have large collections of many kinds of trees, both the common and the rare. Some will sell or give away seeds or cuttings of their trees; all will answer questions. Universities and colleges often have botanical gardens with unusual specimens. They, too, may be able to help you find seeds — if they don't have them, they may know a place or organization that does.

Trees for your neighborhood

The best advice we've heard on trees for a neighborhood is this: think of yourself as a part-owner of the trees in your community. You are!

The challenge in tree planting is in these questions each town and city should ask itself: What distinguishes this town? What trees have given it its character? What trees are best in its soils, climate? What trees remind you of its history — its backgrounds? What trees to make parking lots more attractive? What trees to screen out junkyards and other ugly spots? What trees for greenways through new subdivisions? Where can we find open space for the great landmark trees? — trees too big for small lots and narrow streets? — trees that reach far above the rooftops, high into the sky? What trees for the new expressways? — freeways?

The towns and cities that have made the greatest progress in beautification (and increase in land values) are the ones that have made a three-way tree drive:

1. Planted trees to fit conditions as they found them. Downtown: No natural place for trees, no building setbacks or very narrow planting strips. In established residential areas: narrow planting strips, narrow streets, overhead and underground utilities.

2. Taken steps to provide tree planting space in every type of land use: screen planting between residential and industrial areas; landscaping in industrial parks; encouraging building setbacks for street planting; in greenway easements in subdivisions; in wide planting strips between sidewalk and residential property rather than curb and sidewalk; center parkway planting on wide avenues.

3. Done all they could to preserve existing trees: wih good maintenance; saving valuable old trees by making them historical landmarks; planning developments and streets to by-pass trees.

New trees for old cities

When selecting trees for adverse city situations your choice is, of course, far more limited than when trees are planted in open spaces. With the increased demand for trees for special situations, an increasing number of growers have been selecting trees for special form and growth characteristics — such as narrow top, globe-shaped head, compact growth that fits beneath utility wires, better fall color, no messy fruit or pods. These selected trees are then propagated vegetatively (by grafting, budding, or stem cuttings rather than by seed). Such trees are called "cultivars," short for cultivated variety, and are set off by single quotes elsewhere in this book. The trees produced in this fashion have the same form and growth habits as the mother plant.

If the selected form is distinctly different, a patent is usually applied for or the grower's name for the tree will be trademarked. There has been some criticism of this special naming on the grounds that in some cases the differences between the standard variety and the named variety were too slight to single out the tree.

Nevertheless, through the naming of special trees we now have guidelines to predictable performance — ginkgoes that don't produce fruit; ashes that are seedless. Norway maples and honey locust, for instance, now come in a variety of shapes and sizes undreamed of by the people who first planted our cities. Note the number of nursery-named varieties in the following lists.

The choice of trees has exploded with the introduction of new varieties. Today, with the many selected forms, what was once one tree (ash, oak, whatever) may now be eight. This proliferation makes generalizations about the size and form of a tree meaningless. You must now ask, how big is which selected variety? Attitudes toward certain trees change, too. Bad qualities can be weeded out. For example, the old honey locusts were often blacklisted because of their sharp thorns — most of the new introductions are thornless.

However, the new varieties have risks that the old seed-grown trees did not have. Seedlings of the same species vary greatly in many ways, including their resistance to pests and diseases. A few trees in a batch of seedlings might escape cleanly from a problem that plagues all the others. Not so with selected trees grown from cuttings or grafts of one parent. They share the same weaknesses as well as strengths. A weakness to a certain disease could destroy all the trees of that variety in a community. Good advice continues to be: Don't limit tree planting to one kind. (Don't put all your eggs in one basket.) Plant a mixed variety of trees suitable to the area.

Check list for street-tree planters

Choosing a community's trees is no simple task. Here is what to consider when making selections:

How much space is there between sidewalk and curb? How good is the soil — depth, drainage, fertility, moisture, aeration? Can it be improved?

What about overhead lines or underground utilities or sewers?

Will trees interfere with street lighting or parking?

What kind of street is it — residential, expressway, business? Is the street likely to stay the same size or be widened?

Is the tree the right shape and size for the site?

Can it tolerate adverse conditions at the site?

Is it hardy enough for the area?

Does it make a lot of work for maintenance men?

Will it get the water, pruning, feeding, and cleanup it may need?

Does the tree do something special for the street — flowers, fruit, shade, shape?

The off-street planting concept

Off-street planting solves many a street problem. Richard Harris, Professor of Landscape Horticulture, Univ. of Calif. at Davis, says it this way: "Public utilities, city street departments, and home owners have been faced with a street design that includes a planting strip between the curb and sidewalk which at best is usually much too narrow. This has resulted in more frequent pruning for size control; in many cases unsightly trees and street scenes due to severe pruning; and damaged curbs, gutters, and sidewalks which are hazardous and costly to repair.

"Trees planted behind the sidewalk, particularly if there are no overhead wires along the street, will require little or no pruning for size control of either the top or the roots. With the off-street planting of trees, roots will be less restricted and further removed from the possibility of damage from salt used for ice control on the streets.

"Off-street plantings that are to provide variey of tree species and planting arrangements must be carefully planned and developed to provide a pleasing street landscape

Where trees come from: Row after row of trees at a commercial tree nursery in Oregon are ready to be dug and shipped to retail nurseries.

that is reasonable to maintain. The fairly recent planned-unit developments that are now provided for by most cities through their subdivision ordinances allow for the greatest flexibility of sidewalk, house and tree placement."

Keep looking

Another built-in shortcoming of many lists of approved trees is that the selections are made by a consensus of several tree experts covering wide areas. Excellent trees infrequently planted in some areas may be excluded. Often valuable, locally adapted trees fail to make the general lists.

No approved list for any city should be frozen. New introductions, new selections of old trees must be considered. The more trials, the more surprises in climate adaptation.

Tree shortage

The supply of trees follows demand, but with caution. The trees grown in greatest quantity will always be the trees planted in the greatest quantity in the previous ten years. "New" trees, whether they are rediscovered old trees, or new forms of old trees, or trees new to an area, or new introductions, are invariably in short supply for a few years after their introduction. Communities that select special trees to be planted in quantity may not be able to find them.

The New Jersey Federation of Shade Tree Commissions (College of Agriculture, Rutgers University) has available a plan for buying trees not currently available. The city places funds in escrow to cover a contract with a tree grower to grow and deliver special trees in two to five years.

The search for trees to solve a problem

Selection of trees for your city may now be in the hands of some municipal authority. You may have a tree ordinance. Regardless of how your tree problems are being handled, the more attention and support the program receives from the citizens, the more effective will be the program. One way to bring greater participation into a tree program is to establish a "Tree Commission" through a tree ordinance. A copy of such an ordinance can be obtained by writing to the New Jersey Federation of Shade Tree Commissions, Rutgers University College of Agriculture, New Brunswick, New Jersey.

A greater appreciation of trees can be established with the help of the city government.

Which trees?

Which tree will you plant? Which tree deserves special care? Which trees for the neighborhood? Which trees are best suited to your climate?

This book is intended as a problem-solving guide for the many who are concerned about "which tree."

The homeowner. The homeowner has many reasons to be concerned about which trees to plant for aesthetic value and for use. One use that is often overlooked is the important function of trees in the conservation of energy. By the use of trees, you can reduce the use of energy for summer cooling and winter heating. Trees provide insulation that keeps down summer heat, and they also reduce wind velocity.

The concerned citizen. We have provided many suggestions and cautions for those concerned citizens who want to initiate a tree-planting drive for the betterment of their neighborhood. To start such a drive is not enough; it must be done with responsibility. We have offered advice and guidance in this book, but we suggest you also consult with the arborist in your area and anyone else with a knowledge of trees.

The newspaper editor. He is in a position to make his readers aware of the good planting which has been done and also what still remains to be done. He has the tools to produce this awareness, by letting people know what trees are planted in their city or town, on the streets, on the freeways, and in the parks. If people know the names of the trees that are there and can recognize them, they will appreciate and enjoy them more fully.

◊

Picture perfect: Summer Sundays spent sketching in a grove of willows.

Members of the park and recreation departments. Whoever is responsible for the planting in the parks and other recreation areas has a special role to play. Parks should be looked on as a test area to experiment and to grow special trees that have no place in the home garden, either because they will be too tall, because they need a lot of room to develop, or because they are too slow-growing for the homeowner who plants them to enjoy in his lifetime. In other words, the trees of the future. These trees should be tested in the parks, and planted so present and future generations can enjoy them.

Viewpoint

This book is divided into three editions. It is regionalized for the North, the South, and the West. In it we have brought together 36 contributing authors and consultants. The viewpoint of each has been care-fully noted. We have been careful not to make blanket recommendations, but to consider always the viewpoint of the expert being quoted, each in his own locality. We have asked each to nominate "Trees that need a friend." Their nominations far exceeded the limits of the space allotted, and we have quoted freely from them in the encyclopedia.

We received multiple endorsements of a number of trees, not only in the same region, but from different parts of the country. For example, Amelanchier was nominated 4 times. *Nyssa sylvatica* was nominated in both East and West. These are certainly trees that deserve more attention.

Updating

This book is concerned with updating the evaluations of trees. Trees are constantly being reevaluated in the arboretums, botanical gardens and by growers. From them we bring

Dogwood puts on a spectacular spring performance.

Above: *Hickory trees frame a playground.*
Below: *Large water oaks give this street a special cathedral quality.*

you the very latest update on tree performance.

These are the sources of our information:

The University of Washington Arboretum, Seattle, Washington

North Willamette Experiment Station of Oregon State University

J. Frank Schmidt and Son, Co., Boring, Oregon

Saratoga Horticultural Foundation, Saratoga, California

University of California, Davis, California

Los Angeles State and County Arboretum, Arcadia, California

Secrest Arboretum, Ohio Agricultural Research and Development Center, Wooster, Ohio

American Garden-Cole, Circleville, Ohio

Princeton Nurseries, Princeton, New Jersey

Callaway Gardens, Pine Mountain, Georgia

Each grower listed has growing acreage of approximately 1,000 acres. His judgment is particularly important, as he must gamble on which trees will be saleable 3 or 4 years after planting.

The pattern

As you leaf through this book, you will see a pattern, a sequence to follow, and one that we hope will help you to decide on "which trees."

First, you must know your individual climate. The climate discussions, and the maps that follow are, at best, generalities.

Next come the lists of trees for both aesthetic and functional values (pages 18 to 27). They are intended to be clues for further searching.

The lists are followed by a cross reference of common names to botanical names (pages 28 and 29). Next, the encyclopedia, with specific information on each tree. The encyclopedia is incomplete without "Trees that need a friend" (pages 80 to 84). This section contains recommendations and descriptions of trees that should be given a closer look.

Finally, from page 85 on, we discuss modern tree care, authored by Richard W. Harris, Professor of Landscape Horticulture, University of California, Davis, California.

Tree language

You do not have to take a refresher course in botany to read this book.

Technical terms are described as we go — in illustrations, photographs, and words. You may have to reach for the dictionary occasionally, but that's as far as it goes.

There are a few words used very often that we will explain here.

"Clone" and "cultivar." These words are used interchangeably; however, there are technical differences. A clone is propagated solely by asexual means, while a cultivar can be propagated by seed as well. Both refer to a group of uniform individuals with superior or unique qualities.

Translate racemes, umbels, and panicles as flower clusters, or as an inflorescence. Florets are the individual flowers.

Tree climates of the North

The North is big (zones 1-7 mapped on the following pages). According to the USDA map, zones change from north to south only by minimum temperatures, but tree climates will vary within zones for a number of reasons. Large bodies of water, snow-cover, soil types, slope of the land, elevation, and air drainage will influence tree climates.

South- and west-facing slopes, warmer than north and east slopes because they absorb more of the sun's radiant energy, are important to cold-tender plants and those which grow best on hot, sunny sites. Thermal belts are localized, warm micro-climates that develop on sloping land above valleys and other lowlands. Winters are distinctly colder both below and above these bands of mild temperatures. Therefore, if your garden is in a warm thermal belt, you will probably be able to grow a number of plants considered too cold-tender for the general area.

Structural walls, plant hedges, and screens can act as a dam, and trap cold air on the uphill side, creating a frost pocket. If arranged to deflect the downhill flow of cold air around gardens and outdoor living areas, they provide shelter and protection.

Buildings, automobiles, large expanses of concrete, and other heat-absorbing surfaces all contribute to making cities and towns warmer than outlying areas. Likewise, the warmest areas in the garden are usually beside paved surfaces such as sidewalks, driveways, patios, and sunny south and west walls. Besides reflecting

some of the sun's heat, light, and glare, these surfaces store heat during daylight hours and radiate it back into the atmosphere at night. Dark surfaces also absorb more heat than light-colored ones.

Each side of a building has its own microclimate, which strongly influences plant growth. The cool, shaded, north side is best for cold-tolerant plants and those which do not grow well in full sunlight. A wall that faces south receives maximum sunlight throughout the year and plants that tolerate intense heat and brilliant sunlight do well here. Both east- and west-facing walls are exposed to a half day of sun, but high afternoon temperatures create a much hotter microclimate against the west wall.

Even in the coldest winter climates, there are ways to work with the weather so that storm damage is reduced and the really low temperatures are foiled. Snow, for example, is the finest mulch against cold. It holds a lot of air and insulates against temperatures below freezing. Still, the weight of heavy snow can be a menace on the foliage of evergreens, snapping branches or deforming the shape of the tree. Knock or shake snow off evergreens whenever you can.

Drought is a major menace in winter, so water thoroughly before the ground freezes. Good watering and mulching will prevent a lot of cold burn and will keep roots from heaving out of the ground in freeze-and-thaw cycles.

Wind is the chief menace in winter, especially in the Great Plains. It breaks snow-laden branches, dries exposed branches and foliage, and increases existing cold. Your best answer is a permanent windbreak of hardy trees. A windbreak is only effective if some of the wind can blow straight through. This creates a leeward turbulence, holding the main force up above your garden. Good shelterbelt trees are listed below:

Hackberry	*Celtis occidentalis*
Russian olive	*Elaeagnus angustifolia*
Buckthorn	*Rhamnus cathartica*
Smooth sumac	*Rhus glabra*
Chokecherry	*Prunus virginiana*
Eastern red cedar	*Juniperus virginiana*

Great Lakes

The influence of the Great Lakes is complex, resulting in great climate variation between locations on opposite shores. For example, Lake Michigan (like all large bodies of water) responds to temperature changes slowly, delaying the onset of seasonal weather. Predominantly westerly winds sweep across the lake and buffer the eastern shores against extremes.

Autumn is typically cloudy on eastern shores when moisture-laden air condenses as it moves inland. Thus Madison, Wisconsin, receives an average of 42% possible sunshine in January while Lansing, Michigan, receives only 27%. Precipitation also varies from east to west. In winter, Milwaukee, Wisconsin, can expect precipitation on the average of every 5 days, while Muskegon, Michigan, averages every other day.

Each lake has its own influence on nearby areas in the United States and Canada. For example, as one moves north in Ohio towards Lake Erie, the growing season, is longer. In Cleveland, along the southern shore, the growing season is 195 days. Away from the lake influence, in the Ohio River valleys, the season is reduced to as low as 140 days.

Snow-cover varies throughout the entire Great Lakes region. Lake influence creates what is often called a snow belt, which extends along the eastern and southern portions of the Great Lakes from Chicago to Buffalo and is notorious for high winter snowfall.

Hardiness

Hardiness is of increasing importance the farther north you go. Gregory N. Brown, professor of forestry at the University of Missouri, Columbia, talks about winter hardiness this way:

"Early fall freezes, late spring freezes and severe freezes during winter months often press trees beyond their limits of survival. Usually a tree can handle freezing weather, when prepared for it — a process called winter hardiness, frost hardiness, cold hardiness or numerous other names. Trees can read environmental changes such as shortening days and cooler temperatures in the fall. These signals are interpreted, and preparation for winter hardiness follows. Different tree species have differing capacities to prepare themselves for freezing weather."

The following trees are listed as extremely hardy (less than −40° C).

Betula papyrifera	*Pinus resinosa*
Fraxinus nigra	*Pinus strobus*
Larix laricina	*Populus balsamifera*
Picea abies	*Populus tremuloides*
Picea mariana	*Prunus pensylvanica*
Pinus banksiana	*Robinia pseudoacacia*
	Ulmus americana

Above: *Close-up of a corkscrew willow leaf and a mature tree in a patio.* Below: *A beautiful example of the deodar cedar.*

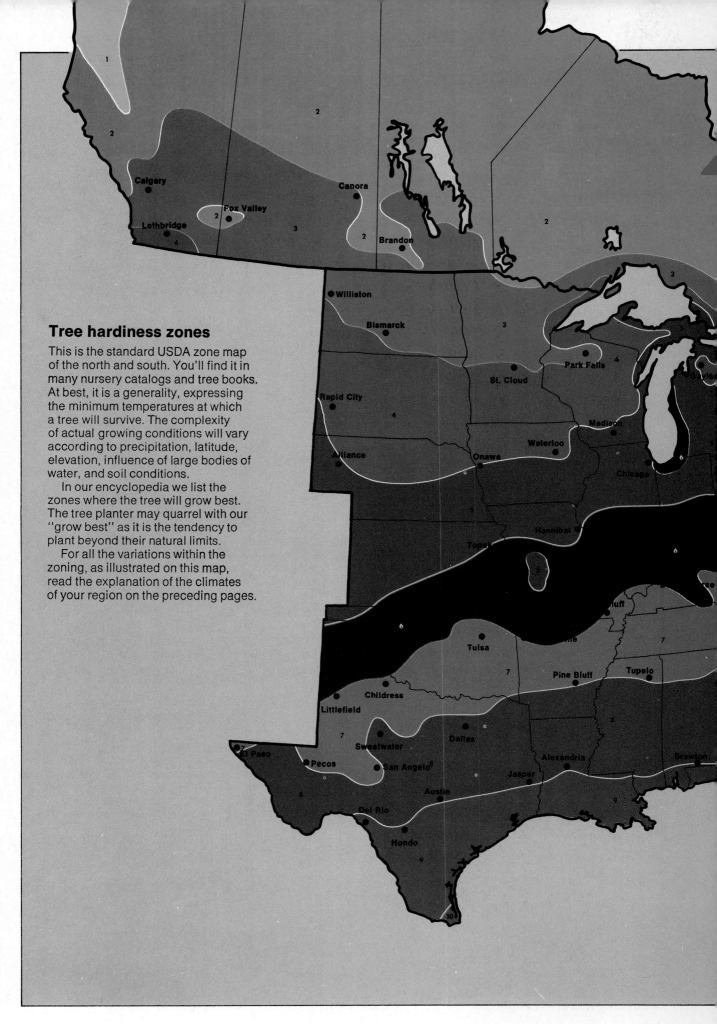

Tree hardiness zones

This is the standard USDA zone map of the north and south. You'll find it in many nursery catalogs and tree books. At best, it is a generality, expressing the minimum temperatures at which a tree will survive. The complexity of actual growing conditions will vary according to precipitation, latitude, elevation, influence of large bodies of water, and soil conditions.

In our encyclopedia we list the zones where the tree will grow best. The tree planter may quarrel with our "grow best" as it is the tendency to plant beyond their natural limits.

For all the variations within the zoning, as illustrated on this map, read the explanation of the climates of your region on the preceding pages.

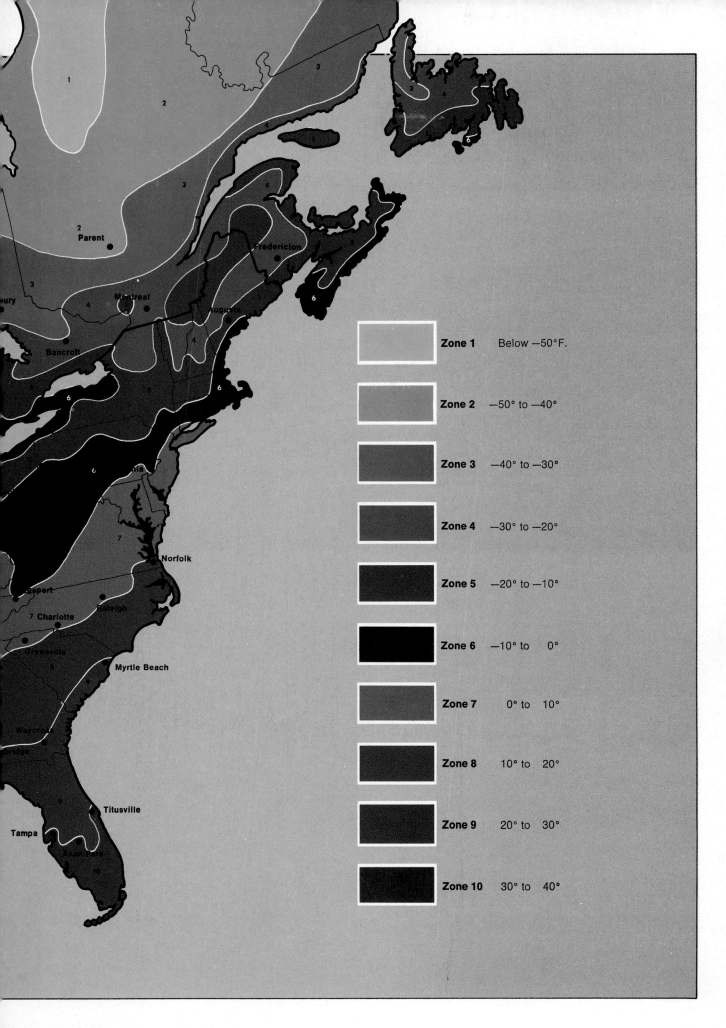

Zone 1   Below −50°F.

Zone 2   −50° to −40°

Zone 3   −40° to −30°

Zone 4   −30° to −20°

Zone 5   −20° to −10°

Zone 6   −10° to   0°

Zone 7   0° to   10°

Zone 8   10° to   20°

Zone 9   20° to   30°

Zone 10   30° to   40°

Seasonal color is a consideration when choosing a tree. Top: *Flowering fruit trees* (Prunus *species) are among the most spectacular spring bloomers.* Bottom: *The well-known ash (Fraxinus* species) *is noted both for its form and fall color.*

The tree guide posts
Selecting trees for problem solving and aesthetic values

Out of the great world of trees, we have chosen a few to serve as a guide. We list some trees by their attributes or characteristics and others by their functions. Each list is but a fraction of all the trees that could be included in that category. However, we think they are the choice of the lot and good guideposts in the search for the tree you are looking for.

If you consider a tree for the patio, also consider it for summer flowers, fall color, winter form, color in more than one season, fruits and berries, fragrant flowers, interesting bark or leaf shapes. No one tree will fit all categories, but it may have the characteristics most important to you.

Trees solve problems

Think of trees in terms of solving problems rather than trees that stand alone. Trees become very useful plants in many situations. Consider the air-conditioning savings of trees espaliered informally against the west wall of the house. Consider the trees that screen out the neighbors. Consider the wall tree that adds its grace to the straightforward condominium. Trees can cover a fence more quickly than most permanent vines. Giant trees can be held in check by pruning (see page 102). Trees can be miniaturized, and held in pots or tubs for years if space is limited. There are also trees for problem sites: trees that will stand flooding, that will grow along the coast, and that can stand up to the harshest city conditions.

Use these lists as your first guide into the encyclopedic listings of trees (see page 30) and "Trees that need a friend" (see page 80).

We have zoned the trees for your guidance but remember that zoning, at best, is only a generality. Tree performance varies by location. Check with your local nurseryman or County Extension Agent.

Some trees, like this evergreen pear (Pyrus kawakami) can cover a fence more quickly than most permanent vines.

Here fall color combines with unique leaf shape to make the ginkgo an eye catcher.

Indoor trees

Under greenhouse conditions most trees can be grown indoors for a time. Here we list a few outdoor trees suitable for common indoor conditions.

Botanical name	Common name	Zone
Araucaria heterophylla	Norfolk Island pine	9-10
Cedrus spp.	Cedar	*
Chamaecyparis spp.	False cypress	*
Citrus spp.	Citrus	
Ficus spp.	Fig	*
Laurus nobilis	Grecian laurel	8-10
Ligustrum spp.	Privet	*
Nerium oleander	Oleander	9-10
Olea europaea 'Swan Hill'	Fruitless olive	9-10
Palms	Palms	*
Persea americana	Avocado	
Pittosporum spp.	Pittosporum	*
Podocarpus spp.	Yew pine, Fern pine	*

*See encyclopedia

Fiddle-leaf fig.

Trees that can be miniaturized

Many shrubs and trees can be miniaturized in bonsai style. We can dwarf trees naturally by restricting their roots to a small container, and by pruning.

Botanical name	Common name	Zone
Acer spp.	Maple	*
Cedrus spp.	Cedar	*
Cercidiphyllum japonicum	Katsura tree	4-8
Chamaecyparis spp.	False cypress	*
Cotinus coggygria	Smoke tree	5-9
Cydonia oblonga	Quince	5-9
Fagus spp.	Beech	*
Ginkgo biloba	Maidenhair tree	6-9
Laurus nobilis	Grecian laurel	8-10
Malus spp.	Crabapple	*
Pinus spp.	Pine	*
Zelkova serrata	Saw-leaf zelkova	5-9

*See encyclopedia

Left: Pine species
Right: European fern-leaf beech.

Trees that can be sheared

Few trees escape the pruning shears of the home gardener. They're sheared and shaped into many forms. The following are some of the trees that can be sheared.

Botanical name	Common name	Zone
Ailanthus altissima	Tree-of-heaven	5-10
Cedrus spp.	Cedar	*
Cupressocyparis leylandii	Leyand cypress	6-9
Cupressus spp.	Cypress	*
Ginkgo biloba	Maidenhair tree	5-9
Ilex spp.	Holly	*
Laurus nobilis	Grecian laurel	8-10
Ligustrum spp.	Privet	*
Malus spp.	Crabapple	*
Platanus acerifolia	London plane tree	5-9
Platycladus orientalis	Oriental arborvitae	7-10
Podocarpus spp.	Yew pine, Fern pine	*
Psuedotsuga menziesii	Douglas fir	6-8
Thuja spp.	Arborvitae	*

*See encyclopedia

Top and bottom: Sheared arborvitae

Trees that stand city conditions

These trees vary in local adaptation but all are resistant to city conditions such as air pollution, reflected heat, and limited open soil surface for air and water.

Botanical name	Common name	Zone
Acer spp.	Maple	*
Aesculus carnea	Red horse chestnut	5-9
Carpinus betulus	European hornbeam	5-9
Catalpa speciosa	Northern catalpa	5-9
Celtis occidentalis	Common hackberry	3-8
Cotinus coggygria	Smoke tree	5-8
Crataegus phaenopyrum	Washington thorn	5-9
Fraxinus spp.	Ash	*
Ginkgo biloba	Maidenhair tree	5-9
Gleditsia triacanthos · inermis	Thornless honey locust	5-9
Ilex opaca	American holly	5-9
Koelreuteria paniculata	Golden-rain tree	5-7
Malus spp.	Crabapple	*
Ostrya virginiana	Hop hornbeam	4-9
Phellodendron amurense	Amur cork tree	4-8
Pinus nigra	Austrian pine	4-8
Pinus sylvestris	Scotch pine	2-7
Platanus acerifolia	London plane tree	5-9
Pyrus calleryana	Callery pear	5-9
Quercus spp.	Oak	*
Sophora japonica 'Regent'	Japanese pagoda tree	5-8
Tilia cordata	Littleleaf linden	4-8
Ulmus parvifolia	Chinese elm	5-9
Zelkova serrata	Saw-leaf zelkova	5-9

*See encyclopedia

Top: Crabapple (foreground) and honey locust.
Bottom left: Callery pear.
Bottom right: Littleleaf linden.

Small garden and patio trees

These are small, well-behaved trees that you can live with comfortably. They provide shade and seasonal show while allowing for patio and garden activities.

Botanical name	Common name	Zone
Acer spp.	Maple	*
Amelanchier spp.	Serviceberry	*
Betula populifolia	Gray birch	4-6
Cercidiphyllum japonicum	Katsura tree	4-8
Cercis canadensis	Eastern redbud	5-8
Chionanthus virginicus	Fringe tree	5-9
Cornus spp.	Dogwood	*
Cotinus coggygria	Smoke tree	5-8
Crataegus spp.	Hawthorn	*
Halesia carolina	Snowdrop tree	5-8
Koelreuteria paniculata	Golden-rain tree	5-7
Magnolia spp.	Magnolia	*
Malus spp.	Crabapple	*
Ostrya virginiana	Hop hornbeam	4-9
Oxydendrum arboreum	Sourwood	5-9
Prunus spp.	Flowering fruit trees	*
Pyrus calleryana 'Faureri'	Faureri Callery pear	5-9
Styrax japonicus	Japanese snowbell	6-9
Syringa amurensis japonica	Japanese tree lilac	5-8
Viburnum sieboldii	Siebold viburnum	5-8

*See encyclopedia

Top: left: Eastern redbud.
Top right: Golden-rain tree.
Bottom left: Hawthorn.
Bottom right: Flowering cherry.

Trees with attractive winter silhouette

Leafless, these trees provide a handsome outline against the open sky or a background of evergreens. They are winter's visual delights.

Botanical name	Common name	Zone
Acer spp.	Maple	*
Aesculus hippocastanum	Horse chestnut	3-7
Betula spp.	Birch	*
Carya ovata	Shagbark hickory	5-9
Cercidiphyllum japonicum	Katsura tree	4-8
Cladrastis lutea	Yellowwood	5-7
Cornus florida	Flowering dogwood	5-9
Fagus grandifolia	American beech	4-9
Ginkgo biloba	Maidenhair tree	5-9
Gleditsia triacanthos inermis	Thornless honey locust	5-9
Gymnocladus dioica	Kentucky coffee tree	5-8
Ilex opaca	American holly	5-9
Liquidambar styraciflua	Sweet gum	5-9
Liriodendron tulipifera	Tulip tree	5-9
Magnolia spp.	Magnolia	*
Malus spp.	Crabapple	*
Nyssa sylvatica	Sour gum	5-9
Phellodendron amurense	Amur cork tree	4-8
Platanus spp.	Sycamore	*
Populus spp.	Poplar	*
Quercus spp.	Oak	*
Salix spp.	Willow	*

*See encyclopedia

Top: Willows in winter.
Middle: The same willows in summer.
Bottom left: Sour gum.
Bottom right: Sycamore.

Trees with excellent fall color

In many parts of the North, trees and fall color are inseparable. Listed below are trees that come across with reliable fall color.

Botanical name	Common name	Zone
Acer spp.	Maple	*
Amelanchier spp.	Serviceberry	*
Betula spp.	Birch	*
Carpinus caroliniana	Hornbeam	4-8
Carya ovata	Shagbark hickory	5-9
Cercidiphyllum japonicum	Katsura tree	4-8
Cornus florida	Flowering dogwood	5-9
Cotinus coggygria	Smoke tree	5-8
Diospyros virginiana	American persimmon	5-9
Fraxinus spp.	Ash	*
Ginkgo biloba	Maidenhair tree	5-9
Larix leptolepis	Japanese larch	5-8
Liquidambar styraciflua	Sweet gum	5-9
Liriodendron tulipifera	Tulip tree	5-9
Nyssa sylvatica	Sour gum	5-9
Oxydendrum arboreum	Sourwood	5-9
Populus spp.	Poplar	*
Pyrus calleryana	Callery pear	5-9
Quercus spp.	Oak	*
Rhus typhina	Sumac	3-8
Sassafras albidum	Sassafras	5-9
Zelkova serrata	Saw-leaf zelkova	5-9

*See encyclopedia

Top left: Sweet gum.
Top right: Japanese maple.
Bottom left: Ginkgo.
Bottom right: Sour gum.

Summer-flowering trees

Many trees are colorful long after the first spring blooms are over. Here are some summer-flowering trees.

Botanical name	Common name	Zone
Albizia julibrissin	Silk tree	7-10
Catalpa spp.	Catalpa	*
Chionanthus virginicus	Fringe tree	5-9
Cladrastis lutea	Yellowwood	5-7
Cornus kousa	Kousa dogwood	5-8
Cotinus coggygria	Smoke tree	5-8
Crataegus phaenopyrum	Washington thorn	5-9
Franklinia alatamaha	Franklinia	6-8
Koelreuteria paniculata	Golden-rain tree	5-7
Laburnum watereri 'Vossii'	Golden-chain tree	6-7
Liriodendron tulipifera	Tulip tree	5-9
Oxydendrum arboreum	Sourwood	5-9
Sophora japonica	Japanese pagoda tree	5-8
Syringa amurensis japonica	Japanese lilac tree	5-8

*See encyclopedia

Kousa dogwood tree and a closer look at its flowers.

Trees with color in more than one season

These trees provide interest and enjoyment over a long period of time, with their flowers, fruits, autumn color, or bark.

Botanical name	Common name	Zone
Amelanchier spp.	Serviceberry	*
Betula spp.	Birch	*
Cercis canadensis	Eastern redbud	5-9
Chionanthus virginicus	Fringe tree	5-9
Cornus spp.	Dogwood	*
Crataegus spp.	Hawthorn	*
Halesia carolina	Snowdrop tree — Carolina silver-bell	5-8
Malus spp.	Crabapple	*
Oxydendrum arboreum	Sourwood	5-9
Prunus spp.	Flowering fruits	*
Styrax japonicus	Japanese snowbell	6-9

*See encyclopedia

Left: Sourwood tree in June.
Top right: Another sourwood tree in October.
Bottom right: The fall color of the sourwood's leaves and flower.

Trees with attractive fruits or berries

Bright colors are not limited to foliage and flowers. Fruits and berries, edible and inedible, can be just as attractive and sometimes last longer.

Botanical name	Common name	Zone
Amelanchier spp.	Serviceberry	*
Chionanthus virginicus	Fringe tree	5-9
Cornus spp.	Dogwood	*
Crataegus spp.	Hawthorn	*
Elaeagnus angustifolia	Russian olive	3-8
Ilex spp.	Holly	*
Malus spp.	Crabapple	*
Oxydendrum arboreum	Sourwood	5-9
Prunus spp.	Flowering fruit	*
Sorbus aucuparia	European mountain ash	4-6

*See encyclopedia

Left: European mountain ash.
Right: Its attractive berries are edible.

Dual-purpose trees

These are the ornamental edibles — trees that are decorative in the garden, with the added bonus of providing edible fruit.

Botanical name	Common name	Zone
Amelanchier spp.	Serviceberry	*
Carya ovata	Shagbark hickory	5-9
Castanea mollissima	Chinese chestnut	5-9
Corylus americana	American filbert	4-9
Corylus avellana	European filbert	4-7
Cydonia oblonga	Quince	5-9
Diospyros virginiana	American persimmon	5-9
Juglans cinerea	Butternut	4-7
Juglans nigra	Black walnut	4-9
Juglans regia	Carpathian English walnut	6-7
Malus spp.	Crabapple	*
Prunus spp.	Flowering fruits	*

*See encyclopedia

Top left: Apple trees.
Top right: Shagbark hickory.
Bottom: Chinese chestnut.

Trees for fragrance

Although some of these trees have flowers that are inconspicuous, their presence in the garden is a pleasure. In this list, trees whose crushed leaves are fragrant are omitted.

Botanical name	Common name	Zone
Acer ginnala	Amur maple	3-8
Chionanthus virginicus	Fringe tree	5-9
Cladrastis lutea	Yellowwood	5-7
Elaeagnus angustifolia	Russian olive	3-8
Magnolia spp.	Magnolia	*
Malus spp.	Crabapple	
Oxydendrum arboreum	Sourwood	5-9
Prunus spp.	Flowering fruits	*
Robinia psuedoacacia	Black locust	4-9
Tilia spp.	Linden	*

*See encyclopedia

Left: Magnolia.
Right: Japanese pagoda tree.

Trees with interesting bark

Texture, color, and patterns of bark are important considerations when selecting landscape trees.

Botanical name	Common name	Zone
Acer griseum	Paperbark maple	6-8
Betula spp.	Birch	*
Carpinus caroliniana	American hornbeam	4-9
Carya ovata	Shagbark hickory	5-9
Cladrastis lutea	Yellowwood	5-7
Diospyros virginiana	American persimmon	5-9
Fagus grandifolia	American beech	4-9
Ostrya virginiana	Hop hornbeam	4-9
Pinus bungeana	Lacebark pine	5-7
Platanus spp.	Sycamore	*
Populus spp.	Cottonwood	*
Prunus serrula	Birch bark cherry	5-7
Salix alba tristis	Golden weeping willow	3-9

*See encyclopedia

Top left: Birch bark cherry.
Top right: River birch.
Bottom: Paperbark maple.

Trees that tolerate seashore conditions

Use these trees as your first line of defense along the coast. Many will lose their natural habit of growth and become artistically shaped by the ocean winds.

Botanical name	Common name	Zone
Acer platanoides	Norway maple	3-7
Acer pseudoplatanus	Sycamore maple	5-8
Acer rubrum	Red maple	4-9
Ailanthus altissima	Tree-of-heaven	5-10
Betula populifolia	Gray birch	4-6
Carpinus betulus	European hornbeam	5-9
Cryptomeria japonica	Cryptomeria	7-9
Juniperus virginiana	Eastern red cedar	4-9
Nyssa sylvatica	Sour gum	5-9
Picea glauca	White spruce	2-5
Pinus nigra	Austrian pine	5-8
Pinus thunbergii	Japanese black pine	5-8
Platanus acerifolia	London plane tree	5-9
Populus deltoides	Cottonwood	3-9
Salix alba	White willow	3-9
Sciadopitys verticillata	Umbrella pine	6-7

*See encyclopedia

A properly selected tree will adapt to coastal conditions.

Wall trees

Trees on this list have well-behaved root systems and habits that allow for close planting to walls; ideal for softening the side of a one- to two-story building.

Botanical name	Common name	Zone
Acer spp.	Maple (columnar forms)	*
Betula spp.	Birch	*
Carpinus betulus 'Fastigiata'	Columnar European hornbeam	5-9
Chamaecyparis lawsoniana	Lawson cypress	6-9
Crataegus phaenopyrum	Washington thorn	5-9
Ginkgo biloba 'Fastigiata'	Sentry ginkgo	5-9
Ilex opaca	American holly	5-9
Malus spp.	Crabapple	*
Picea glauca	White spruce	2-5
Pyrus calleryana	Callery pear	5-9
Quercus robur 'Fastigiata'	Upright English oak	5-7

*See encyclopedia

Left: Live oak.
Right: Crabapple.

Skyline trees

These are the stately giants, to be seen for blocks, that need lots of space to grow in and be appreciated.

Botanical name	Common name	Zone
Acer spp.	Maple	*
Carya ovata	Shagbark hickory	4-9
Fagus grandifolia	American beech	4-9
Gleditsia triacanthos inermis	Thornless honey locust	5-9
Liquidambar styraciflua	Sweet gum	5-9
Liriodendron tulipifera	Tulip tree	5-9
Picea spp.	Spruce	*
Pinus spp.	Pine	*
Quercus spp.	Oak	*
Taxodium distichum	Bald cypress	5-10
Tsuga canadensis	Canada hemlock	4-8

*See encyclopedia

Left: Bald cypress.
Right: Copper beech.

Trees for screens and buffers

These trees are selected for their ability to hide unattractive, but necessary areas.

Botanical name	Common name	Zone
Abies spp.	Fir	*
Carpinus betulus 'Fastigiata'	Upright European hornbeam	5-9
Cedrus deodara	Deodar cedar	7-9
Cupressocyparis leylandii	Leyland cypress	6-10
Juniperus spp.	Juniper (columnar form)	*
Ilex spp.	Holly	*
Picea spp.	Spruce	*
Pinus spp.	Pine	*
Populus spp.	Poplar	*
Rhamnus frangula 'Columnaris'	Tallhedge buckthorn	2-7
Taxus spp.	Yew	
Thuja occidentalis	American arborvitae	3-8
Tsuga canadensis	Canadian hemlock	4-8

*See encyclopedia

Left: Lombardy poplars.
Right: Arborvitae.

Quick-growing temporary trees

These trees supply quick landscape effect. Some may be considered "weed trees," but they can be interplanted with "desirables" and removed as the slower trees reach functional size.

Botanical name	Common name	Zone
Acer saccharinum	Silver maple	4-9
Ailanthus altissima	Tree-of-heaven	5-10
Albizia julibrissin	Silk tree	7-10
Alnus glutinosa	Black alder	4-9
Catalpa spp.	Catalpa	*
Paulownia tomentosa	Empress tree	6-9
Populus spp.	Poplar	*
Robinia pseudoacacia	Black locust	4-9
Salix spp.	Willow	
Ulmus spp.	Elm	*

*See encyclopedia

Top left: Silk tree.
Bottom left: Catalpa.
Right: Chinese elm.

Trees that will stand abuse

Whether you call some of these trees "undesirables" or not won't stop them from growing where all else fails.

Botanical name	Common name	Zone
Ailanthus altissima	Tree-of-heaven	5-10
Elaeagnus angustifolia	Russian olive	3-8
Fraxinus spp.	Ash	*
Ginkgo biloba	Maidenhair tree	5-9
Gleditsia triacanthos inermis	Thornless honey locust	5-9
Juniperus virginiana	Eastern red cedar	4-9
Maclura pomifera	Osage orange	5-9
Malus spp.	Crabapple	*
Melia azedarach	Chinaberry	7-9
Morus alba	Mulberry	5-9
Platanus	Sycamore	*
Populus spp.	Poplar	*
Robinia pseudoacacia	Black locust	4-9
Salix spp.	Willow	*
Ulmus spp.	Elm	*

*See encyclopedia

Russian olive.

Trees essentially pest-free

Choose a tree for more reasons than just freedom from pests. "Pest-free" is a relative term depending on locality. These trees are pest-free where well-adapted.

Botanical name	Common name	Zone
Carpinus betulus	European hornbeam	5-9
Cedrus spp.	Cedar	*
Cercidiphyllum japonicum	Katsura tree	4-8
Chionanthus virginicus	Fringe tree	5-9
Ginkgo biloba	Maidenhair tree	5-9
Gymnocladus dioica	Kentucky coffee tree	5-8
Koelreuteria paniculata	Golden-rain tree	5-7
Metasequoia glyptostroboides	Dawn redwood	5-9
Ostrya virginiana	Hop hornbeam	4-9
Phellodendron amurense	Amur cork tree	4-8
Pseudolarix kaempferi	Golden larch	5-7
Taxodium distichum	Bald cypress	5-10

*See encyclopedia

Left: Katsura tree.
Right: Atlas cedar.

Shrubs that can be trained into trees

These plants are commonly thought of as shrubs but by suppressing branches you don't want and encouraging growth upward, they will develop into trees.

Botanical name	Common name	Zone
Cornus kousa	Japanese dogwood	5-8
Cotinus coggygria	Smoke tree	5-8
Euonymus alata	Winged euonymus	4-7
Hamamelis mollis	Chinese witch hazel	5-9
Hibiscus syriacus	Rose-of-Sharon	5-9
Hydrangea spp.	Hydrangea	5-9
Ilex verticillata	Winterberry holly	3-9
Syringa amurensis japonica	Japanese tree lilac	5-8
Wisteria spp.	Wisteria	5-9

*See encyclopedia

Left: Wisteria.
Right: Hydrangea.

Trees that attract birds

All trees attract birds, but because these trees provide abundant fruit as well as cover, they attract birds in flocks.

Botanical name	Common name	Zone
Amelanchier spp.	Serviceberry	*
Cornus spp.	Dogwood	*
Crataegus spp.	Hawthorn	*
Elaeagnus angustifolia	Russian olive	3-8
Elaeagnus umbellata	Wild olive	
Ilex spp.	Holly	*
Juniperus virginiana	Eastern red cedar	4-9
Malus spp.	Crabapple	*
Morus spp.	Mulberry	5-9
Prunus spp.	Cherry	*
Viburnum sieboldii	Siebold viburnum	5-8

*See encyclopedia

Left: Dogwood variety 'Cloud Nine.'
Top right: Its attractive fruit is fine for preserves or jelly.
Bottom right: Flowering cherry.

Ornamental edibles

To get our information, we went to a lot of different people living in a lot of different places throughout the North. People with all sorts of growing spaces — urban balconies, suburban backyards, and rural farmyards. We asked lots of questions like these: "Have you ever planted a tree?" "What kind; how many?" "What kinds of trees do you have in your yard — on your street?" "What trees do you notice on the skyline?" "What are your favorite trees?" "How do you rank yourself when it comes to trees: expert, non-expert (likes trees but doesn't know their names), or somewhere in between?"

At every level of expertise, one feeling came through clear and strong: the trend toward dual-purpose trees. One northern man spoke for them all when he said, "I like trees that have fruits or nuts."

More and more people are planting fruit and nut trees as part of the ornamental landscape, incorporating the orchard with the backyard.

The hardy English walnut and the black walnut are beautiful trees with attractive foliage and give dense summer shade as well as delicious fruit. The American filbert is a lovely landscape small tree or shrub with brilliant scarlet and bronze fall foliage. Another favorite, the butternut, is fast-growing and will bear within two or three years after planting. And one of our correspondents writes this about the Chinese chestnut: "It forms a dense, rounded tree, much like a big apple tree in shape, and soon begins to bear large sweet nuts in abundance each fall. More of these trees should be planted so that our children can enjoy the pleasures of gathering and roasting chestnuts in the fall as our grandparents used to do."

An edible peach with showy flowers can be a garden tree, a lawn tree, and even a patio tree.

Some of the flowering plums can also produce good fruit. Flowering plums that bear no fruit are best as street trees, but the homeowner who wants fruit will select types like *Prunus cerasifera* 'Atropurpurea' and *Prunus cerasifera* 'Thundercloud.' They have dark coppery leaves, light pink to white flowers, and bear small red plums.

One man wrote, "Hopa and Dolgo crabs are poor street trees because of oversized fruit, but both are excellent jelly crabs in the yard of a suburban or farm home."

Another decorative flowering tree with useful fruits is the cornelian cherry *(Cornus mas)*. This dogwood bears clusters of yellow flowers on bare twigs very early in the year. The leaves turn yellow to red in the fall, and although the bright scarlet fruits are too acid to eat, they make fine preserves or jelly.

Any espaliered fruit tree is a great decorative addition to the garden. The blossoms need not be showy, as the form of the tree is attractive, especially when the branches are bare and the fruits show off to best advantage. Apples and pears are the easiest.

The American persimmon *(Diospyros virginiana)* would be much more widely used if gardeners realized the great value of both tree and fruit. A medium-sized tree with large leaves that turn yellow, pink, and red in the fall, it is very effective as an informal espalier against a wall. The fruit is puckery until fully ripe, then it is sweet and delicious — excellent in cooking.

The fruiting quince *(Cydonia oblonga)* is a small tree that is generally overlooked and should be grown more. It bears lovely fragrant pink and white flowers at the branch tips and has an attractive winter pattern of gnarled and twisted branches. The fruits are large and round or pear-shaped and are covered with down. They can't be eaten raw, but nothing makes a better jelly.

Some ornamental natives provide edible fruit. Elderberry and mountain ash have spectacular blooms and attractive berries that make excellent jelly. And don't forget elderberry wine.

One man passed on this recommendation, "Shadblow, or serviceberry is an excellent tree with white flowers in the spring and berries that make fine jelly. Personally, I prefer *Amelanchier alnifolia,* the Oregon serviceberry. The flowers are bigger, and it's a cleaner tree." But another man suggests the Allegheny serviceberry *Amelanchier laevis,* "a very attractive small tree that flowers in spring and usually has a reddish fall color. The fruit resembles tiny blue-purple crabapples (cream-colored to red to nearly black) with the flavor of blueberries when fully ripe. Can be eaten fresh or dried, canned or baked in a pie, and they're rich in vitamin C.

What you grow depends on where you are. Climate restrictions can be circumvented by planting in tubs and moving them to sheltered spots during periods of extreme heat or cold.

For specific recommendations as to fruits suitable for specific areas, see the Ortho book "All About Growing Fruits and Berries."

The shadblow or serviceberry tree (Amelanchier species).

Ripe fruit of the Oregon serviceberry (Amelanchier alnifolia) has the flavor of blueberries.

Some of the flowering plum trees produce good crops of edible plums.

What's in a common name

Plants have many common names, but just one botanical name. If you're looking for a tree, but don't know the botanical name, these pages will be important to you.

Frank Mackaness, technical advisor to the Schmidt and Son Nursery in Boring, Oregon, gives us some interesting sidelights on the origin of some of the common names of trees. He says:

"Common names tell a story. Blue ash, *(Fraxinus quadrangulata)*, got its name because the inner bark was used by the pioneers to make a blue dye.

"The *Nyssa* species — sour gum — owes its name to the fact that when the leaves are crushed they exude a resinous gum that has a distinctive and pleasant odor. It was one of the original American chewing gums.

"There are two versions of how the dogwood *(Cornus* spp.) got its name. One is that dogwood was used as a cure for dogs' mange. The other is that dogwood was used for making meat skewers or 'dags' and in time, 'dagwood' became dog-wood. I don't know which is valid — maybe both are.

"The name wych elm *(Ulmus glabra)* dates back to the days of tree worship, which was outlawed by Saxon King Edgar. A sprig of elm was used in the butter churn to prevent bewitching and the delaying of buttering. Wych elm was also the favored protection against witches.

"The weeping willow *(Salix babylonica)* has been the symbol of grief since the exiled children of Israel wept beside the waters of Babylon and hung their harps upon the willows in the midst of their grief.

Common name	Botanical name
A	
Alaska yellow cedar	*Chamaeocyparis nootkatensis*
Alder	*Alnus* spp.
Alder buckthorn	*Rhamnus frangula*
Amur cork tree	*Phellodendron amurense*
Arborvitae	*Thuja* spp.
Ash	*Fraxinus* spp.
Aspen	*Populus* spp.
Atlas cedar	*Cedrus atlantica*
B	
Bald cypress	*Taxodium distichum*
Basswood	*Tilia americana*
Beech	*Fagus* spp.
Birch	*Betula* spp.
Black gum	*Nyssa sylvatica*
Blackhaw	*Viburnum rufidulum*
Blue elderberry	*Sambucus caerulea*
Box elder	*Acer negundo*
Buckeye	*Aesculus* spp.
Bull bay	*Magnolia grandiflora*
C	
Catalpa	*Catalpa* spp.
Chinaberry	*Melia azedarach*
Chinese scholar tree	*Sophora japonica*
Cornelian cherry	*Cornus mas*
Cottonwood	*Populus* spp.
Crape myrtle	*Lagerstroemia* spp.
Cucumber tree	*Magnolia acuminata*
Cypress	*Cupressus* spp.
D	
Dawn redwood	*Metasequoia glyptostroboides*
Deodar cedar	*Cedrus deodara*
Dogwood	*Cornus* spp.
Douglas fir	*Pseudotsuga menziesii*
E	
Elm	*Ulmus* spp.
Empress tree	*Paulownia tomentosa*
European mountain ash	*Sorbus aucuparia*
F	
False cypress	*Chamaecyparis* spp.
Fir	*Abies* spp.
Flowering cherry	*Prunus* spp.
Flowering crabapple	*Malus* spp.

Common name	Botanical name
Flowering peach	*Prunus persica*
Flowering plum	*Prunus* spp.
Franklinia	*Franklinia alatamaha*
Fringe tree	*Chionanthus* spp.
G	
Golden-chain tree	*Laburnum* spp.
Golden-rain tree	*Koelreuteria paniculata*
H	
Hackberry	*Celtis* spp.
Hawthorn	*Crataegus* spp.
Hemlock	*Tsuga* spp.
Holly	*Ilex* spp.
Honey locust	*Gleditsia triacanthos*
Hornbeam	*Carpinus* spp.
I	
Indian bean	*Catalpa* spp.
Ironwood	*Carpinus caroliniana*
J	
Japanese pagoda tree	*Sophora japonica*
Japanese snowbell	*Styrax japonicus*
Japanese snowdrop tree	*Styrax japonicus*
Japanese tree lilac	*Syringa amurensis japonica*
Juneberry	*Amelanchier* spp.
K	
Katsura tree	*Cercidiphyllum japanicum*
Kentucky coffee tree	*Gymnocladus dioica*
L	
Larch	*Larix* spp.
Lebanon cedar	*Cedrus libani*
Linden	*Tilia* spp.
Locust	*Robinia* spp.
M	
Maidenhair tree	*Ginkgo biloba*
Maple	*Acer* spp.
Mescal bean	*Sophora secundiflora*
Mimosa	*Albizia julibrissin*
Mulberry	*Morus* spp.
O	
Oak	*Quercus* spp.
Oriental arborvitae	*Platycladus orientalis*
Ornamental pear	*Pyrus* spp.
Osage orange	*Maclura pomifera*

Common name	Botanical name
P	
Pecan	*Carya illinoinesis*
Pepperidge	*Nyssa sylvatica*
Persimmon	*Diospyros* spp.
Pine	*Pinus* spp.
Plane tree	*Platanus* spp.
Princess tree	*Paulownia* ssp.
Q	
Quince	*Cydonia oblonga*
R	
Redbud	*Cercis* spp.
Red horse chestnut	*Aesculus carnea*
Russian olive	*Elaeagnus angustifolia*
S	
Serviceberry	*Amelanchier* spp.
Shadblow, shadbush	*Amelanchier* spp.
Shagbark hickory	*Carya ovata*
Silk tree	*Albizia julibrissin*
Silver-bell	*Halesia carolina*
Smoke tree	*Cotinus coggygria*
Snowdrop tree	*Halesia carolina*
Sorrel tree	*Oxydendrum arboreum*
Sour gum	*Nyssa sylvatica*
Sourwood	*Oxydendrum arboreum*
Spruce	*Picea* spp.
Sugarberry	*Celtis* spp.
Sumac	*Rhus* spp.
Sweet gum	*Liquidambar styraciflua*
Sycamore	*Platanus* spp.
T	
Tamarisk	*Tamarix* spp.
Texas umbrella tree	*Melia azedarach* 'Umbraculifera'
Tree-of-heaven	*Ailanthus altissima*
Tulip tree	*Liriodendron tulipifera*
Tupelo	*Nyssa sylvatica*
U	
Umbrella pine	*Sciadopitys verticillata*
W	
Washington thorn	*Crataegus phaenopyrum*
Western red cedar	*Thuja plicata*
Willow	*Salix* spp.
Y	
Yellowwood	*Cladrastis lutea*
Yew	*Taxus* spp.

"The Kentucky coffee tree (*Gymnocladus dioica*) got its name when the pioneers, in an effort to be self-supporting, tried several kinds of 'beans' as a coffee substitute. (I'll bet they only tried it once, but the name stuck.)

"As for the horse chestnut (*Aesculus* spp.), horses won't eat them, but the nuts are reputed to be a cure for broken-winded horses."

John Ford, Curator of the Secrest Arboretum, Wooster, Ohio, adds these comments:

"Inkberry holly is called gallberry in the Southeast. During the winter, the black fruits are one of the favorite foods of wintering robins who eat so many of the berries that their flesh becomes 'bitter as gall.'

"Arborvitae (*Thuja* spp.) originated when Jacques Cartier was exploring the St. Lawrence River. Many of his men came down with scurvy in the winter of 1535. Twenty-five died before the local Indians made a tea or soup from the leaves of a tree and gave this decoction to the other men. The French were so impressed with the results that they named the tree *l'arbre de vie,* tree of life, the name later being latinized to arborvitae.

"The name of the hop hornbeam (*Ostrya virginiana*) comes from the clusters of seed pods that resemble hops, and from the wood, which is hard as horn.

"Names are not always what they seem. The witch in witchhazel (*Hamamelis virginiana*) does not refer to the Hallowe'en witch, but to an old Anglo-Saxon word, wick or wicken. It means pliant, springy, or quick and alive.

"The common hop tree (*Ptelea trifoliata*) derived its name from claims that the fruits were used as a substitute for hops in brewing beer."

Sour gum.

The leaves of the Kentucky coffee tree.

Weeping willow.

The form of the Kentucky coffee tree.

Cryptomeria japonica. *Japanese cryptomeria.*

Aesculus hippocastanum. *Common horsechestnut.*

Araucaria heterophylla. *Norfolk Island pine.*

Above: Salix matsudana *'Navajo.' Globe Navajo willow.*
Below: Populus nigra *'Italica.' Lombardy poplar.*

Maclura pomifera. *Osage orange.*

The encyclopedia

Here, and in the next 50 pages, is our encyclopedia of trees. It does not contain all the trees in the great world of trees. We have selected only those we think you should be aware of. The encyclopedia is incomplete without "Trees that need a friend" on pages 80-84.

Trees are listed alphabetically by botanic names (the way they should be listed in the nursery). If you do not know the botanical name, see common names on pages 28 and 29.

The botanical name is given in the following way. First comes the genus, always written in italics, with the first letter capitalized, like this:

Gleditsia

This is followed by species, which is also italicized but not capitalized,

Gleditsia triacanthos

The variety is next, also in italics. These are plants that differ slightly from the species and occur in the wild.

Gleditsia triacanthos inermis

Finally, the cultivars and clones are capitalized and in single quotes,

G. t. i. 'Sunburst'

Hortus III is our authority on botanical nomenclature. If Hortus III has changed the name of a tree, we have noted it in parenthesis after the presently accepted name.

The next information we give is whether the tree is evergreen, deciduous, or a needled evergreen; the country or region of its origin; the zones in which it grows; and finally its growth habit, which includes rate of growth, height, and form.

All these terms, of course, are relative. *Fast-growing,* for example, may have different meanings in different locales. To generalize, for all regions, in our book fast-growing will mean an annual growth of more than 2 feet in height.

Moderate-growing, in relation to our definition of fast-growing, means a growth of 1 to 2 feet in height per year.

Slow-growing, in relation to the terms used above, means a growth of less than one foot in height per year.

Height is also relative. It depends on soil, water, and other environmental factors. A Douglas fir, for example, that matures at 200 feet in an Oregon forest, will attain only 20 feet at maturity in the Chisos Mountains of the Big Bend country of Texas. If the tree stands among other trees, it may have no other way to go except up. We give the height the tree should grow to in one's lifetime (50-60 years), as if it were standing alone.

Since trees vary greatly in form, many words are used to describe them. See standard forms below.

Abies. Fir.

There are many species of fir available in the eastern United States, varying according to location. All form perfectly pyramidal trees that need a good deal of room to develop.

Best used in open lawns, parks, or golf courses. Grown best in moist, well-drained, non-alkaline, soils, protected from high winds. Poor choice for hot dry areas. Grow naturally in cold-climate conifer forests where they may reach 200 feet.

Most widely adapted and available firs are *Abies concolor* and *Abies nordmanniana.*

Abies concolor. White fir (Needled Evergreen).

NATIVE TO: Western United States. ZONES: 4-8. HABIT: Slow to moderate growth to 55 feet in 60 years at the Secrest Arboretum, Wooster, Ohio.

The White fir is more tolerant of heat, drought, and city conditions than other species. Needles are attractive blue-green or gray-green about 2 inches long. Branches are in horizontal tiers; upright cylindrical cones are clustered on upper branches. Smooth gray bark on younger trees. Suitable for containers when young. Good, fragrant Christmas tree.

Abies nordmanniana. Nordmann fir (Needled Evergreen).

NATIVE TO: Asia Minor and Mediterranean. ZONES: 5-7. HABIT: Slow to moderate growth to 65 feet in 57 years at Secrest Arboretum, Wooster, Ohio.

Rated as one of the best firs at Secrest. Needles are dark, shiny green with silver underside, and densely cover the horizontal branches.

Like *Abies concolor,* can be grown in a container for several years. Makes an excellent Christmas tree.

Douglas fir. See *Pseudotsuga menziesii.*

Acer. Maple.

The maples are generally trees of the north. Bob Ticknor, North Willamette Experiment Station, Aurora, Oregon, discusses the genus Acer on pages 32-35.

Acer palmatum is praised in "Trees that need a friend" on pages 80-84.

Drip or honeydew-causing insects are common pests of the Maples. You know these pests if the leaves become coated black or if a car parked underneath becomes sticky. Read how to control on page 85.

Aesculus.

A genus that includes several american natives, some of which are useful garden and street trees.

Aesculus carnea. Red horse-chestnut (Deciduous).

NATIVE TO: Hybrid of *A. hippocastanum* of southeast Europe and *A. pavia* of southeastern United States. ZONES: 5-8. HABIT: Slow to moderate growth rate to 30-50 feet by 30 feet. Pyramidal when young, erect with round crown when mature.

A spectacular flowering tree at its best in midspring when it bears upright 8- to 10-inch-long red-to-pink flower spikes. Five-fingered leaves are light to dark bright green; tropical looking. A very manageable garden or street tree. Excellent for parks. Casts dense shade. Subject to leaf scorch in hot, dry winds; best in cool-

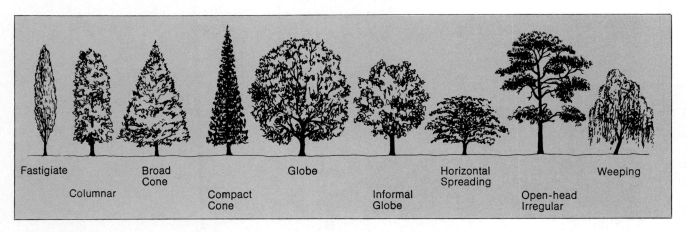

Fastigiate   Columnar   Broad Cone   Compact Cone   Globe   Informal Globe   Horizontal Spreading   Open-head Irregular   Weeping

moist summer areas and protected locations. 'Briotii' has bright red flowers in clusters up to 9 inches long.

Aesculus pavia. Red buckeye (Deciduous).
NATIVE TO: Eastern United States and Texas. ZONES: 5-8. HABIT: Slow to moderate growth rate to 30 feet. Round headed.

To quote William Flemer III, Princeton Nursery, Princeton, New Jersey, ''This native is one of our most colorful small trees. It blooms in mid-May, when it is full of rich red upright clusters of flowers. The foliage is a shiny, dark green color, compound with five leaflets, and unlike most other horse chestnuts it is immune to the disfiguring leaf scorch disease. It can be grown as a large shrub with several stems or it can be trimmed into a rounded, single-trunk tree. Unlike its larger relatives, it blooms very early in life, so the home gardener need not wait very long for the first display of flowers.''

Both *Aesculus carnea* and *Aesculus pavia* are more manageable for the street and home than either *Aesculus hippocastanum* or *Aesculus glabra,* the latter being the state tree of Ohio.

Ailanthus altissima. Tree-of-heaven (Deciduous).

NATIVE TO: China. BEST ADAPTED: Zones 5-9, can be grown 4-10. HABIT: Fast-growing with open broad form. Will eventually reach 60 feet with a spread of about 40 feet.

Long, 18-36-inch, dark green divided leaves, tinged brownish-red as they unfold, have a tropical look. Inconspicuous flowers are followed on female trees by incredible amounts of inedible, papery-winged, orange-red fruits that gradually turn light brown as they last through winter.

Seeds germinate everywhere. Suckers freely and widely. Start with one and, unless controlled, you'll end up with a thicket.

This is the ''tree that grows in Brooklyn.'' It is both praised and damned. It's a weed tree-chain saw tree to some observers, but where few trees can be grown, it is an excellent choice. Observing it in coastal

Acer — Maple

Variety (in size, foliage and color) is the key feature of the maples, both among and within the 90 species. Plant size ranges from 100-foot giants to low shrubs, while the leaves vary from broad 12-inch specimens to palmate ribbons 3 inches wide. White, yellow, many shades of green, pink, and maroon-red are found in the summer foliage, while the fall colors of yellow, orange, and red are legendary. Even the bark can be colorful: red, cinnamon, green-and-white-striped, and silver as well as the usual gray-brown.

Although maples are a varied lot, certain characteristics are true to all varieties: samaras (winged seeds), and opposite leaves and branches.

Maples are Northern Hemisphere trees found primarily in temperate climates with adequate rainfall. Only a few species occur in cold or hot areas. In dry areas, maples are associated with streams.

While some diseases such as verticillium wilt and nectria canker do occur, they are not virulent. Aphid drip may also be a problem. A more irritating problem for a gardener is the fertility of some species and cultivars. Wind disperses the samaras, or winged seeds, over a wide area. Fortunately, although most maples produce quantities of seed, only a few are exceptionally fertile.

Acer buergeranum — Trident maple.
The sharp, three-pointed leaves explain the common name of this 25-foot-tall, round headed maple. It often grows with multiple stems and branches low, but can be trained to a single stem and pruned for head clearance. The 3-inch leaves are glossy green, turning yellow to red in the fall. It grows in zones 6-8

A. campestre — Hedge maple. In its native Europe, this species is often trained as a hedge. A slow-to-medium growing tree to a height of 25-30 feet with a spread of 20-25 feet, useful as a small street tree. Although it grows best in well-drained soil, it will tolerate dry, poor, or sandy soils. The small 2- to 4-inch dull green leaves turn yellow in the fall. It will grow in zones 5-8.

A. ginnala — Amur maple. A native of Siberia, it is cold-tolerant (zones 3-8) and wind-tolerant. A broad oval or globe-shape, 20 feet tall and 20-feet wide, is the normal habit of this usually multiple-stemmed tree. Its fragrant flowers are a novelty among maples. Summer color is provided by the bright red fruit. Later the foliage also turns bright red. It is useful as a substitute for the Japanese maple in cold regions.

A. griseum — Paperbark maple. If propagation were easier, this would be one of the most popular of the small maples. Shiny, cinnamon-colored bark identifies this 25-foot, roundheaded tree that will grow in zones 5-8. Even the leaves are different,

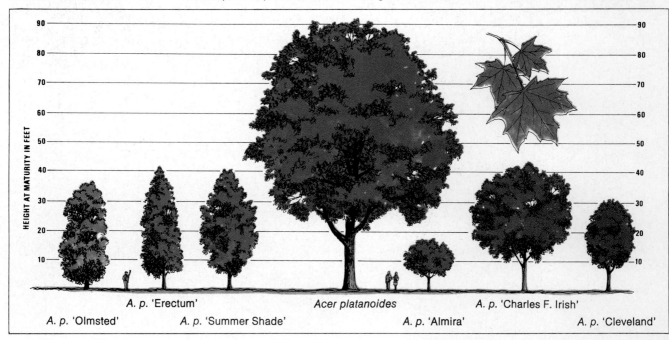

A. p. 'Olmsted'   A. p. 'Erectum'   A. p. 'Summer Shade'   Acer platanoides   A. p. 'Almira'   A. p. 'Charles F. Irish'   A. p. 'Cleveland'

areas, Raymond Korbobo of Rutgers University, Princeton, N.J. said, "When we really get close to the shore, you would throw your arms around this tree for its ability to grow, in spite of all odds, to relatively good size and in good condition, almost right down to the dunes."

Russell Beatty, Landscape Architect, University of California, Berkeley, theorizes that anyone who could find a sterile form of this tree should be offered $50,000. See his, "In defense of weed trees," page 110.

Albizia julibrissin. Silk tree, mimosa (Deciduous).
NATIVE TO: Asia, from Iran to Japan.
BEST ADAPTED: Zones 7-10, can be grown 6. HABIT: Fast to 25-40 feet, wider than high. Arching branches form a beautiful umbrellalike canopy, sometimes twice as wide as tall. Most useful multi-trunked.

Most beautiful in summer when the showy pink powder-pufflike flowers are held above the fernlike, almost feathery, light green leaves. Light-sensitive foliage folds at night.

Silk tree can be anything from a street tree to a hedge depending on how it's pruned. Prune so the branches begin at about 8 feet, and you have a pleasant umbrella. When pruned to branch near the ground the tree spreads low and wide. Excellent filtered shade for the patio, although falling leaves and seed pods that follow flowers should be considered. Good in a lawn, or plant in a container.

Because of the way the flowers are held above the foliage, they are best looked down on from a balcony or hill. Flowers best in high summer heat. Takes alkaline soils.

A note of caution from William Collins, American Garden-Cole, Circleville, Ohio, "It is popular with homeowners who, unfortunately, always seem to want to grow it just north of where it is reliably bloom-hardy."

'Rosea' with rich pink flowers is the hardiest form. 'Charlotte' and 'Tryon' are wilt-resistant. Besides wilt, other problems are short life, weak wood, and twig girdlers. Pruning will help relieve weight on wide-spreading branches.

having three leaflets instead of being lobed. The upper surface is dark green and the lower surface silver. Fall color is scarlet.

A. palmatum — Japanese maple.
An extremely variable species that can be a low mound or a slow-growing small tree 20 feet tall and 20 feet wide. The 2- to 4-inch leaves, which have 5-inch lobes, can be almost round with small lobes or little more than leaf veins. Leaf color ranges from yellow-green to dark maroon-red in solid colors and includes white and pink in variegated forms.

The color develops best in full sun but where hot, dry winds are a problem it may be necessary to grow this species in light shade. It will grow in protected areas of zone 5 as well as zones 6-8.

Some of the selected forms are: 'Atropurpureum' — one of the hardiest, which has five-lobed leaves that remain red all summer; 'Osakazuki' with 7-lobed green leaves and bright red fall color; 'Dissectum' — finely divided cutleaf forms available with green or red leaves; 'Senkaki' — a green-leafed type with coral bark that is very attractive in the winter landscape.

A. platanoides—Norway maple. Over 20 selections of this variable, hardy species (zone 3-7) have been named. Many were selected for growth form, others for foliage color. The yellow flowers produce a good display. The species will grow 40-50 feet tall with a 65-75 foot spread in cultivation, producing very dense shade. It has a vigorous surface root system so that growing grass or other plants beneath it is difficult.

'Cleveland' is quite columnar as a young tree, eventually forming a broad oval, 50 feet tall by 25-30 feet wide. The dark green leaves turn yellow in the fall.

'Crimson King' is probably the best-known variety of Norway maple. The leaves remain maroon-red throughout the season. Growth is somewhat slower than the green-leafed types, forming a tree 35-40 feet tall and 50 feet wide.

'Drummondii,' with white and green leaves, gives a cool appearance on a hot day, although the white areas are apt to burn. It will form a tree 40-50 feet tall by 35-45 feet wide.

'Emerald Queen' is a fast-growing selection with an upright, spreading form. It can be expected to grow 50 feet tall and 50 feet wide. One of the best cultivars for yellow fall color.

'Globe' is a very dense, spreading form. The ultimate height is determined by grafting height. When grafted at 6-7 feet, it will grow 20-25 feet tall and 35-45 feet wide. More susceptible to aphids than other cultivars.

'Summer Shade' is a fast-growing selection that should grow to 45-50 feet with a 60-70

A. platanoides 'Erectum'.

A. rubrum 'Bowhall'.

A. rubrum 'Red Sunset'.

Alnus glutinosa. Black or European alder (Deciduous).

NATIVE TO: Europe, North Africa, and Asia. ZONES: 3-9. HABIT: Fast growth to 40-50 feet, upright, irregular form.

A problem-solver where a quick effect is needed or soils are poorly drained. Rich, glossy-green leaves turn yellow in fall. Neither flowers nor fruit are particularly effective.

Best used in wet soils, near ponds or low-lying areas. Good quick screen. Attractive multi-trunked form in groves. Roots can be invasive with shallow irrigation.

William Collins describes 'Aurea' in, "Trees that need a friend" on pages 80-84.

Amelanchier.
Here's a tree that has many common names: saskatoon, serviceberry, sarviceberry, shadblow, shadbush, or juneberry. The botanist as well as the nurseryman is never sure which species you'll be offered. It doesn't make much difference. The trees hybridize readily.

Actually there are many amelanchiers: *A. arborea, A. alnifolia, A. canadensis, A* x *grandiflora, A. laevis,* and the list goes on. They are generally adapted to zones 5-8, with *A. alnifolia* being 1-5.

New experiments are being carried out, notably in western Canada, to select varieties with larger fruits.

Birds and tree lovers appreciate the amelanchiers. See "Trees that need a friend," pages 80 to 84.

Araucaria.
A group of trees that eventually become tall enough to provide an interesting outline on the skyline the year round.

Araucaria araucana. Monkey-puzzle tree (Needled Evergreen).

NATIVE TO: Chile. ZONES: 7-10. HABIT: Slow to moderate growth rate to 60-70 feet by 30-35 feet spread. Erect, pyramidal with branches in regular whorls.

More of an oddity than an effective landscape tree. Dark green, stiff, and sharp, the large needles arm the upward sweeping branches giving them a tubular look, often called exotic. Gets its name because, once

Acer — Maple

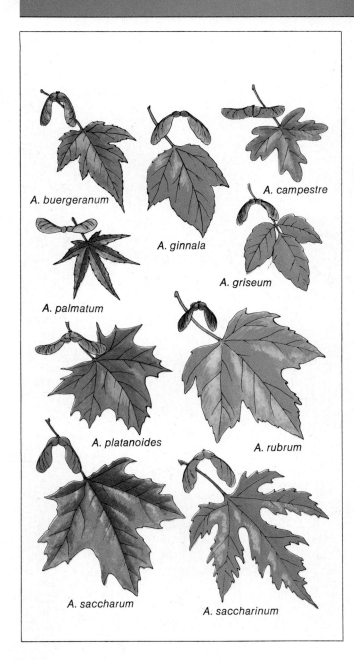

A. buergeranum
A. ginnala
A. palmatum
A. campestre
A. griseum
A. platanoides
A. rubrum
A. saccharum
A. saccharinum

foot spread. With heavy-textured leaves, it is more heat-tolerant than the species.

A. rubrum —
Red or swamp maple.
A fast-growing species with relatively small leaves, it does not produce as dense shade as the other large maples. The common names indicate two features of this species: its attractive, small red flowers in early spring, and its ability to grow in wet as well as normal soil, developing fall color under both conditions. When raised from northern seed, it is very hardy and grows in zones 4-9. The species normally develops as a symmetrical, spreading, pyramidal tree to a height of 50-60 feet and a spread of 40-60 feet. Many selections have been made for growth, form, and fall color.

'Autumn Flame' forms a roundheaded tree, 30-40 feet tall and wide. This selection consistently colors orange-red 1 to 2 weeks before the others. Leaf fall is also 1 to 2 weeks earlier. In areas of short growing seasons, fall color occurs before frost.

'Bowhall' is a narrow, pyramidal form, 45 feet tall and 15 feet wide that develops good fall color. It is useful near buildings and streets where spreading limbs could be hazardous. 'Scanlon' has the same characteristics and might be identical.

'Red Sunset' is also a broad, pyramidal tree, 50-60 feet tall and 30-40 feet wide. Heavy production of red flowers in spring and midseason and red

fall foliage make this one of the most colorful selections.

A. saccharinum —
Silver or soft maple.
Zones 4-9. A fast-growing tree with a broad, open crown 70 feet wide. Limb breakage in wind or ice storms is the problem with this species. Heat and dry winds have less adverse effect than on other maples, so it is used for quick shade where other trees fail. Some cities have prohibited planting silver maple as a street tree. Check local ordinances.

A. saccharum —
Sugar or rock maple.
Grown in the open, it forms a majestic tree 80-100 feet tall and 60-80 feet wide, with yellow-to-orange-to-red fall coloring. This maple, which supplies much of the fall color in New England, is the source of maple syrup and the lumber for maple furniture. It is a hardy tree adapted to zones 4-9, but does not grow well in inner city or hot, dry conditions.

The best selections of this species are the narrow columnar form: 'Newton Sentry,' which develops a central leader, and 'Temple's Upright,' which does not. Both were reported to be 50 feet tall and 12 feet wide after 40 and 75 years respectively at the Arnold Arboretum, Mass.

'Green Mountain' has the typical broad, oval shape of the species, but the dark green leaves are resistant to adverse conditions.

he's gotten up, it's the only tree a monkey can't climb down.

Needs room to develop; lower branches often die out. Likes a well-drained soil with lots of water. Like other araucarias, bears dangerously large cones, up to 13 to 15 pounds.

Araucaria bidwilli. Bunya-bunya (Needled Evergreen).

NATIVE TO: Australia. BEST ADAPTED: Zones 9-10, can be grown warmer parts of 8. HABIT: Moderate growth rate to 30-50 feet, spread 35-55 feet. Dense pyramidal, round top, broader with age.

Needles are dark green; sharp and stiff. Branches curving with upsweeping tips. Same culture and restrictions as monkey-puzzle tree. More widely used in the western United States.

Araucaria heterophylla. Norfolk Island pine (Needled Evergreen).

NATIVE TO: Norfolk Island (1000 miles east of Australia). BEST ADAPTED: Zone 10, can be grown 9. HABIT: Moderate growth rate to 60-70 feet, spreads half as wide. Formal pyramid with symmetrical branching in horizontal tiers.

Most widely known as a container tree in Victorian times. Recently reintroduced as an indoor plant. Legend has it that the tree was introduced by Captain Blight of "Mutiny on the Bounty" fame.

Truly a softly formal character. Gets quite large in the landscape. Possible as an indoor Christmas tree. Same culture and restrictions as other araucarias.

Arbutus unedo. Strawberry tree (Evergreen).

NATIVE TO: Mediterranean and Ireland. ZONES: 8-9. HABIT: Slow to moderate growth rate to 10-25 feet, spreads as wide as tall. Irregular rounding habit.

A handsome, shrubby plant that needs pruning shears to make a well-formed tree (suckers readily). Leaves are dark green with red stems. Small white urn-shaped flowers are followed by fruit that resemble strawberries.

The twisting, almost bonsailike habit of the tree becomes more attractive with age. Bark is smooth, deep-red to brownish red.

Best used when it can be looked up into; on the patio or lawn. Widely adaptable to soil and climate.

A. saccharum. *Sugar or rock maple.*

A. ginnala. *Amur maple.*

A. platanoides *'Globe'.*

A. palmatum. *Japanese maple.*

Betula. Birch.
Evaluated by John Ford, Secrest Arboretum, Wooster, OH. See page 38.

River Birch, *Betula nigra,* has received multiple endorsement from our authors and consultants. It is discussed by John Ford in "Trees that need a friend" on pages 80-84.

The messiest pest of birches is The honeydew-dripping aphid. Another pest, the bronze birch borer, can be damaging particularly to older birches. Read about controlling these pests on page 85.

The birch leafminer can be very damaging. Gray, paper, and European white birches are most susceptible. The damage they cause shows up as blotches or blisters on newly developing leaves. It's caused by the larva of the black sawfly as they feed between the two surfaces of the leaf. Look for them about the time the leaves are half open. There are later (but less damaging) generations, the second one appearing the end of June. The insecticides Cygon or Orthene can control these pests. Read the label for complete directions.

Carpinus betulus. European hornbeam (Deciduous).

NATIVE TO: Europe and Asia Minor. ZONES: 5-9. HABIT: Most available and preferred variety is 'Fastigiata.' Slow to moderate growth, 30-40 feet by 10-15 feet. Dense pyramidal form.

Neat, manageable, attractive tree with dark green, elmlike foliage and smooth gray bark. Yellow fall color. Dead leaves retained until spring. Interesting nutlike fruit clusters.

Consistently scores in the top five at the Shade Tree Evaluation Plot, Wooster, Ohio. One of the best trees for hedges and screens (see hedges page 40). Excellent street tree.

Stands soils from dry and rocky to wet but well-drained. Tolerant of air pollution. Sold in the trade as 'Fastigiata' and 'Pyramidalis.' 'Columnaris' is very similar, but more spreading.

Carpinus caroliniana, an American native, has many of the same good qualities, is slightly hardier, and is

---

Trees that look good in a grove

A grove is a group of trees in an open area. It is usually made up of one type of tree, which can be found in a pure stand somewhere in nature. Groves can provide pleasure when seen from a distance, and a tranquil or overwhelming emotional experience up close. Dramatic groves are those of large-growing trees that have prominent trunks and branches and a high foliage canopy such as birch, hemlock, aspen, beech, oak, and pine. Often the trunks of the trees emphasize strong vertical lines. Sunlight coming through the high canopy produces a soft lighting effect that gives some people the impression of being in an outdoor cathedral. People come to groves to rest and meditate and also to picnic and play. Groves can also be groupings of smaller trees, planted for visual effects that suggest larger groves.

Fagus grandifolia. *American beech.*

Nyssa sylvatica. *Sour gum.*

A grove of pines. The trunks emphasize strong vertical lines.

more colorful in the fall. Praised by Kissida and Gould in "Trees that need a friend" (see pages 80-84).

Carya.
Two of the most valuable dual-purpose, trees, the hickory and the pecan, belong to this genus.

Carya illinoinensis. Pecan (Deciduous).

NATIVE TO: Southeastern United States. ZONES: 7-9. HABIT: Moderate growth to 100 feet with an equal spread and rounded crown.

This great native tree needs no praise from us. No tree in the southern landscape contributes more as a shade tree and a food tree. It has held its place in the affection of home gardeners in spite of its suceptibility to diseases — notably scab. Symptoms of scab are round or irregular olive-brown to black spots on leaves and young twigs, and small, dark, circular spots on husks of the nut.

Since the backyard orchardist is not likely to have his tree sprayed, scab resistance is a more important factor for him in variety selection than it is in a commercial orchard.

The Auburn University Gulf Coast Agricultural Substation at Fairhope, Alabama, recommends 'Chickasaw' and 'Kaddo,' among others, as scab-resistant.

In the alkaline soils of arid Texas, pecans should be sprayed for zinc deficiency. Check with your local agricultural extension agent.

Carya ovata. Shagbark hickory (Deciduous).

NATIVE TO: Southeastern United States. ZONES: 5-9. HABIT: Moderate growth rate to 70-80 feet. Irregular oval head.

Like the pecan, a valuable dual-purpose tree. Long yellowish-green leaves, divided into many leaflets, turn yellow in fall. Bark on old trees is attractively shaggy. Nuts ripen from September to October.

Casuarina cunninghamia.
Beefwood, river she-oak (Evergreen).

NATIVE TO: Queensland and New South Wales. ZONES: 9, 10. HABIT: Fast rate of growth to 70 feet. Pinelike with spreading, drooping branches.

A rugged tree, valuable for quick effects. Good on the coast. Long, thin

Populus tremuloides. *Quaking aspen.*

branches with leaves that look like needles. Woody, grayish, conelike fruit. Picturesque silhouette.

Catalpa.

Fast-growing, tough American natives known for their large leaves, beautiful flowers, and ability to stand adverse conditions.

Catalpa bignonioides. Common or southern catalpa, Indian bean, cigar tree (Deciduous).
NATIVE TO: Southeastern United States. ZONES: 5-9. HABIT: Fast-growing to 35-40 feet, spreads nearly as wide. Irregular, broad, rounded crown.

When grown in full sun, it is covered with white trumpet-shaped flowers in late spring to early summer. Flowers are spotted with yellow, purple, and

brown. Blooms are followed by long 13- to 18-inch bean pods which last into winter and can be a nuisance in a lawn. Pods were smoked by Indians, hence the name, Indian bean, or cigar tree. Large heart-shaped leaves.

Widely adapted to soils and climates. Stands city smog. Best used in large areas to accent bold features. Can be drastically pollarded.

Catalpa speciosa. Northern or western catalpa (Deciduous).
NATIVE TO: Eastern United States. ZONES: 5-9. HABIT: Fast-growing to 65-75 feet in 75 years at Secrest Arboretum, Wooster, Ohio. Round headed.

Very similar to *C. bignonioides,* but has larger leaves, fewer flowers and is slightly hardier. It is also larger and

should be used with discretion in small areas.

Cedar. Cedar

Many trees are called cedars. Here we evaluate the true cedars.

Cedrus atlantica. Atlas cedar (Needled evergreen).
NATIVE TO: Middle East and North Africa. BEST ADAPTED: Zones 7-10, can be grown 6. HABIT: Slow to moderate to 40-60 feet by 30-40 feet. Irregular pyramidal when young; wide pyramidal to open, with broadly spreading crown at maturity.

Fine-textured, bluish-green needles in stiff clusters. Picturesque growth habit becomes most spectacular with room and time to mature. Moderately drought resistant. Unsuitable for small

Betula — Birch

The birches are mixed up in nomenclature and through hybridization. The taxonomists have been having a holiday naming and renaming them, adding to the confusion. Below, we list the names of the birches as they appear in "Hortus II." Any changes in "Hortus III" are shown in parentheses.

In general, the white birches *(B. pubescens, B. papyrifera,* and *B. pendula)* are trees of the North. With the exception of *Betula nigra,* birch do not thrive too far south of their hardiness zones except at high elevations. There is evidence in pollen determinations, etc., that birch trees followed the glaciers — being forced south, and then following them back north again. Many birches are found in the Arctic, where they are only a few inches high. There are large areas of birch forest in the north country, not only in North America, but in Europe and Asia. To many people from the northern countries, birch is the hardwood tree they know best.

Betula pendula (often sold as *B. verrucosa,* or *B. alba)—* European white birch. Grows on drier sites than *B. pubescens.* Normal expected height would be about 60 feet. It is distinguished from *B. pubescens* by its rough, warty twigs and the white bark with vertical black markings. Older trees have pendulous branches. Zones 2-5. Some common cultivars are:

Pyramidal European white birch, *Betula pendula* 'Fastigiata.' Columnar and dense when young.

Cutleaf European white birch. *Betula pendula* 'Gracilis.' A finely dissected leaf.

Slender European white birch, *Betula pendula* 'Tristis.' A tall, graceful tree with slender pendulous branches.

Betula pubescens — Hairy birch.
Zones 1-4. Grows to 60 feet tall in northern Europe into Siberia. A variable species with many geographical forms. It differs from *B. pendula,* as its bark is more reddish and the twigs are smooth and downy, hence the name hairy birch. White bark on the trunks has horizontal markings.

Betula populifolia — Gray birch.
Zones 4, 5. Short-lived to 30 feet. A pioneer tree. Grows in full sun. Has a natural tendency to clump and is best used that way. Very similar to *B. pendula.*

Betula nigra — River birch.
Zones 5-9. This is the birch of the South, and the most widely adapted. Young bark is red, gradually becoming an attractive, shaggy, chocolate-brown with age.

Betula papyrifera — Paper birch.
Zones 3-5. Very similar to *B. pendula,* but more open and erect. Reaches 40 to 60 feet. The peeling bark is used by Indians to make canoes.

Betula alleghaniensis — Yellow birch.
Zones 4-7. A versatile tree that deserves to be better known. Widely adapted, reaches 90 to

100 feet though usually smaller. Name derives from the yellowish cast on the bark of young trees. Darkens and peels with age.

In the north country, the birch is often called "the lady of the forest." Its white bark brings a lively grace to a group of needled evergreens, and in

the winter, its white bark and blue-gray branches provide a cheerful and colorful contrast to the typical dark brown of other leafless trees.

The natural habit of the birch is to grow in clumps of several trees. Clump planting is suggested as a variation on the typical spacing of 6 feet.

B. pendula. *European white birch*

B. alleghaniensis. *Yellow birch.*

B. nigra. *River Birch.*

B. nigra. *Young river birch (see copy).*

city lots, but excellent in parks, large gardens, or planted along a wide boulevard. A fine skyline tree. Wherever it can be grown, the atlas cedar, is the most popular of the blue-foliaged conifers. The cultivar 'Glauca' has the richest foliage.

Cedrus deodara. Deodar cedar (Needled evergreen).
NATIVE TO: The Himalayas. BEST ADAPTED: Zones 8-10, can be grown 7. HABIT: Fast to 40-60 feet by 20-30 feet.

Most refined, graceful and softest-textured cedar. Lower branches sweep to the ground; upper branches evenly spaced and well pronounced. The green foliage is in typical cedar clusters but not as stiff. Fastest growing of the cedars.

Nodding tip one of the most recognizable features on the skyline.

Can be used as a screen, but there are better choices. Good in parks. Like other cedars, needs space to be appreciated, but responds to pruning for confinement.

The last of the true cedars is *Cedrus libani,* the cedar of Lebanon, which was admired by King Solomon 3000 years ago when he said, "Now therefore command thou that they hew me cedar trees out of Lebanon." Very similar to *Cedrus atlantica* but has bright green foliage, is slower growing and hardier (zone 6).

Celtis. Hackberry.
There are two hackberries common to the eastern United States: *Celtis laevi-* gata, the sugarberry, or Mississippi hackberry, and the common hackberry, *Celtis occidentalis.* Both are tough trees, standing drought, hot dry wind and city conditions.

Celtis laevigata. Sugar hackberry, Mississsppi hackberry (Deciduous).
NATIVE TO: South central and southeastern United States. ZONES: 5-9. HABIT: Slow to moderate growth rate to 30-50 feet, spread slightly narrower than height.

Dr. L. C. Chadwick of Ohio writes that the *Celtis laevigata,* the sugar hackberry, is "an upright, spreading tree of about 50 feet at maturity. The bark of the trunk and larger branches is gray, like that of the American beech. Normal foliage is dark green with little change in fall color. Tolerant

B. pendula 'Gracilis'. Cutleaf European white birch.

B. pendula 'Fastigiata'. Pyramidal European white birch.

B. papyifera. Paper birch.

B. nigra. River birch.

B. pendula 'Youngii'. Young's weeping birch.

of a wide range of soil conditions. Much less susceptible to 'witches' broom' than the common hackberry.''

Celtis occidentalis. Common hackberry (Deciduous).
NATIVE TO: Central and southeastern United States. BEST ADAPTED: Zones 5-8, can be grown 3, 4. HABIT: Moderate growth rate to 35-45 feet, spread as wide as tall. Irregular to round-headed; spreading, sometimes pendulous branches.

The common hackberry has bright green leaves with finely toothed edges and dark red berries that attract birds. Its one drawback is ''witches' broom,'' a foliage and branch deformation. There appear to be great possibilities for selection of resistant cultivars, as exhibited by the recent introduction 'Prairie Pride.'

A valuable shade tree in tough situations. Used in shelter belts in the Great Plains.

Cercidiphyllum japonicum. Katsura (Deciduous).
NATIVE TO: Japan. ZONES: 4-8. HABIT: Slow growth rate to 40 feet or more, slightly narrower than tall.

Trained as a single-trunked tree, it is upright and narrow, but spreading and vase-shaped with age. Left multi-trunked, it is broad and spreading, branching upward and outward — an excellent tree for filtered shade.

Leaves are lustrous reddish to reddish-purple in spring when they first unfold. In the summer, foliage is neat and crisp. Dark green, heart-shaped leaves showing tints of red, turn scarlet and gold in the fall. Small, dry fruit capsules provide winter ornamentation. Pest-free. Tolerant of moist soil and shade but needs protection from hot sun and drying winds.

C. magnificum is a similar relative with wider leaves.

Cercis canadensis. Eastern redbud (Deciduous).
NATIVE TO: Southern Canada and eastern United States. BEST ADAPTED: Zones 5-7, can be grown 4-8. HABIT: Fast growth to 25-35 feet as wide as it is high with irregular round head and attractive horizontally-tiered branches.

Best known for its pinkish-red, pea-shaped flowers that bloom on bare branches in spring, about the same time as the dogwood — a good combination. All-seasons performer; attractive, green, heart-shaped leaves, yellow fall color, interesting seed pods,

---

Trees for hedges

Frank Mackaness, Schmidt & Son Co., Boring, Oregon, talks of his experiences with trees that can be trimmed into hedges:

"Surprisingly, our local hemlock, *Tsuga heterophylla,* normally a forest tree, makes an excellent hedge. Many years ago; at the Wind River Experiment Station, trees were planted 2 feet apart in a row. All were kept clipped except one specimen adjacent to each gate post. The last time I saw the planting the hedge was still a neat 5 feet and the unclipped specimens were 30 feet!

"English yew *(Taxus baccata)* is by far the most useful hedge plant around Portland, Oregon. It is hardy, pest- and disease-free, needs clipping only once a year (in August) to keep it tidy and within bounds.

"Hawthorn *(Crataegus oxycantha* or *Crataegus laevigata)* and English holly *(Ilex aquifolium)* make a marvelous, stock-proof fence. At intervals of 6 inches, plant 5 hawthorn seedlings, then one holly; repeat for length of desired hedge. Keep them clipped so they grow bushy. Allow them to increase in height a little each year until about 6 feet and you have a permanent, impenetrable hedge that is functional and good-looking. Port Orford Cedar *(Chamaecyparis lawsoniana)* can be clipped without reducing its height. I have seen clipped hedges of this — bordering a driveway for a mile or more — 30 feet high. Magnificent!

"European beech *(Fagus sylvatica)* and the hornbeam *(Carpinus betulus)* both make marvelous hedges. Maintain them at a width of 2 feet and a height of 8 feet. Plant the trees 2 feet apart in a row. The beauty of these species is that they are deciduous, so you get clean, fresh foliage every year. Foliage turns a lovely russet in the fall and hangs on until the new leaves push off the old ones in spring. So there is never a "see through" or naked season.

"Privet — several ligustrum species are used for hedges and I despise them all because of their propensity for getting buggy.

"Cherry laurel *(Prunus laurocerasus* 'Pyramidalis')* makes a fine and very useful hedge of handsome proportions. It is used widely in the Deep South — southern Louisiana and the other Gulf States.

"Tamarisk *(Tamarix gallica)* is an interesting hedge for use close to the coast. It is tolerant of salt air from the ocean, collects the salt on its feathery foliage, and drips brine (when it rains), effectively weed-killing the ground beneath so that the hedge bottom is always clean.

"Hogan's cedar *(Thuja plicata* 'Fastigiata'), a variety of Western red cedar, can be shaped into a bold but neat hedge. Osage orange *(Maclura pomifera)* was used for years in the Middle West for farm hedges. It is excellent if (a) space is no problems (b) you never have to dig it out yourself.

"Mock orange *Pittosporum tobira* and the small tree *Escallonia vubra macrantha* are two good hedge plants for mild areas.

"Tallhedge *(Rhamnus frangula* 'Columnaris') is a tall, narrow shrub that will be less than 2 feet thick when 20 feet tall. It is apt to get leggy and leafless at the base. When it does, cut it down to the ground and let it sprout up again. It is lush in no time and as useful as ever.''

Crataegus oxycantha. English hawthorn.

and attractive reddish-brown bark in winter.

Will grow in sun and shade, acid or alkaline, and moist soils. One of the best trees on the patio, in containers, or anywhere space is limited.

'Forest Pansy' has beautiful purple foliage, best viewed where light can shine through. Red branches. Highly praised by observers throughout the East. 'Oklahoma' has dark red flowers and shiny foliage. Best redbud for high heat and alkaline soils. 'Alba' has white flowers. Susceptible to fire-blight and borers (see page 85).

Chamaecyparis.

A large group of plants. The following are useful as wall trees, lawn speci-mens, and especially as screens or tall hedges. Good tub trees when young. Best adapted to cool coastal conditions, but can take heat if protected from hot, dry winds. Best in moist, well-drained soil. Will take some drought.

Chamaecyparis lawsoniana. Port Orford cedar, Lawson cypress (Needled Evergreen).

NATIVE TO: Southwest Oregon and north-west California. BEST ADAPTED: Zones 6-9, can be grown 5. HABIT: Moderate growth rate to 60-70 feet and a third as wide. Pyramidal with wide-spreading pendulous branches.

A very graceful tree. Branches end in lacy sprays of bright green to blue-green. Scale-like leaves, nodding tip. Soft brown to reddish-brown fibrous bark.

Many varieties available, varying in form and foliage color. Some with widest adaptations include narrow, pyramidal 'Allumii,' with metallic-blue new growth to 30 feet, 'Ellwoodii,' which reaches 8 feet and has silvery-blue foliage, and 'Lutea,' to 30 feet with yellow new foliage.

Chamaecyparis obtusa. Hinoki false cypress (Needled Evergreen).

NATIVE TO: Japan. ZONES 4-9. HABIT: Slow growth to 40-50 feet, spreads 15-25 feet with pyramidal shape.

Foliage is deep, shiny green in thick, horizontally-flattened sprays. Branch tips slightly pendulous.

Many varieties, including useful dwarf forms, are usually more avail-able than the species. Favorites in-

Fagus sylvatica. *Weeping European beech.*

Tamarix gallica. *Tamarisk.*

Above: Pittosporum tobira.
Left: Carpinus betulus *'Fastigiata.' Hornbeam.*

clude 'Crippsii,' with golden new growth, which reaches a height of 30 feet, 'Gracilis,' with very dark, shiny green foliage and somewhat weeping form, which grows to 20 feet by 4-5 feet, and 'Nana Gracilis,' which grew only 9 feet in 66 years at the Secrest Arboretum, Wooster, Ohio.

Chamaecyparis pisifera. Sawara false cypress (Needled Evergreen).

NATIVE TO: Japan. ZONES: 4-9. HABIT: Slow growth to 58 feet in 68 years at Secrest Arboretum, Wooster, Ohio. Pyramidal, spreads half as wide.

Less dense than *Chamaecyparis obtusa.* Loosely arranged, scale-like leaves are bright, glossy green. Loses lower branches early in life, revealing reddish-brown bark, peeling in long strips. Inner branches often die out; encourage new growth with annual pruning.

Many varieties. Some favorites include 'Filifera,' which reaches 20 feet and has long, green, drooping, thread-like young branches (good in oriental gardens) and 'Plumosa,' which reaches 20-30 feet and has a bright green, feathery appearance.

Chionanthus virginicus. Fringe tree (Deciduous).

NATIVE TO: Southeast United States. BEST ADAPTED: Zones 5-9, can be grown 4. HABIT: Slow growing to 20-30 feet with a round crown.

One of our showiest natives. Foliage is heavy textured and bold, almost suggesting a magnolia; it turns yellow in autumn. Late to show its foliage and flowers in the spring, missing late frosts.

Dependable spring bloomer; white threadlike petals form delicate, fleecy clusters. Pendulous clusters of dark blue berries on female trees are a lasting feature in the fall and early winter.

A good tree for a small property, especially near the patio. Deep-rooted and multi-trunked, almost more of a shrub than a tree, it requires special shaping or training if a tree form is desired.

Chionanthus retusus, Chinese fringe tree, a native of China, is slightly smaller (20 feet), less ornamental but has larger flowers and wider adaptation in warmer climates.

Cornus — Dogwood

The dogwoods include plants that range in size from the 6-to 9-inch bunchberry of the northern woodlands to the Pacific dogwoods, which may grow 70 feet or more in height. The shrubby tree dogwoods have some of the showiest flowers, and are among the finest of all flowering trees.

Technically speaking, the spectacular dogwoods have composite blooms. The true flowers are yellow and small, clustered in a tight bundle in the center and surrounded by four (or sometimes 6) white or pink bracts, which look like the petals of a very large flower. They require heat and late summer drought in order to mature the twigs and set abundant flower buds for the next spring.

In general, dogwoods require a slightly acid soil with moderate moisture and good fertility, and they will grow well in full sun or semi-shade.

The dogwoods that grow to tree size are divided into two groups; those with petal-like bracts surrounding a central cluster of true flowers and having their leaves placed opposite each other on the twigs, and those with alternate leaves and flat heads of tiny, white flowers like viburnum blooms.

An example of the second group is *Cornus alternifolia,* also called pagoda dogwood. It is less showy than the species with large bracts, but it is far hardier (zone 3), and is useful in the harsh climate of the midwestern states and adjacent southern portions of Canada. The branches are arranged in distinct, flat tiers, like many other dogwoods, the white flowers are attractive, and the fall color is good. There is a variety with white variegation, but the leaves burn badly in summer heat.

In zone 5 and farther south, a similar, but much preferable species called the giant dogwood *(Cornus controversa),* from Japan and China, is well worth planting. It is also alternate leafed, has huge flat branches with white flowers in May, and lustrous foliage that turns red in the fall. Unfortunately, it is very rare in the nursery trade.

Flowering dogwood, *Cornus florida,* is a lovely little tree, seldom exceeding 30 feet in height, and is surely the queen of them all. It grows wild in an enormous range from Massachusetts to Florida, and west to southern Ontario, Texas, and Mexico. Hardiness varies according to seed source (see page 112). Having been admired and cultivated for so long, many unusual plants have been selected and propagated, so there is an abundance of named selections in the nursery trade. Not all of these really merit naming and only the most distinctive will be discussed below.

The flowering dogwood is a tree with many seasons of interest. The display of flowers in the spring is wonderfully showy. In the fall, the leaves turn a rich brocade of red and crimson. The berries, borne in clusters, are a rich, glossy red, and often persist long after the leaves have fallen. Even in winter, the layered "oriental" branching habit and the myriads of conspicuous flattened flower buds are decorative, especially after a fall of clinging snow. The following selections are among the best of their kind. They are listed in alphabetical order.

'Cherokee Chief' is a relatively new, red-flowering dogwood from Tennessee. It has a much deepened, richer red color than the older *C. florida rubra,* a pink flowering dogwood. The young foliage is also a much more pronounced red in color, so much so that 'Cherokee Chief' can be distinguished from other kinds when not in bloom. Unfortunately, being of Tennessee origin, it is not as winter hardy as the old original pink dogwood which comes from Pennsylvania. In particular, the flower buds are easily injured by cold and, in the north, many malformed flowers with only two bracts instead of the normal four result. In the south it is a fine tree, far superior to the original selection.

'Cherokee Princess' is another variety of southern origin, selected for its abundant white flowers borne even when it is a young tree. It will set many flower buds when only two-years-old in contrast to white dogwoods of seedling origin which may take as long as 10 years to come into bloom. It is a faster and more shapely grower than other grafted strains of white dogwood and just as good a bloomer, all of which makes it hard to surpass in the southern part of the dogwood range.

'Cloud Nine' is an extremely profuse bloomer from Alabama, which is noted for the many flowers borne on even a young tree. It is slow-growing and smaller than most of the other varieties at maturity, which makes it a fine choice for planting wherever space is limited. It is of southern origin and not hardy in areas with cold winters (zone 4).

'Fragrant Cloud' is another white-flowering variety that originated in Tennessee. The delicate fragrance is detectable on a warm day.

'New Hampshire' is one of the hardiest of all the selections of *Cornus florida* and blooms regularly each year in southern Vermont and New Hampshire, where it originated. It "burns up" in the hot southern summers, but it grows well and blooms profusely throughout zone 4, where the lovely southern varieties are not winter-hardy. It is a first choice for planting in southern Canada and the northern tier of states.

Of the many pink forms, one with especially rich color was discovered early, propagated, and named the red flowering dogwood — *Cornus florida rubra.* Its color varies somewhat depending on the soil in which it is grown and the age of the flowers, but newly opened flowers are often a

Chrysolarix amabilis. (Pseudolarix kaempferi). Golden larch (Deciduous conifer).

A beautiful tree praised by John Ford in "Trees that need a friend," pages 80-84.

Cinnamomum camphora.
Camphor tree (Evergreen).

NATIVE TO: China, Japan. ZONES: 8, 9, 12-24. HABIT: Slow-growing to 50 feet or more with wider spread. Round-headed, with limbs spreading upward.

A tree for dense shade. Attractive, aromatic, shiny yellow-green foliage often contrasted with reddish new leaves. Yellow flower clusters are fragrant, though not showy. Does poorly on heavy, alkaline soils. Makes a good street tree if given room.

Cladrastis lutea. Yellowwood (Deciduous).

NATIVE TO: North Carolina and Kentucky. BEST ADAPTED: Zones 3-6, can be grown 7-9. HABIT: Moderate growth rate to 30-35 feet, spreads 20-25 feet. Upright, with spreading branches forming a vase-shaped crown.

William Flemer, III, President of Princeton Nurseries, Princeton, N.J. says this: "It has attractive, smooth gray bark like a beech, and clean foliage that turns clear yellow in fall. Its crowning glory, however, is the wonderful show of pure white, intensely fragrant flowers, pea-shaped and borne in clusters like white wisteria in June. Heavy flowering tends to occur in alternate years and in a good year it is a wonderful experience. Should be planted more."

Brown pods and zigzagging branches are of winter interest. Good lawn, patio, or park tree, although it won't bloom until it's 10 years old.

Withstands prolonged drought, heat and extreme cold. Tolerates alkaline, and wet soils.

Cornus. Dogwood.
Evaluated by William Flemer III, Princeton Nurseries, Princeton, NJ, on page 42.

Kousa dogwood, *Cornus kousa,* is multiply endorsed by our authors and consultants.

A serious disease of dogwood in the eastern states is canker. Recently transplanted or injured trees are most susceptible. Read more about canker disease on page 85.

clear, full red. Most admired when it is planted in combination with white-flowering specimens.

Japanese dogwood, *Cornus kousa,* closely rivals our native *Cornus florida* for the title of the most beautiful flowering small tree. It is described by John Copeland in "Trees that need a friend." There is also *Cornus kousa chinensis* from China, which has wider leaves and broader, overlapping floral bracts. Its thicker leaves make it more scorch-resistant in summer droughts.

Like the Japanese dogwood, 'Summer Stars' has long-lasting flowers. It was discovered in a garden on Long Island, N.Y. The floral bracts of the parent tree last unblemished for two full months. Trees grafted from the parent tree and grown inland do not retain their flowers in perfect condition as long, but they do last longer than the flowers of ordinary trees of seedling origin. Happily, 'Summer Stars' is an exceptionally profuse bloomer as well, and young specimens begin to bloom heavily several years before seedling trees bear even the first flower.

Cornus mas. Cornelian cherry, is a very hardy (zone 4). drought-tolerant small tree that is not readily recognized as a dogwood. The floral bracts are small and inconspicuous, while the cluster of yellow true flowers in the center is the showy part of the inflorescence. It blooms in early April, and makes a good show of clear yellow. The bright red edible fruits are pendulous, borne on stems like cherries. They ripen in late August. There are selections with very large berries that are grown as fruit trees in Russia.

Flowers of Cornus florida. *Flowering dogwood.*

Pink flowering dogwood.

Form of C. florida.

Combination plantings add beauty to any landscape.

Borers are sometimes dogwood problems. They are also discussed on page 85.

Cotinus coggygria. Smoke tree (Deciduous).
NATIVE TO: Southern Europe, central China. ZONES: 5-8. HABIT: Moderate to fast growth to 15-25 feet, equal spread. Broad urn-shape with rounded top.

Actually a shrub, but a little pruning can produce an attractive multi-trunked tree form. Although it blooms at the beginning of summer, the feathery masses of fine-textured inflorescense that develop fine hairs as they fade, give the tree a smokelike appearance throughout the entire summer. Normal leaf color is blue-green. Varieties that complement their bloom with purple foliage include 'Velvet Cloak' and 'Royal Purple.' All have excellent orange-red fall color.

Good patio tree or planted in groups. Widely adaptable but prefers good drainage. Blooms best in infertile, dry soils. Drought-tolerant. Easy to grow.

Crataegus. Hawthorn.
William Flemer III, Princeton Nurseries, Princeton, New Jersey discusses this genus on page 44.

Cryptomeria japonica. Japanese cedar (Needled Evergreen).
NATIVE TO: Japan and China. ZONES: 7-9. HABIT: Moderate to 70-90 feet and half as wide. Pyramidal, open form; rounded top with age.

The small, light green to bluish-green needles and drooping branches combine to give this tree a soft, graceful look. The needles pick up a bronze tinge in winter. Reddish-brown bark peels in strips.

Needs room to develop, eventually reaching skyline status. Good park tree. Likes ample water, a well-drained deep soil, and resents arid climates. Relatively pest-free.

'Elegans' is best described by its often-used common name, plume cedar. Soft, feathery foliage turns coppery-bronze in winter. Slow-growing to a 20-25 foot dense pyramid. Many other cultivars available, including dwarf forms.

Cunninghamia lanceolata. China fir (Needled Evergreen).
NATIVE TO: China. BEST ADAPTED: Zones 7-9, can be grown 5-6. HABIT:

Crataegus — Hawthorn

The hawthorns, the toughest of our flowering trees, form a group of quite similar, thorny, small trees which grow on every continent in the northern hemisphere. With very few exceptions, they all bear white flowers, have showy red or orange fruits, and thrive even in adverse situations: in the inner city, along highways, and at the seashore where salt spray is a hazard to most trees. They are particularly useful for making trespasser-proof hedges where vandalism is a problem, as their sharp thorns will deter even the most determined intruder. Compared to crabapples and cherries, they are difficult to transplant but, once established, they are long-lived and permanent. They bloom in late May after most of the spectacular spring-flowering trees have faded. Many species have fine glossy foliage and the fruits of most are exceptionally long lasting. Their picturesque and wide-spreading habit make them a landscape asset even in the midst of winter. Of the dozens of valid species, the following are among the best for the home garden or city park:

Crataegus crus-galli, cockspur thorn, is one of the toughest of all the species; flat-headed when mature and considerably broader than tall. The fruits are red and long-lasting. The foliage is very glossy, dark green in summer, and orange to scarlet in the fall. It is exceptionally well-adapted to shearing, forming a dense thorny hedge. There is a thornless variety, *C. c. inermis,* which makes a good tree for the small city garden where few other kinds of flowering trees will even survive, let alone thrive. It is hardy in zone 4.

Crataegus lavallei, Lavalle hawthorn, is hardy in zone 5. The flowers are large and abundant and the foliage is glossy green in summer and bronzy-red in the fall. The orange to red fruits last well into the winter.

Crataegus monogyna 'Stricta,' columnar single seed hawthorn, is one of the two species of hawthorns native to England and Europe. Millions of them are used as an understock for the grafted varieties and as a hedge plant. This columnar variety is one of the best narrow trees for urban situations, growing to a height of 35 feet, but only 8 to 9 feet in width. It is hardy in zone 5, is almost completely thornless, and bears single white flowers in small clusters in late May.

Crataegus oxyacantha (C. laevigata), English hawthorn, is the other abundant European species, the most common country hedge plant throughout England. It is also the most variable of all the hawthorns: single and double-flowered trees have been found with white, pink, and red flowers. Unfortunately, the species does poorly in summer heat and humidity. The leaves, being subject to fungus diseases, drop off to leave the twigs bare during most of the summer months. These problems do not seem to be serious along the Pacific Coast where the summers are cool and dry, and even the varieties which are poorest in the East, like 'Paulii,' hold their foliage throughout the summer. The wild species has little to offer our gardens, but some of the varieties are the most beautiful of all hawthorns.

'Alba Plena' is a small (15-foot), wide-spreading tree bearing myriads of double, pure white flowers in late May. Sterile, they last a long time, gradually turning a pale pink. It is a very sparse fruiter, but holds its foliage quite well in the East.

'Autumn Glory' is noted for its very large and long-lasting red fruits. It grows rapidly and reaches 18 feet in height, bearing single white flowers in May. It is hardy in Zone 5.

'Crimson Cloud,' a recent introduction, is the best of the hawthorns with colored flowers for eastern conditions. It bears clouds of bright crimson flowers, each with a white star in the center to give it sparkle. The foliage is leathery, fine textured, and, best of all, highly resistant to leaf spot disease. It grows into a tall, oval tree, 20 feet in height and thrives under city conditions from Zone 4 south. The fruits are glossy red and last well into the winter.

'Paulii,' Paul's scarlet hawthorn is certainly one of the most beautiful varieties wherever the climate suits it. The flowers are fully double and an intense rosy-red color, but are not followed by fruit. It makes a full, rounded tree, hardy in the warmest portions of Zone 4.

Crataegus punctata, the dotted hawthorn, is a hardy native species with attractive silvery bark and abundant fruit. It is one of the few

C. phaenopyrum   *C.o.* 'Autumn Glory'   *C. crus-galli*   *C. orientalis*

Slow to moderate growth to 50-60 feet high by 20-30 feet wide. Pyramidal, branches to the ground.

Distinctive looking conifer. Sharp, stiff, needlelike leaves arranged spirally on the twigs; pale green on top, whitish beneath. Heavy, spreading branches with pendulous twigs and pale color give the tree its character. Picks up a reddish-bronze tint in winter. Attractive cinnamon-brown bark.

Retained dead leaves may be unattractive to some. The odd, round cones form at the end of the branches and often persist several years, when they end up looking as if they had grown from the middle of the twig. Takes alkaline soil. Should be protected from hot, dry winds. Used as a hedge or screen.

'Glauca,' with attractive gray-green foliage is hardier. Used as a southern substitute for the Colorado blue spruce.

Cupressocyparis leylandii.
(Needled Evergreen).
HYBRID: *Chamaecyparis nootkatensis* and *Cupressus macrocarpa*. ZONES: 6-10. HABIT: Fast to 40-50 feet. Columnar, loosely pyramidal with age.

One of the best fast-growing columnar plants for tall hedges and screens. Growth rate reports range from 3 to 5 feet a year.

Graceful branching pattern in horizontal fans of gray-green foliage. Dense when young.

Needs room to develop if used by itself. Tolerates a wide range of soils and climates.

Cupressus sempervirens. Italian
cypress (Needled Evergreen).
NATIVE TO: Southern Europe and Western Asia. ZONES: 8-10. HABIT: Fast 30-40 feet by 3-6 feet. A strict vertical column.

A dominant vertical element in any landscape, and must be used with caution. Too stiff and formal for anything but a large garden or driveway approach. Too many people use them thinking they will stay small but they soon get out of scale.

Tolerates a wide range of soil and drought conditions. Scale-like, dull green leaves are borne on horizontal branches.

Several cultivars are more available than the species. Most have tighter habits and vary in foliage color from bright green to blue.

species that contains individuals bearing yellow, as well as the normal red fruits. 'Ohio Pioneer' is valued because it is virtually thornless, making it useful for garden or street planting. It is hardy in Zone 4.

Crataegus phaenopyrum, Washington thorn, has splendid, glossy foliage that turns a beautiful orange-red in the fall; the best of all the hawthorns for fall coloration. The flowers are abundant and pure white, giving rise to large clusters of scarlet fruit, which are among the longest-lasting of all the species. It is quite narrow and upright when young, broadening with age, and is hardy in Zone 4. It grows exceptionally well in the city and there are specimens which are many decades old but still thriving in "mini-parks" in downtown New York City.

Crataegus 'Toba' is one of the hardiest and most beautiful varieties. It originated in the harsh climate of Manitoba, Canada, and is hardy in Zone 3. The flowers are borne abundantly every year and are a pure white when they first open, gradually deepening to a rose color. They are fully double and the tree fruits rather sparsely. The leathery foliage is a fine, dark green color, immune to leaf spot diseases and lasting throughout the summer. It is almost thornless and hence a most useful flowering garden tree, especially in cold areas where most of the showy flowering

cherries and crabapples are not hardy.

Crataegus viridis 'Winter King,' has distinct green stems with a waxy bloom and fine glossy leaves. Its principal merit is the production of abundant and long-lasting red fruits — making the leafless trees a distinct patch of red in the winter landscape. It has vase-shaped branches when young, forming a full rounded head when mature. It is hardy in Zone 4 and reaches 35 feet in height when grown in rich soil.

Flowers of C. phaenopyrum.

Crataegus phaenopyrum. *Washington thorn.*

Cydonia oblonga. Quince (Deciduous).

NATIVE TO: Asia. ZONES: 5-9. HABIT: Shrubby, usually an umbrellalike, multi-trunked tree, slow-growing to 10-25 feet.

A beautiful dual-purpose tree, often overlooked as an ornamental. Four-season value. White to light pink flowers in spring after the leaves are out. Yellow fall color. The fragrant fruits are large and yellow when ripe. Interesting twisted and knotty branches provide winter appeal. Tolerates moist soils.

Davidia involucrata. Dovetree, handkerchief tree (Deciduous).

NATIVE TO: China. ZONES: 6-8. HABIT: Moderate growth to 30-40 feet. Rounded crown.

An interesting flowering tree that gets its name from the unusual white spring flowers (which are actually modified leaves) that, to some, look like white doves sitting among the bright green leaves, and to others look like handkerchiefs hung out to dry. Flowers are followed by round seedballs lasting into winter.

May take 8-10 years to bloom. Should be protected from heat and wind. Best used alone or with evergreens rather than mixed with spring-flowering trees. A variable tree; room for selection of superior forms.

Diospyros. Persimmon. Dual-purpose trees with attractive features the year round.

Diospyros kaki. Oriental or kaki persimmon (Deciduous).

NATIVE TO: China and Korea. BEST ADAPTED: Zones 7-9, can be grown 6. HABIT: Moderate growth rate to 20-30 feet, similar spread. Low round head.

New foliage is soft, light green, gradually turning a heavier dark green, in the summer, and finally different shades of yellow, red, and orange before dropping in the fall. Then followed by bright orange fruits which light up the bare branches like Christmas tree ornaments. Bark is also attractive. Fruits are sweet, excellent dried or fresh. Choice fruiting varieties include 'Fuyu,' 'Hachiya,' which is also the most valuable as an ornamental tree, and 'Chocolate.'

A fine small garden shade tree. Hardiness can be stretched by planting in portable containers, or as an espalier against a south wall. Few pests. Constant moisture and early spring fertilizing will avoid fruit drop.

Diospyros virginiana. American common persimmon (Deciduous).

NATIVE TO: Eastern United States. BEST ADAPTED: Zones 5-9, can be grown 4. HABIT: Moderate growth rate to 30-50 feet, spreads half as wide. Oval form.

American persimmon has the same good qualities as the Oriental persimmon. Fruits ripen after the first frost, turning from astringent to sweet. Doesn't have the striking show of fruit on bare branches, but does provide the same interesting winter branch silhouette as the Oriental persimmon.

More widely adapted than the Oriental persimmon, tolerating a wide range of soils and climates. Requires male and female trees for fruit production.

Elaeagnus angustifolia. Russian olive, silver berry (Deciduous).

NATIVE TO: Asia and Southern Asia. ZONES: 2-8. HABIT: Fast growth to 20-25 feet, equally wide; shrubby, round-headed as a tree.

A tough tree and a problem-solver, especially in hot dry areas. The leaves are willowlike, olive-green above, silvery beneath. Attractive, shedding, dark-brown bark on the usually crooked, twisted trunk. Thorny branches. Greenish-yellow flowers in early summer are followed by quantities of yellow berries that furnish winter food for many birds.

Widely adaptable to all but poorly drained soils. Resents cool, moist coastal conditions. Excellent hedge, screen, or wind break. A good choice when there is a need for erosion control.

Catalpa blossom.

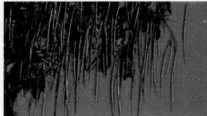

Catalpa seed pod.

Above: Catalpa.
Below: Celtis occidentalis. *Hackberry.*

Above: Firmiana simplex. *Chinese parasol tree.*
Below: *Flower clusters of* F. simplex.

Eriobotrya japonica. Loquat (Evergreen).

NATIVE TO: China and Japan. ZONES: 8-10. HABIT: Upright and moderate growth to 30 feet with equal spread, Broad, round crown — less rounded in the shade.

A dual-purpose tree, very ornamental, with edible fruits. Most striking feature is the very large leaf, 6-12 inches long by 2-4 inches wide, prominently veined and serrated, dark green above with downy, rust-colored underside. Fragrant but small white flowers in the fall are followed by abundant orange to yellow fruits that ripen in late winter or early spring. The fruit has a large seed and is puckery if picked green but has a delicious flavor when ripe.

Amenable to pruning, even as a ground cover, and may be used as a landscape specimen, espalier, or in a container.

Tolerates alkaline soil but needs good drainage and is sometimes subject to fireblight. See *Malus.*

Cercidiphyllum magnificum. *Katsura tree.*

Cercis canadensis. *Eastern redbud.*

Cotinus coggygria. *Purple smoke tree.*

Cunninghamia lanceolata. *China fir.*

Cornus. *Dogwood.*

Seedlings are unpredictable as to fruit, but cultivars are reliable. 'Gold Nugget' and 'Champagne' both produce good fruit.

Eriobotrya deflexa is a non-fruiting species, smaller and more shrubby, but good for espaliers or trained as a small tree. The new growth is bronze-red. Showier than *Eriobotrya japonica.*

Eucommia ulmoides. Hardy rubber tree (Deciduous).

NATIVE TO: Central China. ZONES: 5-7. HABIT: Moderate (4-8 feet in 4 years in shade tree evaluation tests conducted by the Ohio Research and Development Center in Cleveland Ohio), spread equal or exceeding height. Round-headed to broad-spreading.

A consistent high scorer at the Shade Tree Evaluation Plot, Secrest Arboretum, Wooster, Ohio.

Dr. L. C. Chadwick of Ohio describes it as "a small tree of an ultimate height of 25-30 feet with excellent glossy-green foliage, even during the driest of seasons. Extremely drought-resistant. Suited for inner-city environments. It is easy to transplant, but difficult to propagate." No serious pests or diseases. Plant as a lawn tree. This tree is also recommended and used in large areas such as parks or golf courses. It makes an excellent street tree.

Fagus. Beech.

Although our American beech, *Fagus grandifolia,* has paler, more beautiful bark, the European beech *(F. sylvatica)* is more commonly planted. A very slow-growing tree. The true beauty of the beech is rarely seen by those who plant them, as they take from 50 to 100 years to develop fully.

Fagus sylvatica. European beech (Deciduous).

NATIVE TO: Central and Southern Europe. ZONES: 5-8. HABIT: Slow-growing to 70-80 feet, with a spread of 60 feet. Dense pyramidal form.

Prized for its smooth gray bark and glossy, dark green foliage which takes on excellent fall color. Edible nuts attract wildlife.

Raymond Korbobo, of Rutgers University, New Jersey, says of the European beech, "The bark of an old venerable beech can be compared to the hide of an elephant. Parts are smooth, and parts look like wrinkled

Fraxinus — Ash

In the Edda — the sacred book of the ancient Norsemen — it is related that the court of the gods is held beneath a mighty ash whose top reaches the heavens, whose branches overshadow the whole earth, and whose roots penetrate the infernal regions. An eagle surmounts the tree to watch over the land and a squirrel travels up and down the trunk to report what the eagle has seen.

Few trees have been admired for so long .Today, as a versatile shade tree and valuable source of wood, it is on almost every list of top ten trees.

There are about 65 species of ash, with the majority from temperate areas of the Northern Hemisphere (about 17 of which are native to North America).

The wood from the ash is widely used commercially because of its strength, rigidity, and hardness. Tool handles, baseball bats, and tennis rackets are commonly made of ash.

In general, the genus *Fraxinus* is made up of fast-growing, deciduous trees of roundheaded habit. They are widely adapted to climatic conditions and soil types, and are especially able to take wet soils with poor drainage. One glaring weakness of the ash is heavy seed production and resulting seedlings, but this is being eliminated among the wide variety of seedless cultivars available.

One of the main aspects of the ash's beauty lies in its leaves. With few exceptions, they are 6-12 inches long and divided into as many as 12-13 leaflets that can each be several inches long. They combine to form a beautiful soft textured canopy casting a shade light enough to allow grass and other plants to grow beneath. The ashes are great as lawn trees or for any area needing lots of leafy shade.

Although there are many ashes commonly available, several stand out as the most valuable and versatile.

Fraxinus americana — 'Autumn Purple.' White ash.

As the name suggests, this is the ash for fall color, a rich purple. It has a fine oval habit with a round crown and rapidly reaches a height of 65-75 feet. Good adaptability and hardiness (zones 4-9). Besides being seedless, the summer foliage has more substance and a finer texture than the species.

Fraxinus pennsylvanica lanceolata — 'Marshall Seedless.' Green ash. The ash with the widest range of adaptability, the 'Marshall Seedless' is adapted to zones 3-9 and can stand up to the rigors of arid climates, drought, and poor soils. It reaches a height of 45-55 feet, becoming pyramidal and open-headed. The extremely attractive, glossy dark green foliage casts a heavier shade than most ashes, and turns yellow in fall. Compared to the species, it grows faster, is seedless, and hasn't many pest problems.

Fraxinus oxycarpa — 'Flame.' Claret ash.

This ash and the similar cultivar 'Raywood' are hardy in zone 5 and possibly in zone 4. Both will reach a height of 30-40 feet, forming roundheaded trees with small, glossy, dark green leaves that turn wine-red in fall. The spreading habit and light shade make these good selections for the yard.

Fraxinus excelsior — 'Hessei'. European ash.

The single, glossy, dark green, leathery leaves distinguish this cultivar from other ashes. It

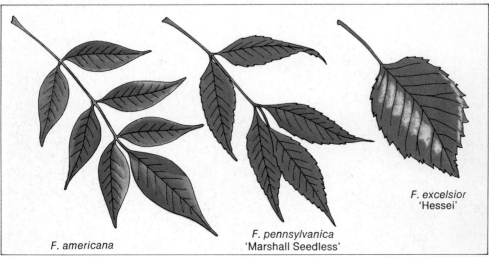

F. americana

F. pennsylvanica 'Marshall Seedless'

F. excelsior 'Hessei'

F. excelsior 'Hessei'. European ash.

skin. The beech, like the huge elephant, needs and demands lots of room. Beeches are usually found growing in groves, and the sight of a beech grove is truly a sight to remember. The silvery gray bark brings a brightness to the area, even on a cloudy day. To do the beech full justice, it should be allowed to sweep the ground with its lower branches — which means a circular area of 50 or 60 feet, and often up to 90 feet. This makes it best suited to parks, golf course, and college campuses, rather than the home garden.''

'Pendula,' the weeping European beech, is the best of all weeping trees. Clean, dark green foliage on graceful pendant branches that sweep the ground.

'Riversii,' River's purple beech, is considered to be the most beautiful of all purple-foliaged trees. Resists drought, and tolerates moist soil conditions.

'Asplenifolia' is a beech that has refined, fernlike foliage.

Feijoa sellowiana. Pineapple guava (Evergreen).
NATIVE TO: South America. BEST ADAPTED: Zones 9, can be grown, 8. HABIT: Grows to 20-25 feet, usually smaller. Open shrub-like habit.

Will need some time and training to develop tree form, but worth the wait and effort. Dual-purpose tree with glossy green leaves and chalky-silver undersides. Fleshy white flowers with showy red stamens in spring, followed by edible, oval, gray-green fruits.

Flavor is described as between that of a pineapple and a guava. One of our consultants referred to this tree as the ''Sculptors' friend'' because it thrives on pruning. It can be espaliered or used as a hedge. It also grows well in a tub or large container.

Fruit flavor varies by plant and climate. Choose varieties selected for fruiting qualities. 'Coolidge' and 'Pineapple Gem' are self-fertile; others require cross-pollination. Heat and drought tolerant.

Firmiana simplex. Chinese parasol tree, varnish tree (Deciduous).
NATIVE TO: China and Japan. ZONES: 8-9. HABIT: Slow growth to 40 feet, spread 15-40 feet, dense, high-branching upright.

This is an exciting looking tree for protected areas like a patio or court-

forms a round-headed, 30- to 50-foot tree which is adapted to zones 4-9. Although no fall color, the leaves stay green late, contrasting nicely with brightly colored trees around it.

Fraxinus ornus —
The flowering ash. Untypical of most ashes, the flowering ash bears fluffy white to greenish-white clusters of fragrant white flowers in late spring. Reaches 35 feet with a round head. Shiny green leaves turn soft lavender or yellow in fall (zones 6-8). Perhaps the flowering ash will receive the attention of growers, and a seedless, early-flowering cultivar will be selected.

Many other species and cultivars of ash are used ornamentally. But because of climate adaptation, lack of availability, or susceptibility to disease (borers, anthracnose, and mistletoe are major problems — severity varying with species and location), the following are not as highly recommended.

Fraxinus americana —
'Rosehill.' White ash. Seedless, upright to 60-70 feet. Bronze-red fall color. Light green summer foliage, zones 5-9.

Fraxinus holotricha —
'Moraine.' Broad upright crown to 30-35 feet. Lighter-textured foliage than most ashes; turns yellow in fall. Zones 5-8. Borer problem in the Midwest.

Fraxinus pennsylvanica lanceolata —
'Summit.' Green ash. Straight, upright habit to 55-60

feet. Yellow fall color. Good hardiness (zones 3-9).

Fraxinus latifolia — Oregon ash. 40-80 feet. Round head, stands winter flooding. Prized in its native northwest.

Fraxinus uhdei —
'Majestic Beauty.' Shamel ash. Much used tree in the southwest. Evergreen in mild climates. Upright, narrow, oval to 50-60 feet.

Fraxinus velutina —
Modesto ash. Upright branching to 50 feet. Weak wood. Bright yellow fall color. Most widely used in California. Anthracnose and mistletoe problems in the West.

Fraxinus velutina —
'Rio Grande.' Fantex ash. Similar to Modesto ash but better adapted to hot, dry, windy locations. Dark green leaves. Zones 8-10.

F. ornus. *The flowering ash.*

F. americana *'Rosehill'. White ash.*

The beauty of ash leaves.

F. pennsylvanica lanceolata. *Green ash.*

yard. Its large lobed leaves will not stand up to wind, but it is unusually hardy for such a tropical looking tree. Even in the winter the upright branches and shiny gray-green bark are quite picturesque. Attractive flowers and seed pods in summer.

Franklinia alatamaha. Franklinia (Deciduous).

NATIVE TO: Georgia. BEST ADAPTED: Zones 6-8, can be grown 5. HABIT: Slow to moderate growth to 20-25 feet. Upright, open pyramid.

Much has been written about the search for this tree. Once thought extinct, it was discovered growing in Georgia in the eighteen hundreds and has not been found in the wild since, although many have looked. It can, however, be found in cultivation and is

well worth growing. Its beautiful, white camellialike flowers are often found on the tree at the same time the leaves are turning briliant orange-red in the fall. People have referred to it as a crazy fall-flowering dogwood. Glossy green foliage.

This tree is somewhat of a challenge to grow, but worth it. It prefers rich acid soil, partial shade and protection from wind. An excellent specimen, lawn, or patio tree.

Fraxinus. Ash.
We evaluate this genus on page 48.

Fraxinus excelsior 'Hessei' has received multiple endorsements from our authors and consultants.

Borers are a major problem to ashes. See page 85.

Ginkgo biloba. Maidenhair tree (Deciduous).

NATIVE TO: China. BEST ADAPTED: Zones 5-8, can be grown 4, 9. HABIT: Slow growth rate (50 feet in 60 years at Secrest Arboretum, Wooster, Ohio). Can reach 60-100 feet but growth rate varies with climate. Usually somewhat conical and sparsely branched in youth, becoming more spreading and denser with age.

One of the oldest living trees; fossil records date back 200 million years. The picturesque, irregular habit of growth is most interesting, as are the bright green, fan-shaped leaves. They turn brilliant yellow in fall and drop all at once — sometimes overnight — a plus for those who like to rake only once.

A remarkably tough tree that stands smoke and air pollution and ranks as

Trees that stand flooding

Flood-tolerant trees are your best choice in many situations. Seasonal floods, occurring because of torrential rains, can inundate areas for extended periods of time. Around reservoirs and lakes, where water levels fluctuate according to rainfall and water usage, shoreline plantings should be adaptable to periodic flooding. In urban landscapes, where excessively wet soils occur, such as low-lying, poorly drained areas, flood-tolerant trees should be planted.

Trees listed here have withstood flooding (water over the ground) for 50 days or more.

Acer saccharinum
Betula nigra
Celtis occidentalis
Diospyros virginiana
Fraxinus pennsylvanica
Gleditsia triacanthos
Liquidambar styraciflua
Nyssa spp.
Platanus acerifolia
Populus spp.
Quercus phellos
Salix spp.
Taxodium distichum

Populus nigra *'Italica.' Lombardy poplar.*

Platanus acerifolia. *London plane tree.*

Salix babylonica. *Weeping willow.*

Salix matsudana. *Globe willow.*

one of the top ten trees for wide streets. Pest-free. Widely adaptable, demanding only a well-drained soil. Needs room to develop. Excellent park or large lawn tree.

Slow to respond after transplanting. Extra watering may be helpful. Seeds are highly valued in China and Japan where they are roasted. They are supposed to aid digestion, and "diminish the effects of wine." Male trees are preferred since seed pods of the female tree have a rancid odor when crushed.

Many good male cultivars are available, including 'Autumn Gold' with consistently brilliant fall color and compact vase-shaped growth, 'Fairmount,' which is pyramid-shaped, and 'Sentry,' with a narrow fastigate form.

Gleditsia. Honey locust.
The honey locust are enjoying unmatched popularity. This genus is discussed by William Collins, American Garden-Cole Nursery, Circleville, Ohio, on page 52.

Gymnocladus dioica. Kentucky coffee tree (Deciduous).
NATIVE TO: Eastern United States. ZONES: 5-8. HABIT: Fast-growth to 65-75 feet, very open-spreading round top.

The common name is said to come from the use of the seed pods as a coffee substitute (see page 28). One wonders how much truth there is in this tale since the leaves and fruit are poisonous. However, the Secrest Arboretum, Wooster, Ohio, reports that Indians have eaten the berries, so possibly cooking destroys the poison.

The Arboretum also notes that, "when the leaves fall in autumn, the tree, with its large branches and stubby twigs, has often been given the descriptive local name of 'stump tree.' "

Deserves to be planted for its contorted branching and wide adaptability to soil and climate. Dark green, compound leaves. Long (6- to 10-inch) pods on male trees.

The combination of furrowed bark, branching pattern and size make this tree especially attractive against the winter skyline. Not a tree for a small garden. However, its open habit provides light shade; great for gardening under. Best used in large areas like parks and golf courses.

Pest-free. Somewhat difficult to transplant. Won't tolerate shade.

Taxodium distichum. *Bald cypress.*

Halesia carolina. Snowdrop tree, silver bell (Deciduous).

NATIVE TO: Southeastern United States. ZONES: 5-8. HABIT: Slow to moderate growth rate to 25-30 feet. Pyramidal in youth, roundheaded with age.

One of the most attractive American natives. William Flemer, III, Princeton Nurseries, Princeton, New Jersey, notes ". . . this pretty little native is very popular in England and on the continent, but is rarely planted here in its country of origin. In mid-May each twig bears a string of one-inch-long white flowers like little wedding bells hanging down on slender stems. It's an open grower, usually in clump form with several stems; a fine shelter plant for combining with an underplanting of azaleas or rhododendrons."

Attractive bark is quite dark and uniquely scaled. Interesting seed pods. Foliage is yellow-green in summer, turning yellow in fall. Definitely a tree that should be used more. Plant as a patio tree or against a dark wall to show off the white flowers. Widely adapted, but does best in a moist, well-drained, rich soil. Will take shade. May need pruning to develop tree form.

Francis Gouin describes a more tree-like form, *Halesia monticola,* in "Trees that need a friend," pages 80-84.

Ilex. Holly.

Trees of this genus are evaluated on page 56 by John Ford, Secrest Arboretum, Wooster, Ohio.

English and American hollies are attacked by two kinds of leaf miners. The most common one makes blotches, the other a serpentine pattern. They are most active from April to mid-May. At that time, use Orthene, Cygon, Diazinon, or a combination spray. Read the labels.

Scale (see page 85) and spider mites are sometimes a problem. Apply a dormant oil spray in winter to control overwintering mite eggs. Use Orthene or a combination spray during the growing season. Read the label for complete directions.

Juniperus. Juniper.

This is a very large group of tough plants that range in size from low-spreading ground covers to tall columnar trees. There can be two

Gleditsia — Honey locust

The honey locust is a native tree over a large part of the eastern and central United States. In addition, it has been extensively planted to the east, north, and west of its original native range. It is grown as a shade and street tree in selected areas in the Rocky Mountains, the Southwest and the West Coast.

The rise in popularity of our native honey locust tree is almost like a Cinderella story. The typical, well-established native or wild tree of the fields and woods usually has small

thorns on the twigs and larger thorns on the branches. Wide, beanlike pods develop from the small, insignificant blossoms, twisting and curling to a length of 10 to 12 or more inches. For years, these characteristics kept the honey locust from becoming a popular landscape tree.

When the seriousness of the Dutch elm disease became evident, concerned tree people immediately began to investigate the landscape qualities of some of our other native species that might fill the void left by the elm. This was a real challenge, because the American elm had already proven itself to be widely adapted, easy to transplant, tolerant of a wide variety of soils, and fast growing. This beautiful tree shaded homes and streets in thousands of cities and

towns in eastern and central United States.

It has been known for years that there were occasional honey locust trees without thorns, some without pods, and a few free of both. Within a relatively short time, several large tree-producing nurseries began seeking and selecting the best tree they could find or develop, free of both thorns and pods. Siebenthaler and Cole in Ohio, and Princeton in New Jersey were the pioneers in this vast undertaking. The early introductions of these firms are still among the leaders, both in popularity and performance. Newer selections appear equally promising and a number of individuals and firms are still trying to develop even better varieties.

The choice of this species was a good one, for few other

native trees possess as many of the desirable growing characteristics as the American elm.

The honey locust leaf is delicate and compound (see drawing) with tiny leaflets, allowing filtered sunlight through. The lacy appearance gives the tree an almost tropical look, a rarity itself among trees hardy in the northern U.S.

Besides its light shade, the honey locust has one other characteristic that favors good lawn growth. Turf is usually most vigorous in the cooler, moister seasons — early spring and late fall. By good fortune, the growth of the honey locust favors lawn development by leafing out late in the spring and dropping its golden leaflets early in the fall. The leaflets require a minimum of raking.

With all its advantages, the honey locust does have some

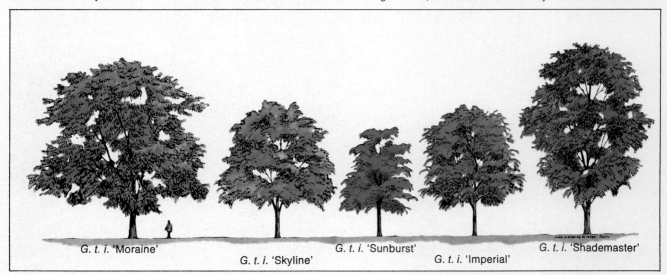

G. t. i. 'Moraine'   *G. t. i.* 'Skyline'   *G. t. i.* 'Sunburst'   *G. t. i.* 'Imperial'   *G. t. i.* 'Shademaster'

types of foliage: short, needlelike, juvenile leaves and scalelike, twig-hugging, mature foliage. Which juniper tree you choose depends on your climate. Differences between the species that form trees is slight. There is wide variety in the selections within the species. Here we look at two simlar forms with different adaptations.

Juniperus scopulorum. Rocky Mountain juniper (Needled Evergreen).

NATIVE TO: The Rocky Mountains. ZONES: 5-9. HABIT: Slow growth to 35-45 feet. Broad pyramidal form becomes round-topped with age.

The best juniper for areas of heat and drought like Texas and the Great Plains. A poor performer in areas of high summer rainfall or humidity.

Blue-gray foliage, brownish-red bark. Excellent tall hedge, screen, or windbreak.

Many selections available varying in foliage color and form.

Juniperus virginiana. Eastern red cedar (Needled evergreen).

NATIVE TO: Eastern United States. BEST ADAPTED: Zones 4-8, can be grown 3. HABIT: Slow growth to 34-45 feet. Pyramidal.

Adaptable to a remarkable range of soils and climates in the eastern United States. Unlike *J. scopulorum,* it will take summer rain, but not hot dry winds. Normally bright green foliage, but several selected varieties vary both in foliage color and form. May turn plum colored in cold winter weather. Attractive blue berries are a favorite

winter bird food. Excellent, long-lived, tall hedge, screen, or windbreak.

Other common tree junipers include the Swedish juniper, *J. communis* 'Suecica' and the alligator juniper, *J. deppeana pachylaea,* named for its deeply fissured bark.

Koelreuteria paniculata. Golden-rain tree (Deciduous).

NATIVE TO: China, Japan, Korea. ZONES: 5-8. HABIT: Moderate to 25-35 feet. Rounded outline, wide-spreading open branches, eventually to a flat top.

Roland Roberts from Lubbock, Texas, who loves the tree, wrote us: "Without a doubt the golden-rain tree is our favorite. It is well adapted to this climate and tolerates the high winds, alkaline soil, long periods without much water, and low temperatures in

problems. Although subject to almost no widespread serious diseases, in certain southern localities mimosa webworm, pod gall, and plant bugs, for example, can be troublesome, so check locally to determine if these insects are prevalent in your area.

Honey locust has performed especially well in difficult, inner-city plantings. It is tolerant to a high degree of various environmental stresses, including air pollution and highway salting.

Landscape architects frequently specify the honey locust for municipal and industrial plantings. In many areas it is one of the most popular street trees. Architects (and homeowners) like it because the foliage is not dense, allowing the architectural features to be seen through the trees.

It also permits more light to reach building interiors.

Honey locust trees are quite resistant to wind damage. The upright branching habit, especially of young trees, allows them to survive much ice storm damage resulting from ice build-up on the twigs.

Occasionally, the vigor of these essentially thornless, podless varieties results in quite long new growth on twigs and branches of young trees — even to the state of being "weepy." If this happens, about one-half of the new growth should be cut off in midsummer. New branches will develop in the latter part of the summer and the tree will have stronger branches and a better shape. This technique is particularly rewarding on the 'Sunburst' (yellow leaves) and 'Rubylace' (reddish leaves).

Older trees, whose vigor is re-duced because of age or site, should be pruned quite se-verely once every 2 to 4 years. The vigor and foliage color will be impressive, almost as if the trees had been heavily fertilized.

Here are some of the forms that have been developed:

'Imperial' — Moderate growth rate to 35 feet. Symmetrical, spreading round crown. Bright green foliage. Heavier shade than others because of closely spaced leaves and dense branching.

'Majestic' — Fast growth rate to 45 to 55 feet. Compact (not as dense as 'Skyline' or 'Imperial') spreading crown. Dark green foliage.

'Moraine' — The first cultivar to be patented. Fast-growing. Vase-shaped, to 40-50 feet.

Green foliage. Trunk may be curved when young, requiring more training.

'Rubylace' — Fast-growing, spreading habit that reaches 30-35 feet. New foliage is purplish-bronze, then green. Of controversial beauty. Try to see an older one before buying. May need extra prun-ing in youth.

'Shademaster' — Fast growth to 40-50 feet. Upright, spread-ing branches form wineglass shape. Holds dark green foliage longer than other selections.

'Skyline' — Fast growth to 40-45 feet. Pyramidal form. Leaves are dark green, compact, leathery, and larger than the others.

'Sunburst.' — Fast growth to 30-35 feet. Upright, spreading habit. New foliage is yellow, gradually turning green.

'Majestic' honey locust.

'Sunburst' honey locust.

'Skyline' honey locust.

Above: Halesia carolina. *Snowdrop tree,* silver bell.
Below: Koelreuteria paniculata. *Golden-rain tree.*

Ginkgo biloba. *Maidenhair tree.*

winter. It is a well-behaved tree. The deep root system and the open branching habit permit grass to grow beneath the branches. Starting in April, the new leaves develop quickly and cover the tree with soft, medium-green, divided leaves. By late spring the flower spikes begin to open and the tree is completely covered with a mass of beautiful yellow flowers, enthusiastically visited by the honey-bees. If the tree is kept watered, the flowers set small fruits, which develop an outer papery husk very much like a husk tomato. Later in the summer, the fruits mature to a dark copper-tan and hang in clusters. The tree appears to be full of little Japanese lanterns, which last through fall. In the winter the characteristic angular branch growth gives the tree an interesting form even without leaves.

"The golden-rain tree grows fast while young and, by the age of fifteen or twenty years, displays a mature, well-proportioned form that requires little or no pruning to maintain a pleasant symmetry. We have not had any trouble with wind damage or salt injury and there appear to be no problems of trace element deficiency, insects, or disease."

Laburnum watereri 'Vossii.'
Vossii laburnum. Golden-chain tree
(Deciduous).

HYBRID OF *L. alpinum* and *L. anagy-roides.* ZONES: 5-7. HABIT: Moderate
growth rate to 20-30 feet. Dense upright
vase-shaped crown.

All of our observers agree that the
only reason to choose this tree is for
the flowers. In May it bears 18-inch,
tapering clusters of rich yellow, pea-
shaped flowers that look a good deal
like wisteria blooms. Not spectacular
out of bloom. Leaves, fruits, and
flowers are all very poisonous.
Resents hot climates.

Lagerstroemia. Crape myrtle.
Includes two of the most reliable and
spectacular summer-flowering trees.
One is very common, the other is
a tree that needs a friend.

Lagerstroemia fauriei. Japanese
crape myrtle (Deciduous).

NATIVE TO: Taiwan and China. ZONES:
7-9. HABIT: Slow growth to 12-15 feet.
Vase-shaped.

Very similar to *Lagerstroemia
indica,* but with smaller white blossoms and no fall color. Bark is
attractive, peeling brown and red.

Outstanding feature of this species
is its resistance to powdery mildew,
which rules out *L. indica* in cool, moist,
coastal areas.

Larix *Larch.*

Lagerstroemia indica. Crape myrtle
(Deciduous).

NATIVE TO: China. ZONES: 7-9. HABIT:
Slow growth to 10-30 feet. Vase-shaped as
a multi-trunked tree, roundheaded when
trained to a single stem.

Best known for its late summer
profusion of showy flowers in electric
shades of pink, red, lavender, or
white. The flowers are crinkled and
ruffled like crêpe-paper and held high
above the foliage. The bark is attractive
year-round, but especially in winter,
when the peeling red and brown
mottled trunk is quite striking. Most
dramatic on multi-trunked trees.
Good but inconsistent fall color.

Excellent small street, lawn, or
patio tree. Grows well in containers.
Best adapted to a hot dry climate; will
mildew in moist coastal locations.

The National Arboretum has introduced several cultivars of greater
hardiness, mildew-resistance, and
vigor, collectively called Indian Tribe
crape myrtles. Notable selections
include 'Catawba' with good orange-
red fall color and dark purple blossoms, 'Cherokee' with open spreading
habit and rich red flowers, and
'Seminole' with large pink blossoms.

Larix. Larch.

These feathery conifers stand out from
others by being deciduous and

Lagerstroemia indica. Crape myrtle.

providing good fall color.

Larix decidua. European larch
(Deciduous).

NATIVE TO: Northern and central Europe.
ZONES: 3-7. HABIT: Moderate to fast
growth, from 27 feet to 60 feet in 60 years.
at the Secrest Arboretum, Wooster, Ohio.
Slender pyramidal form, widening with age.

Beautiful in spring when it breaks
dormancy with thousands of pale
green, feathery tufts. Foliage remains
soft green all summer, turns yellow
to orange in fall. Interesting reddish
cones last into winter dotting the
bare branches. Widely adapted,
tolerates most soils.

Larix leptolepis. (L. kaempferi).
Japanese larch (Deciduous).

NATIVE TO: Japan. ZONES: 5-8. HABIT:
Fast growth from 20 feet to 68 feet in
40 years at Secrest Arboretum. Spreads
25-40 feet in pyramidal form.

Broader and hardier than the
European larch. Blue-green foliage,
excellent yellow-orange fall color.

Laurus nobilis. Sweet bay,
Grecian laurel (Evergreen).

NATIVE TO: The Mediterranean. ZONES:
8-10. HABIT: Slow growth to 12-30 feet,
compact conical form.

This is a well-behaved, indoor-
outdoor tree. Has a very sophisticated
look and takes well to shearing into
hedges, screens, or formal shapes.
Aromatic, dark green leaves. Insignificant flowers are followed by small
dark berries, which attract birds.
Stands city conditions, requires well-
drained soil. Works well as a wall tree.

Ligustrum lucidum. Glossy privet (Evergreen).

NATIVE TO: China, Korea, Japan. ZONES: 8, 9. HABIT: Fast growing to 35-40 feet by 15-20 feet. Roundheaded, often multi-trunked.

The dense head, glossy, deep green foliage and ability to take shearing make this a very popular hedge or screen plant. Feathery clusters of milky white flowers in summer are followed by heavy clusters of small, berrylike, blue-black fruits. Tolerates salt winds and a wide variety of soils. A good tree where root space is restricted. Makes a handsome container specimen. Equally useful as a small shade tree in a lawn or as a street tree, although the falling fruit may be messy on sidewalks.

Liquidambar styraciflua. American sweet gum (Deciduous).

NATIVE TO: Eastern and southern United States and Mexico. ZONES: 5-9. HABIT: Moderate- to slow-growing to 90 feet. A symmetrical pyramid when young, spreading to irregular with maturity.

One of the most reliable trees for autumn color even in warm climates. The star-shaped leaves, which somewhat resemble maple leaves, turn rich shades of crimson to purple in the fall. Color lasts as long as six weeks. Fruits, which mature in the fall, are the size of golf balls and prickly like burrs. May be a nuisance when they drop. Corky ridges on the uniquely horizontal branches yield winter interest. A good skyline tree.

Will grow on a variety of sites, but does best in rich clay or loam soils.

Its symmetrical beauty is an asset to the home grounds as well as the street.

Cultivars selected for fall color include: 'Burgundy,' leaves purplish in autumn, holding late; 'Festival,' narrow upright tree with pink and orange fall color; 'Moraine,' red fall color, and 'Palo Alto' which turns orange-red in fall.

Liriodendron tulipifera. Tulip tree, yellow poplar, tulip poplar (Deciduous).

NATIVE to: Eastern United States. ZONES: 5-9. HABIT: Fast-growing to 60-70 feet in 70 years at the Secrest Arboretum, Wooster, Ohio.

This is the tallest of our eastern hardwoods and needs plenty of room to develop properly. Its beauty lies in

Ilex — Holly

There are some 300 different species of hollies growing in the temperate and tropical regions of both hemispheres. Hollies are evergreen or deciduous, trees or shrubs.

Some hollies have spiny leaves while other types have leaves with smooth margins. The fruit is black, red, yellow, or orange, depending upon the species or variety. Usually, both male and female plants are required to obtain a set of berries. One male will normally pollinate 16 to 19 females within 900 feet.

Most hollies thrive best on an acid soil. The trees will grow in full sunlight or partial shade but become leggy in dense shade.

Hollies have been used since prehistoric times by widely diverse peoples, either as decorations or in connection with religious ceremonies.

Ilex opaca — American holly. Native in eastern United States. Through the use of hardy cultivars, this holly has been successfully grown in zones 5 and 6, north of its original home. Hardy cultivars have withstood temperatures of -24°F or even

colder. The pyramid-shaped tree can grow to 45 or 50 feet. Foliage is evergreen and leaves are normally spiny. The color of the berries varies from red through orange to yellow, but the normal color is red.

When this tree is planted north of its original home it becomes more selective in its site requirements. In the southeast, American holly will grow on moist or wet sites. In the north, it requires good drainage and protection from severe winds.

Over a thousand selections of American holly have been named. Hardy red-berried forms include 'Angelica,' 'Arlene Leach,' 'Betty Pride,' 'Carnival,' 'Cumberland,' 'Mary Holman,' 'Red Flush,' and 'Valentine.' 'Jersey Knight,' and 'Santa Claus' are two hardy males. If you want yellow berries, plant 'Canary' or 'Morgan Gold.'

A smooth-leafed variety is 'Kentucky Smoothleaf' which is somewhat tender, so plant in zone 6 — south. A southern smooth-leafed holly is 'East Palatka.' 'Savannah' is another southern selection, prized for its heavy set of red berries.

I. aquifolium. *English holly. Female (left) and male (right).*

I. aquifolium *'Wilsonii.'*

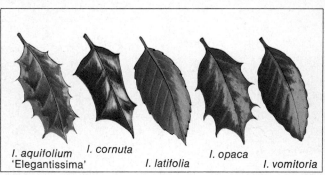

I. aquifolium 'Elegantissima'   *I. cornuta*   *I. latifolia*   *I. opaca*   *I. vomitoria*

its uniquely shaped bright green leaves that create a beautiful, light canopy (see photo, page 60). Looks somewhat like a very clean sycamore from a distance. Yellow fall color. Bears large, tulip-shaped, greenish-yellow flowers with an orange blotch at the base in late spring. Flowers are best viewed up close, since they tend to blend into the foliage from a distance.

At the Secrest Arboretum, the wood has been found to be somewhat brittle in wind and ice storms. The roots can be invasive. Does poorly in drought and alkaline soils. Subject to aphid attack. For control, see page 85.

Best used in open areas, parks, and golf courses. Good in a large lawn.

Great skyline tree. Smaller cultivars like 'Fastigiata,' which reaches only 35 feet with a narrow columnar form, expands this tree's possible uses to include smaller homes and gardens.

Maclura pomifera. Osage orange (Deciduous).

NATIVE TO: South central United States. ZONES: 5-9. HABIT: Fast growth to 50-60 feet, spreading, open form.

A tough tree for problem areas. Tolerates heat, cold, wind, drought, and alkaline soils. Pest free. Female trees have fruit resembling lumpy green oranges. Glossy green foliage and durable wood. Plant with caution; it has invasive, shallow roots and spreads quickly into thickets if not cared for. Valuable hedge plant.

Magnolia. Magnolia.
William Collins, American Garden — Cole Nursery, Circleville, Ohio, discusses this genus on page 58.

The most frequent pests of magnolias are scales. Read about how to control them on page 85.

Malus. Crabapple.
Trees of this genus have been evaluated on page 62.

Fireblight often infects crabapples. This is a bacterial disease that survives in cankers, leaves and fruits previously blighted. It is usually spread by insects during the bloom period, gaining entry through flowers and wounds. Symptoms are the sudden wilting of leaves which then turn dark, as if burned. Leaves hang on rather than fall.

Ilex aquifolium — English holly. Native in southern Europe, northern Africa, and Asia. To 60 feet tall. Hardy zones 6 and 7. Mostly grown in the Pacific Northwest. Cultivated since ancient times. Lustrous foliage, dense growth, bright red fruit. Requires moist, cool site and wind protection. Over 200 types in U.S. Variegated forms are available, such as 'Argenteo-marginata' with white margins. 'Golden Beam' is a male selection with golden variegations. 'Green Knight' is a male form. 'Yellow Beam' has golden fruits. The cultivar 'Angustifolia' has small, narrow leaves.

Ilex cornuta — Chinese holly. Native of China. Shrubs or small trees to 15 feet tall. Zones 6 or 7. Large, spiny leaves, glossy, and dark green. Evergreen. Large red berries on female. 'Burfordii' is quite common and desirable with spine only at tip of leaf. Abundant red berries. The selection 'D'or' is a yellow-fruited type. Many Chinese hollies will set sterile fruit without males.

Ilex latifolia — Luster-leaf holly. From eastern China and Japan. To 60 feet tall. Has large, thick, leathery, glossy, sawtoothed leaves to 7 inches long. Red berries. Should be planted on protected sites even in the South. Zones 7-10.

Ilex vomitoria — Yaupon. Native to South Georgia. To 12 or 15 feet tall. Small, shiny red berries. Zones 7-10. Can be used as a tall sheared hedge. Will grow on wet sites.

Ilex pedunculosa — Longstalk holly.
To 15 feet. Zone 5. Evergreen spineless leaves. Bright red berries on long stalks. Hardy.

Ilex decidua — Possum haw holly.
To 20 feet. Zone 5. Red berries retained well into winter. Deciduous. Wide range of

sites. Does best with abundant moisture and good drainage.

New hybrid hollies:
'Nellie R. Stevens.' Zones 6-8. To 25 feet, fast-growing. Large red berries. Evergreen.

'Poster No. 2.' Zones 6-8. Narrow, spiny, dark green leaves. Bright red berries. Use for a hedge or specimen plant.

Holly berries.

I. opaca. *American holly.*

I. vomitoria. *Yaupon holly.*

For control, apply a weak bordeaux, copper or streptomycin spray during bloom. First spray when 10% of the flowers are open, repeating every 5 days. Prune out diseased wood, cutting several inches below the infected parts into healthy wood. Sterilizing pruning tools in a strong solution of household bleach can prevent spreading the disease when pruning.

Melia azedarach. China-berry (Deciduous).

NATIVE TO: Asia. ZONES: 7-9. HABIT: Fast growth to 30-40 feet with equal spread. Spreading umbrellalike crown.

Valuable tree for desert regions of the South. Purple flowers followed by poisonous berries. Suckers and has weak wood, but still useful where most other trees won't grow.

More common than the species is 'Umbraculifera,' the Texas umbrella tree, which is praised by James Foret in ''Trees that need a friend,'' pages 80-84.

Metasequoia glyptostroboides. Dawn redwood.

A tree with multiple endorsements from our authors and consultants, described by Roger R. Huff, Virginia Beach, Virginia: ''The Dawn redwood existed in North America over 15 million years ago and became extinct. In 1945, Dr. E. D. Merrill of the Arnold Arboretum, was documenting vegetation in central China. Upon his return to the United States, he re-introduced the tree and found it to be hardy. There are now hundreds of dawn redwoods growing in the United States.

''The dawn redwood is a fossil-age conifer that is deciduous in habit and has a fast rate of growth. It somewhat resembles the deciduous bald cypress in foliage character, although its flat needles are closer to the size of the hemlock, which is a northern tree. Its framework has a regular appearance with horizontal penduolus branches. The bark of *M. glyptostroboides* is reddish brown with orange-brown twig bark. Summer color is light green and then turns yellow in the fall.

''There is a selected form of dawn redwood, known as *M. glypostroboides* 'National,' which can grow to a height of 35 feet in 10 years. When fully grown, it will reach a height of 65 to 79 feet. This tree should do extremely well in our area.''

Magnolia — The Magnolias

Magnolia blossom

The enthusiasm of those who know or grow magnolias is aptly described by Hugh Johnson in ''The International Book of Trees'': ''Every magnolia is the apple of someone's eye. To be conspicuous but to manage an air of frailty is a good recipe.''

So it is with many gardeners who have not included magnolias as a part of their landscaping. They have the idea that any tree (some magnolias are no bigger than large shrubs) that produces such large exotic flowers on a bold-leafed plant just must be difficult to grow. Not true. Even if you live in a climate one or two zones colder than the zone listed for the species, you might wish to try one of them if you have a suitably sheltered site. Some of the hardiest species are among the following:

Anise magnolia . . . Zone 5.
Magnolia salicifolia

Merrill magnolia . . . Zone 5.
Magnolia loebneri 'Merrill'

Saucer magnolia . . . Zone 5.
Magnolia soulangiana

Star magnolia . . . Zone 6.
Magnolia stellata

Sweet bay
Magnolia virginiana . . Zone 6.

Magnolia species are frequently placed in one of three categories. One is the evergreen type, such as the southern magnolia. The second type is the deciduous magnolia that develops blooms after the leaves appear. The lily-flowered magnolia is one of these. The third group includes the kind that flower before the leaves appear, such as the saucer magnolia. Some are variable, depending on where grown. The sweet bay magnolia is evergreen in the South, deciduous in the colder climates.

Magnolias are woody plants possessing fleshy roots and therefore should be transplanted balled and burlapped or in containers, except for the very smallest and youngest sizes, which can be handled bareroot. Some of the specialty growers are able to furnish young magnolias bareroot, the only practical way to ship cross-country.

Spring planting is generally preferred. Sometimes, in years when there is a very early spring, the flowers of the star magnolia and other early-flowering kinds do get caught by spring frosts. This possibility suggests that you plant the early-flowering species in as sheltered and protected a location as is available.

The bark of magnolias is softer than that of most other trees and is easily injured. For this reason it has not been planted much as a highheaded street tree. However, planted on a wide median strip, the lower branches can act as a barrier to trunk damage. Work is now underway at the National Arboretum, Washington, D.C. to breed and select superior, single-stem, tree-form magnolias that may be the street tree type of the future.

The popularity of the saucer, star, and loebneri magnolias is evident from the number of varieties of each one that have been named and introduced. They vary from a few kinds in loebneri to a dozen or more of the saucer varieties. A few are not generally available except from specialty magnolia growers, or perhaps the local nurseryman who introduced it.

Chances are that the saucer magnolia is the most widely planted and best known. It is a very popular photographic subject. Colors of the different varieties range from white to dark reddish-purple. Part of their popularity is due to their blooming well while still small, a trait that also favors the anise and star magnolias. Saucer magnolias are capable of reaching a height of 25 feet with the same spread. They are sometimes planted where a more erect-growing tree should have been placed, so allow the space needed for development of normal shape or form. As for foliage, they are not among the best-looking magnolias after the flowers have faded.

Too often overlooked is the anise magnolia. The fragrant, 5-inch, white, 6-petal flowers and the willowlike 2- to 4-inch leaves are beautifully staged on a conical tree making it one of the best for the small garden.

M. veitchii

M. soulangiana

M. stellata

M. grandiflora

Morus alba. White mulberry (Deciduous).

NATIVE TO: China. ZONES: 5-9. HABIT: Fast-growing to 35-40 feet and about as wide. Spreading head.

The species has small, blackberry-like fruit. Attractive to birds. Of the fruitless varieties, 'Kingan' is the hardiest. Somewhat less hardy are 'Stribling,' 'Fan San,' and 'Cutleaf.'

Unless properly cared for, may only have a life of 20 years. Its spreading branches should be cut back annually. City crews sometimes thin drastically, giving it a tallish, rather airy shape. The usual procedure of dehorning or stubbing will shorten its life.

Not a street tree for small areas because it buckles sidewalks. It is a tree for hot climates, surviving desert sun and heat. A valuable temporary tree.

Nyssa sylvatica. Black tupelo, black gum, sour gum, pepperidge (Deciduous).

NATIVE TO: Eastern United States. ZONES: 5-9. HABIT: Moderate growth rate to 30-50 feet, spreads about half as wide.

This tree has as many endorsements from our authors and consultants as it does common names. Praised by John Kissida and William Gould in "Trees that need a friend," pages 80-84.

Ostrya virginiana. American hop-hornbeam.

NATIVE TO: Eastern United States. ZONES: 4-9.

A tree with multiple endorsements from our authors and consultants. We quote L. C. Chadwick, Columbus, Ohio: "A slow-growing, round-headed small tree of 30-35 feet. The bark of the trunk and larger branches is platelkie and sheddy. The foliage is dull green, usually with a fair reddish autumn color. It is somewhat difficult to transplant, but is tolerant of a wide range of soils. It has done well under adverse inner-city conditions."

Oxydendrum arboreum. Sourwood, sorrel tree (Deciduous).
NATIVE TO: Eastern United States. ZONES: 5-9. HABIT: Slow growth to 30-40 feet. Pyramidal form.

Ths tree is highly recommended by many of our authors and consultants. The common name, sourwood,

If planting space is limited, you will need to stay with more of the smaller shrubby types to capture greater variety in flower color and leaf. Choose the lily-flowered magnolia, *Magnolia liliiflora (quinquepeta)* or its cultivar 'Nigra,' or one of the several new selections now available of the star magnolia.

The magnificent, evergreen, southern magnolia, *Magnolia grandiflora* (zones 7-9), is a legend in the southern United States. To see the large (8 inches plus), fragrant, creamy white flowers and lustrous heavy-textured, 5 to 8 inch long leaves is to enjoy one of the world's finest flowering trees. Selected forms include 'St. Mary's,' a smaller tree (20 feet) known for its abundant bloom and predictable shape and 'Samuel Sommer,' which has flowers up to 14 inches wide.

Only if an area is available that is well protected from prevailing winds, such as a ravine edged with evergreens, then you should try one of the really unusual and rare big-leafed magnolias: umbrella magnolia *(Magnolia tripetala)* or the big-leaf magnolia *(Magnolia macrophylla)*. Perhaps they are for the gardening connoisseur who is willing to accept a real challenge.

With the exception of the southern magnolia (70'-90'), we have described only the small and medium-sized kinds, the more usable landscape species.

Where space permits, there are fine, large, tree types suitable for some northern areas. The cucumber tree (*Magnolia acuminata,* zone 5), the most stately of the hardier magnolias, is a vigorous, fast-growing tree native to eastern United States. It needs room to develop properly. The common name is derived from the shape and color of its fruit clusters.

The sweet bay magnolia, *Magnolia virginiana,* zone 6), growing to almost 40 feet in the South, is also one of the most popular in the colder areas, where it develops into a tall shrub. However, it comes close to suggesting a miniature version of the southern magnolia with its smaller, fragrant, creamy white, globular flowers and smaller (5") leaves, glossy above, blue-white beneath. It blooms from late spring to early fall on favorable growing sites. Being native to lowlands, it prefers rich moist soil.

If available, don't overlook two other quite hardy tree forms: *Magnolia denudata (M. heptapeta)*, the Yulan magnolia (zone 5), and *Magnolia kobus,* (Kobus magnolia, zone 5).

If your local suppliers are unable to furnish the kinds you want, you can get help in locating some of the splendid new sorts by contacting the Secretary, American Magnolia Society, Box 347A, Jackson, Tenn. 38301.

M. grandiflora. *Southern magnolia.*
M. grandiflora *'St. Marys'.*

M. loebneri.
M. soulangiana.

comes from the very sour tasting foliage. A woodsman's remedy for thirst is to chew sourwood leaves. Praised by Raymond Korbobo and James Foret in "Trees that need a friend," pages 80-84.

Parkinsonia aculeata. Jerusalem thorn, Mexican palo verde (Deciduous).
NATIVE TO: Mexico. ZONES: 8-10. HABIT: Fast-growing to 20-40 feet with a similar spread.

A tree most valued in hot areas with alkaline soil. We quote Francis Dean, Newport Beach, California, "a delicate, beautiful tree with diminutive leaves; better in dryer areas. Beautiful yellow flowers in spring when not overwatered."

Phellodendron amurense. Amur corktree (Deciduous).
NATIVE TO: Northern China and Manchuria. ZONES: 4-8. HABIT: Moderate to fast to 30-45 feet, round-headed, open form.

Liquidambar styraciflua. *Sweet gum.*

This fascinating tree is a good performer in areas with hot, dry summers and cold winters. Requires little care. Corky bark, twisted limbs and dark green, compound leaves give it a coarse, wild texture. In fall, the leaves turn yellow and drop early. Needs space to develop. A good candidate for large open areas, such as parks, where its beauty can be enjoyed at at distance as well as close up.

Widely acclaimed as a top tree for city conditions. Recent studies at the Morris Arboretum, Philadelphia, Pennsylvania, have found this to be true only when it is planted in open lawn areas. Planting strips along streets have yielded poor results.

Picea. Spruce.
William Collins, American Garden-Cole Nursery, Circleville, Ohio, evaluates this genus on page 66.

Serbian spruce, *Picea omorika,* is a tree that has received multiple endorsement from our authors and consultants. It is praised by John Ford in "Trees that need a friend," pages 80-84.

Spruce spider mites and the Cooley spruce gall aphid are common spruce pests. The mites are colored dark green to black, produce copious amounts of webbing, and turn the tree grayish. Control with Orthene.

Cooley spruce gall aphids cause cone-like galls to form at ends of twigs. Galls are green to reddish purple in spring, then turn brown, dry and hard in summer. Spray Cygon, Diazinon, or other insecticides labeled for this pest.

Pinus. Pine.
John Ford, Secrest Arboretum, Wooster, Ohio, and Fred Galle, Callaway Gardens, Pine Mountain, Georgia, collaborate on pines of the north and south on page 68.

Pistacia chinensis. Chinese pistachio (Deciduous).
NATIVE TO: China. ZONES: 7-9. HABIT: Moderate growth to 50-60 feet, and as wide. Spreading umbrellalike crown.

One of the best trees for filtered shade. The long (up to 12 inches), bright green leaves are divided into graceful leaflets. New leaves have a pink tinge, turn brilliant shades of

Above: Liriodendron tulipifera. *Tulip tree.*
Below: *Tulip shaped leaves and flowers.*

yellow to orange and red in fall. Attractive zigzag branching pattern.

Widely adapted, grows best with summer heat. Excellent lawn or street tree, although female tree will produce berries when a male tree is nearby. No disease problems. May need a little extra pruning when young to deveolp best form.

'Keith Davey' is a fruitless male selection with especially glossy foliage and predictably brilliant red fall color.

Platanus.

This genus contains the very popular London plane tree and several native sycamores. The American sycamore, *Platanus occidentalis,* is limited in value due to its size and susceptibility to anthracnose (see tree problems, page 85). *Platanus acerifolia*, the London plane tree, is the most useful of the species but is considered by many of our observers to be over-planted.

Prosopis glandulosa torreyana. *Mesquite.*

Platanus acerifolia. London plane tree (Deciduous).

HYBRID: *P. occidentalis* and *P. orientalis.* ZONES: 5-9. HABIT: One of the fastest-growing trees at the Secrest Arboretum, Wooster, Ohio; grew from 9 feet 8 inches to 18 feet 6 inches in five years. Eventually reaches 40-60 feet with an open spreading crown.

Metasequoia glyptostroboides. *Dawn redwood.*
Below: Morus alba. *Mulberry.*

Podocarpus gracilior. *Fern pine.*

Versatile, widely adapted tree; can take harsh city conditions, drought, and tough soils. Can be severely pruned. Widely used as a street tree and in malls. Large-lobed leaves are bright green. No fall color. The brown, ball-shaped fruits are borne two to a cluster. Most attractive feature is the striking green and white flaking bark. To one observer, the bark gives the impression of dappled sunlight. Of all the sycamores, it is the most resistant to anthracnose.

'Bloodgood' has consistently rated in the top 20 at the Shade Tree Evaluation Plot, Wooster, Ohio. Has better anthracnose resistance than the species. 'Pyramidalis' has a narrower habit.

Platycladus orientalis. (Often sold as *Thuja orientalis*). Oriental arborvitae (Needled Evergreen).

NATIVE TO: China, Japan, and Korea. BEST ADAPTED: Zones 6-9, can be grown 5. HABIT: Moderate to 25-50 feet, spread of 10-30 feet, pyramidal.

Forms a dense, candle-flame shaped tree. Upward ascending branches with foliage in vertical plates. Foliage is bright green above, yellow-green beneath.

Makes an especially tough windbreak, screen, or buffer. Takes heat, drought and wind. Grows best in moist, well-drained soil.

Many selections available, with varying foliage colors and heights. Some are small shrubs.

Podocarpus macrophyllus. Yew pine (Evergreen).

NATIVE TO: Japan. BEST ADAPTED: Zones 8-10, can be grown 6, 7. HABIT: Slow growth to 50-60 feet. Erect columnar form.

Valuable indoor-outdoor plant with graceful oriental character. Long, narrow, rather stiff, bright green leaves on slightly drooping branches. Pest-free. Widely adapted but may show chlorosis in alkaline or heavy soils. Protected locations will extend hardiness. Great for entryways or containers. Makes a fine hedge or espalier. *P. m. maki* is a slower growing, smaller plant often grown in containers.

The fern pine ,*Podocarpus gracilor,* is quite similar but has a softer leaf and character, and is best adapted outdoors to zone 9. Foliage varies on seedling grown trees.

Populus. Poplar.

Trees of this genus have been evaluated by William Flemer, III, Princeton Nurseries, Princeton, New Jersey, on page 72.

Populus alba 'Richardii' is championed by William Collins in "Trees that need a friend," pages 80-84.

Two of the major pests of poplars are canker disease and insect borers. Read more about them on page 85.

Prosopis glandulosa torreyana.
Mesquite (Deciduous).
NATIVE TO: Southwestern United States. ZONES: 7-10. HABIT: To 30 feet with loose-spreading crown. Usually multi-trunked.

A tree for the hot, dry regions of Texas. Gray-green foliage casts light filtered shade. Greenish-yellow flowers in spring and summer attract bees.

Drought-tolerant. Takes alkaline soils. Can be used as a screen or windbreak.

Prunus. Flowering fruits.

John Ford, Secrest Arboretum, Wooster, Ohio, writes about the large genus, *Prunus:*

The stone fruits, such as almonds, apricots, cherries, peaches and plums, are all in this genus.

A great many plants are dual purpose trees, being ornamental and furnishing fruit. Most of the fruit trees have a pronounced display of spring flowers. Some, such as Sapa plum, usually sold as a dwarf plum, have such fragrant flowers that it is worthwhile to grow them for this.

CHERRIES.

The cherries can be divided into three groups: the European, the American and the Oriental. In general, the Oriental types are less hardy than the others.

Prunus avium. Sweet Cherry. Zones 4-8. European. To 60 feet tall. Attractive bark becoming mahogany-red. Flowers white; the ancestor of most sweet cherries. Can be planted where Oriental cherries are not hardy.

Malus —
Flowering crabapple

More than 600 species and varieties of flowering crabapples are being grown in the United States and Canada. It is the most widely adapted of the flowering trees. Like all hardy flowering fruits, it requires a period of winter chilling and is not adapted to the mild-winter areas of the South and Southern California.

In some localities the tree's resistance to apple scab is all-important. In 1973 apple scab was so serious in south-

eastern Wisconsin that thousands of trees were completely defoliated. In Massachusetts, New Jersey, New York, Ohio, Pennsylvania, Rhode Island, and the District of Columbia, annual surveys have been made to determine which varieties are resistant to scab, cedar apple rust, mildew, and fire blight. Records of the surveys have been kept and constantly up-dated by Lester Nichols of the University of Pennsylvania.

The following list of recommended varieties is made up from reports of these evaluations. Some of the most popular crabapples proved to be most susceptible and are not included. Noteworthy for their absence are 'Almey', 'Flame', 'Eleyi', and 'Hopa'.

In the following list we have noted those that have usable, good-sized fruit and are commonly used to make jams & jellies.

M. floribunda. Deep pink

buds are pinkish-white in full flower, followed by small reddish-yellow fruit. Flowers profusely. Grows to 20 feet with graceful arching spread. Resistant to scab but will get some fire blight.

'Profusion.' Small, single flowers, deep red in bud, open purplish-red, fading to purplish-pink. Upright, spreading, growth habit, slow to 15 feet. Usable fruit. Disease-resistant, but moderately susceptible to powdery mildew.

Malus floribunda. *Crabapple.*

'Red Jewel.'

'Red Jade'.

The cultivar 'Plena,' the double flowered Mazzard cherry, has white flowers with up to 30 petals. Blooms a week before the double flowered Orientals. Grown for 2½ centuries.

Prunus cerasus. Sour cherry, Zones 4-8. European. Hardier than *P. avium.* To 30 feet tall. Many different cultivars used for fruit. The dwarf cultivars 'North Star' (to 10 feet) and 'Meteor' (to 16 feet) have attractive form and bark and can be used as small ornamentals. 'Rhex' sour cherry is a double flowered cultivar that can be planted farther north than *P. avium* 'Plena.'

Prunus sargentii. Sargent cherry. Zones 5-7. Oriental. To 75 feet tall. Hardiest of Oriental cherries. Deep pink flowers bloom before the double

Japanese cherries. One of the largest of Oriental cherries.

Prunus serotina. Black cherry. Zones 4-9. 80-100 feet tall. Native species. White, fragrant flowers in clusters 2 to 6 inches long. Fruit is black and especially relished by birds but not by man. When grown in the open as a specimen, it develops a huge, rounded crown. Branches partially drooping.

Prunus serrulata. Japanese Flowering Cherry. Zones 6-8. 20-25 feet tall. Oriental. Not completely hardy Zone 5. Over 100 cultivars have been developed. 'Amanogawa' cherry to 20 feet, most narrow and upright of Japanese cherries, flowers pale pink. 'Kwanzan' most popular and hardy of double flowered Oriental cherries, 12 to 18 feet, flowers deep pink. Used with

Prunus yedoensis in the famous Washington, D.C. plantings.

Prunus subhirtella. Higan cherry. Zones 6-8, to 25 feet. Oriental. Not completely hardy Zone 5. Unknown in wild. Intolerant of smog. Flowers pink and early. 'Autumnalis,' 15 to 30 feet, blooms during warm falls and again in spring; 'Pendula,' the most popular of higan weeping forms, having long pendulous branches. A double flowered form is available.

Prunus virginiana 'Shubert.' Shubert choke cherry. Zones 3-7. American. Red leaves all summer. Black fruits against red foliage are quite striking.

Prunus yedoensis. Yoshino Cherry. Japan. Zones 6-8, to 40 feet. Warmer parts of Zone 5. One of the most rapid

'Red Jade'. Gets its name from the color of its fruit. Small white flowers in great profusion on long, irregular, weeping branches in the spring. Heavy yield of usable fruit lasts late into the fall. Grows 15 to 20 feet. Reasonably disease-resistant, but will get some scab.

'Red Jewel.' One of the finest red-fruited, white-flowering crabapples. Bright cherry-red fruit persists to spring. Dark, rich green foliage and

excellent limb structure with horizontal branching. Grows to 15 feet. Good disease resistance.

M. sargentii. Profuse clusters of small, white flowers are fragrant, followed by masses of small, dark-red fruit. A dwarf, spreading variety. Slow growth to 8 feet. Good disease resistance.

Siberian crab *(M. bacatta mandshurica).* This heavy bearer of usable fruit has

1-inch, fragrant, white flowers in early spring. Grows vase-shaped to 15 to 30 feet tall. Reasonably disease resistant.

'Van Eseltine'. Flowers are borne in clusters. Buds are red, becoming pink as they open, and changing to white when fully open. Small, inedible fruits are golden yellow. Vase-shaped, growing to 18 feet. Resistant to scab, but susceptible to fire blight.

'White Angel'. Pure white

blossoms in the spring followed by cherrylike fruit clustered along the length of each branch, that last through the winter. A strong grower to 20 feet. Good disease resistance.

M. zumi calocarpa. Pink buds open to fragrant, pure white flowers. Red fruit persists through the winter. Moderate growth to 20 feet. Pyramidal habit with weeping branchlets. Resistant to scale, but will get some fire blight.

'Profusion'.

'Profusion.'

Siberian crabapple.

growing cherries. A flat-topped, wide spreading tree. Single white flowers are borne in abundance early in the season. This cherry comprises the main part of the cherry display in the Washington, D.C. tidal basin.

PLUMS.

The plums, like cherries, include three varieties: American, Euroasiatic, and Sino-Japanese. Most plums are dual-purpose trees, having heavy spring blooms and furnishing edible fruit as well. Plum trees can be mere shrubs or small trees which seldom exceed 30 feet in height. There are many species of American plums, from the small fruited cherry-plums to types with fruit an inch or more in length. The original range of most American plums is not known since they had been spread over wide areas of the country long before the advent of European settlements. One, the Chickasaw plum, was named after the Chickasaw Indians. Indian legend has it that this plum was originally brought from west of the Mississippi River. It is now common throughout the South. Many of the plums are quite hardy and some of the shrubby species can be found growing north into Zone 2. Many plums have a tendency to form thickets. A number of plums require two seedling trees or two different varieties for cross pollination to obtain a good set of fruit.

Prunus americana. Wild plum. Zones 4-9. To 30 feet. A coarse tree with shaggy bark, often thorny. Some form thickets. Abundant white to pink flowers. Fruit is yellow to purplish red. Good for preserves. A number of improved cultivars have been developed, such as 'Blackhawk,' 'Hawkeye' and 'De Soto.'

Prunus angustifolia. Chickasaw plum. Zones 6-9. To 16 feet. Small tree with spreading top. Forms thickets. Has thorny branchlets. Flowers are white and borne before the leaves. Fruit small, sweet, and edible. May be red or yellow. A number of

Pistacia chinensis. *Chinese pistache.*

Above: Prunus subhirtella pendula. *Weeping cherry.*
Below: Prunus cerasifera *'Thundercloud.'* Purple leaf plum.

Pyrus calleryana. *Callery pear.*

cultivars have been developed for better fruit such as 'Newman' and 'Lone Star.'

Prunus blireiana. Blireiana plum. Zones 5-7. To 24 feet tall. A widely planted tree with reddish-purple foliage. Flowers pink. Grows rapidly when young.

Prunus cerasifera. Cherry plum. Zones 4-8. To 25 feet tall. Flowers white. Fruit sweet, yellow or reddish. Cultivar 'Atropurpurea' has purple leaves and pale rose flowers. 'Thundercloud' has pale pink flowers and purple leaves that appear almost black.

Prunus munsoniana. Wild goose plum. Zones 6-8. To 30 feet tall. A good sized tree. Often cultivated. Fruit bright red, rarely yellow, sweet and juicy. Ripens in June and July.

CHERRY LAURELS.

The cherry laurels, or laurel cherries, are grown for their attractive, evergreen leaves. The fruit is small and is eaten by birds. These plants are used as hedges, screens, background plants, and as specimen plants. They make their best growth in the Coastal plain and lower Piedmont sections of the South.

Prunus caroliniana. Cherry laurel. Zones 7-10. 18 to 40 feet tall. Large shrub or small tree native from North Carolina to Texas, often forming dense thickets. May reach a trunk diameter of one foot. Flowers white. The plant has been widely spread by birds who favor the ½-inch black fruit. Can withstand heavy shearing. Relatively free from insects and disease.

Prunus laurocerasus. Cherry laurel, English laurel. Zones 7-9. To 30 feet tall. Original home is Eastern Europe and Asia Minor. Grown and naturalized in England since 1576. Has erect axillary and terminal white flowers in clusters five inches long. Fruit is red at first, turning black. Tolerant of shade and drip from overhanging trees. A great many cultivars have been developed. 'Angustifolia' has narrow

Rhus glabra. *Sumac.*

leaves; 'Caucasica' grows upright; 'Latifolia' is a large-leafed form; 'Schipkaensis' is one of the hardiest and very free flowering.

Prunus lusitanica. Portugal laurel. Zones 7-10. To 60 feet tall. Original home Spain, Portugal, and the Canary Islands. A beautiful specimen when allowed to develop naturally. Flowers small, white in clusters to 10 inches. Fruit is red turning dark purple. Hardier and will withstand more sun, heat and wind than *P. laurocerasus.* A num-

ber of cultivars have been developed, such as 'Myrtifolia' with smaller leaves and 'Variegata' with white in leaves.

A number of species and types of *Prunus,* primarily developed as fruit trees, can also be used as ornamentals — especially the dwarf trees. The bloom of the peach tree *(Prunus persica)* has been spectacular enough to inspire the poets. Peach trees grow in Zones 5-9 and will grow to be 20 feet in height. Many cultivars have been selected as orna-

Prunus persica. *Flowering peach.*

Prunus caroliniana. *Cherry laurel.*

mentals such as 'Double White,' 'Double Red, and 'Peppermint Stick,' these names describing the flowers.

Strains of almond, such as Hall's almond, have been developed that are hardy in the same areas as peaches. The apricot (Prunus armeniaca), although only reliable for fruit production in Zones 8 and 9, has hardy types on the market, such as 'Moongold' and 'Sungold' that are hardy to Zone 5. They flower so early that the blossom and developing fruit are usually killed by late frosts. Nevertheless, the bloom can be quite heavy and make a good display. The hardy apricots are worth growing since the tree itself has clean-looking green leaves and interesting, unusual-looking bark.

Pseudotsuga menziesii. Douglas fir (Needled evergreen).
NATIVE TO: Alaska through western United States into Mexico. BEST ADAPTED: Zones 6-9, can be grown 4-9. HABIT: Fast-growing. Can reach 200 feet, usually less. Spread 30-60 feet.

The Douglas fir is unmatched as a timber tree. It produces more lumber than any other single species in the United States. It also has merit as a landscape tree. Uniform pyramid shape when young makes it an ideal Christmas tree.

Stiff branches droop on lower part of tree, extend upward and outward on upper part. Soft, flat, bluish-green needles arranged spirally on twig. New growth in spring is attractive apple-green. Always fragrant, fresh smelling.

Although native to the moist Northwest where it can reach 200 feet, it is widely adapted to soils and climate. Size varies with moisture. When grown in areas with a high water table, the roots can pancake. Roots of a 60-foot tree may only be 12-18 inches deep. Many times, in new housing developments, areas are cleared leaving just a few firs around the homes. Without the mutual support and protection of other trees, they blow over in the first big wind.

Pyrus calleryana. Callery pear (Deciduous).
NATIVE TO: Eurasia, North Africa. ZONES: 4-9. HABIT: Moderate growth rate to 25-35 feet with a spread of 15-20 feet. Form varies by cultivar from broad-base oval to conical.

Picea — Spruce

You could name the colors of the American flag with spruce trees. Some of the species have the common names, red spruce, white spruce and blue spruce. Most of the spruce of North America are native to the northern areas of the continent: Canada, Alaska, and the northern parts of the United States from Minnesota and Wisconsin to New England.

Native to the east are the black spruce (Picea mariana), white spruce (Picea glauca), and the red spruce (Picea rubens). The Engelmann spruce (Picea engelmannii), occurs in parts of the Rocky Mountains, mostly west and north of Colorado. Also from the Rocky Mountain area come the very popular Colorado spruce (Picea pungens), and especially the named varieties and selected seedlings that have bluish-green needles. They are collectively called Colorado blue spruce, Picea pungens 'Glauca,' with variety names tacked on it if they are vegetatively propagated.

Tree breeders are working to further improve the vigor and form of certain spruce species.

The most widely adapted spruce, the Norway spruce (Picea abies), is not a native. It was brought from Europe early in this country's history. Pioneers moving West, espe-

cially in the near-treeless Prairie States, wanted trees that would remind them of their homeland. The Norway spruce was one of these and, surprisingly, was found to be quite well adapted to these grasslands. It was already finding its niche in the Colonial States.

You will find these beautiful, pyramidal evergreens actually becoming more attractive as they age, because the branchlets gradually become more pendulous. They are now planted around homes all across the country, and for the most part, they are vigorous and growing well. Norway spruce make excellent windbreaks and tall screens.

One characteristic that has made them so popular is their natural ability to retain their lower branches and needles, a direct contrast with some of the spruce, which may, as they mature, have their lower branches (and needles) shaded out.

Where space permits, Norway spruce is a good landscape specimen. Do not plant on poor sites; avoid dry ridges and slopes where soils are likely to be low in fertility. On preferred sites (cool and moist), it has reached a height of 100 feet with a trunk diameter of 2 feet. Under most landscaping situations, these dimensions should probably be cut in half.

Besides all its other fine features, they have large (for a spruce) and attractive seed-bearing cones, 4"-7" long.

Norway spruce has produced many "sports" — unu-

sual forms — that range from dwarf to weeping, compact to spreading. Many, especially the weeping forms, will require staking to bring them up to the desired height.

Availability of these odd or different types varies from year to year and in different parts of the country. As many as a dozen different types have been offered for sale.

Where space isn't available for large spruce like the Norway, you are likely to find seedling trees of the Colorado spruce, with green or slightly bluish needles. Selected seedling trees with a pronouncedly bluish-green color may be called Colorado blue spruce, but for the bluist needles buy the named, grafted varieties, such as 'Koster.'

For over 50 years the Colorado blue spruce almost has been a status symbol among the evergreens, especially in the eastern and midwestern United States. As a young tree it is beautiful, vigorous, and fast-growing. Its major fault is its tendency to lose its lower branches, detracting from its beauty. Nurserymen propagate several forms with pronounced whitish-blue needles. Most likely to be available are the varieties 'Koster,' 'Moerheimii,' and 'Hoopsii.' Some plantsmen describe these bluish types as so different as to require careful placement in a landscape, or they will dominate, even to their own disadvantage.

The white spruce has furnished a very popular, compact selection. It is the dwarf Alberta spruce, Picea glauca

Koster blue spruce.

P. pungens 'Pendens'.

If any one tree illustrates what can be done through selection, it's the Callery pear. The species has many good qualities: abundant early spring bloom, brilliant crimson-red fall color, shiny dark green leaves with scalloped edges, and amazing adaptability. It has three basic problems: thorns, susceptibility to fireblight, and messy, inedible fruits. With the development of cultivars like 'Bradford,' which are thornless, fireblight resistant, and have small fruits of no inconvenience, this tree has become one of the most attractive specimens available. Add to this the difference in form between cultivars and you also have one of the most versatile.

All cultivars have the good qualities of the species. The difference lies in the form. 'Bradford' grows to 50 feet by 30 feet, oval-shaped with spreading upright branches, thornless and usually fruitless, with spectacular fall color. 'Chanticleer' is narrower, closer to pyramidal. 'Aristocrat,' most similar to 'Bradford,' is pyramidal with wide-spaced, horizontal branches. It also has a glossier leaf with wavier edges. 'Faureri,' a fourth cultivar, sometimes available, is a dwarf form (20 feet) with an oval habit, known primarily for its profuse flower show.

All cultivars are extremely adaptable. They stand up to pollution and other stresses of the city and can take wind, even on the coast. They are demanding as to soil type and they are drought resistant, require little maintenance, and are relatively pest free.

Exceptionally fine street trees, receiving consistently high scores at the Shade Tree Evaluation Plot, Secrest Arboretum, Wooster, Ohio. Also valuable as shade and specimen trees.

Pyrus kawakamii. Evergreen pear (Evergreen).
NATIVE TO: Taiwan. ZONES: 8-10.
HABIT: Moderate growth rate to 30 feet; open, irregular habit.

One of the most widely used trees in California. Naturally a spreading shrub but most commonly used as a single or multi-trunked tree. White, late winter to spring blossoms. Shiny, light green leaves with wavy edges. Adaptable to many soil types and needs minimum care.

Easy to espalier, good in containers, near the patio, or on the street.

'Conica.' Refined, dense, and compact, its appearance is formal. Slow-growing and stays small. Prefers a somewhat sheltered position. In north central United States there may be a preference for the slower-growing, more compact form of white spruce, called the Black Hills spruce, *Picea glauca* 'Densata.'

The spire-like Serbian spruce *(Picea omorika)* deserves much wider use than its availability would indicate. The glossy, dark green needles are borne on a slender-trunked tree having short ascending (sometimes drooping) branches, the net result being a very narrow pyramidal head like that of the Norway spruce. The tree usually retains its lower branches, a most valuable trait in a specimen tree that is expected to retain its beauty throughout its lifetime. For its height, no spruce is likely to use less

ground area, a fact that permits it to be used with discretion on quite small landscaped areas.

Occasionally available are the tigertail spruce, *Picea torana,* a potentially large-growing, handsome and hardy evergreen from Japan, and the Oriental spruce *(Picea orientalis),* a tall, graceful tree from Asia minor.

While we have not discussed all the interesting and useful kinds of spruce for ornamental plantings, those most generally available have been covered.

One parting thought about identifying spruce trees. The needles (leaves) of nearly all spruce are squarish in cross-section and can be rolled between the thumb and index finger. Fir and hemlock needles are flatish and do not roll easily like those of spruce.

P. pungens and P. pungens 'Glauca.' Colorado green and blue spruce.

P. omorika. Serbian spruce.

Quercus. Oak.

One of the most familiar group of trees, the oaks, are discussed in general by William Collins, American Garden-Cole Nursery, Circleville, Ohio, on page 74.

Commonly available deciduous species are: *Quercus alba* (White oak), *Quercus acutissima* (Sawtooth Oak), *Quercus palustris* (Pin Oak), *Quercus phellos* (Willow oak), *Quercus robur* (English oak), *Quercus rubra* (Northern red oak).

Evergreen species include: *Quercus virginiana* (Southern live oak).

Rhamnus frangula. Alder buckthorn (Deciduous).

NATIVE TO: Europe, Asia, North Africa. BEST ADAPTED: Zones 5-7, can be grown zones 2-7. HABIT: Fast-growing to 15-18 feet by 8-12 feet wide. Upright, spreading, oval in form. Can be multi-trunked or trained to a single trunk.

Most highly valued as a quick hedge or screen in cold winter climates. Glossy green foliage takes well to shearing. Insignificant flower clusters followed by red fruit that gradually turns black. They attract the attention of birds more than they do people.

Preferred form is 'Colmnaris,' the tallhedge buckthorn, which makes a good tight hedge. See "Hedges" on page 40.

Rhus. Sumac.

This is a large group of evergreen shrubs and trees that includes poison oak and poison ivy. Two very similar forms in this group are useful trees in the eastern United States.

Rhus glabra. Smooth sumac (Deciduous).

NATIVE TO: Eastern United States. ZONES: 3-9. HABIT: Moderate to fast growth rate to 20 feet with an equal spread. Irregular in form.

The large, divided, tropical-looking leaves are deep green above, whitish underneath, and take on brilliant red to red-purple fall color. This and the clusters of red fruit that last into the winter are outstanding characteristics.

A very tough, durable American native that can grow in a wide range of conditions. It is most valuable in dry, infertile soils. Useful as a small single-stemmed tree for patio or garden. Can be grown in large containers.

Pinus — Pine

Here are the northern pines as seen by John Ford.

Pinus aristata. Bristlecone pine. Zones 5-6. Needles 5 in a bundle, 1 to 1½ inches long, usually flecked with white dots of resin. Needles will remain on twigs 20 to 30 years, giving the ends of the branches a bushy or brushlike appearance. Cones 3½ inches long. Tree grows slowly to 45 feet tall. May only average 3 inches increase in height a year. Original home in mountains of southwestern United States, where some specimens are approaching 5000 years old — the oldest living trees in the world. Will grow on very dry and exposed sites. Dwarf and picturesque. Use as specimen or in rock garden wheer years will pass before it outgrows its place.

Pinus banksiana. Jack pine. Zones 2-5. Needles 2 in a bundle, ¾ to 1½ inches long, twisted and spreading apart. Needles turn yellow in winter. Cones 1 to 2 inches long, without stalks, usually curved and pointed. Tree can grow to be 70 feet tall. Will grow on poorer sites than most pines. Usually found naturally on deep, dry sands. Poor growth on heavy soils. It grows farther north than any other American pine. Recommended on sites in the North where other pines might not grow.

Pinus bungeana. Lacebark pine. Zones 5-6. Needles 3 in a bundle, 3 inches long, usually dense. Cones 2 to 3 inches long. Tree to 75 feet tall. Original home, China. Bark most interesting when scaling off like that of a plane tree, leaving chalky, white patches. Holds its needles 5 years or longer. Often with several trunks, spreading. Very picturesque. Grow as specimen plant. Overlooked but very desirable ornamental pine.

Pinus griffithii (P. wallichiana). Himalayan pine. Zones 6-7. Needles 5 in a bundle, 6 to 8 inches long. Cones 6 to 10 inches long. Tree can reach 150 feet but usually grows to half this height. Long, drooping, blue-green needles are most attractive. Native of Himalayas. Grows best on sandy loam. Resembles native white pine but needles and cones are usually longer. Grow as specimen tree but give it room in which to develop a spread of 40 feet or more.

Pinus nigra. Austrian pine. Zones 4-7. Needles 2 in a bundle, slender and stiff, 4 to 6 inches long. Cones 2 to 3 inches long. Tree 60 to 100 feet tall. Original home is Central and Southern Europe. The tree will stand heat and drought. Widely planted as ornamental and for windbreaks. Grows on wide variety of soils. Variety *caramanica*. Crimean pine. Zones 5-7. Crown much more dense than species, branches more ascending. Makes a much more uniform, better looking species, branches more Appears to be more tender than species. To 100 feet tall. Variety *maritima*. Corsican Pine. Zones 5-7. Needles slightly longer and faster growing than species, but slightly more tender.

Pinus parviflora. Japanese white pine. Zones 6-7. Needles 5 in a bundle, 1½ to 2½ inches long. Cones 2 to 3 inches long, can remain on tree 6 to 7 years. Tree to 90 feet tall, grows slowly. Will grow in zone 5 on protected sites. Crown can spread almost as wide as tree is tall, so give it ample room in which to develop. Excellent specimen tree that should be more widely used. Grows on sandy loam to silty clay. 'Glauca', Silver Japanese white pine. Needles silver-blue, more striking-looking tree than the species.

Pinus resinosa. Red pine. Zones 2-5. Needles 2 in a bundle, 4 to 6 inches long. Cones 2 inches long. Tree to 75 feet tall, forming extensive forests in Newfoundland and Quebec to Manitoba, south to Lake States and mountains of Pennsylvania. Bark reddish-brown; when the sun shines on the bark in a forest stand, there is often a reddish haze. Crown is pyramidal, becoming round-topped on old trees. Makes best growth on sandy type of soils. An excellent ornamental tree in the cooler sections of the country.

Pinus strobus. Eastern white pine. Zones 2-8. Needles 5 in a bundle, 3 to 5 inches long. Tree to 150 feet tall. In original forest, some trees grew to be 200 feet tall. A tree of the North, following the Appalachian Mountains south to north Georgia. Grows best on well-drained, sandy loams or silty soils but will grow

P. thunbergii. *Japanese black pine.*

P. nigra. *Austrian pine.*

Rhus typhina. Staghorn sumac, velvet sumac (Deciduous).

NATIVE TO: North America. ZONES: 3-8. Habit: Fast to 15-30 feet, wider than high. Upright, wide-spreading and irregular in form.

Distinguished from *Rhus glabra* principally by having hairy branches and slightly lower growth.

Robinia. Locust.

Robinias can be quite attractive but unfortunately they are subject to several pests, most notably the locust borer (see page 85 for control), and should be used only as a last resort in very tough situations. They are fast-growing, widely adapted trees commonly found on undesirable lists because of heavy thorns, invasive roots and weak wood.

Robinia pseudoacacia. Black locust (Deciduous).

NATIVE TO: East central United States. ZONES: 4-9. HABIT: Fast-growing to 40-75 feet by 30-60 feet wide. Often multi-stemmed, umbrellalike in form with sparse, open branches.

Young leaflets are silvery gray-green turning dark green with age, and yellow in fall. Fragrant, pea-shaped flowers grow in long pendant clusters and are attractive to bees. Flowers are followed by thin, flat brown pods that persists through the winter. Thorny with rough, deeply furrowed bark.

A good choice for difficult situations. Takes heat, drought, all types of soil, and neglect. This is a quick-growing temporary tree.

Many selections have been made, some with more manageable form, some with colored flowers and some with no thorns. Because of hybridization, there is confusion as to which species the following belong.

Hortus III lists 'Frisia' and 'Globe' as *R. pseudoacacia,* and 'Decaisne-ana' and 'Idahoensis' as *R. x ambigua.*

'Frisia' has orange new growth, eventually turning red. 'Globe' has a formal globe shape. 'Decaisneana' is a more widely planted form with fragrant pink flowers. 'Idahoensis' is a more shapely tree to 40 feet with deep rose flowers.

Salix. Willow.

There are many willows ranging in size from small shrubs to large trees. Childhood memories of the huge

on most soils. A long-lived tree that can survive to be 450 years old or more. Has been widely planted in refor-estation projects and as orna-mentals, often as screens. One of the most widely planted and best-known pines in the Northeast. A number of horticultural cultivars have been developed for special planting situations. Three of the most common are: 'Fastigiata'. Pyramidal white pine. A narrow, upright columnar tree. Useful in con-fined planting areas as screens. 'Nana'. Dwarf white pine. Grows 6 to 10 feet tall with spread of 10 feet or more. Very compact. Sometimes listed as the cultivar 'Radiata', which is what the taxonomist calls it. 'Pendula'. Weeping white pine. Pendulous branches touch the ground.

Pinus sylvestris. Scotch or Scot's Pine. Zones 2-8. Twisted needles, 2 in a bundle, 1½ to 3 inches long. Cones 2 inches long. Tree to 75 feet tall. Bark at first reddish-orange in color. Has been extensively planted in the North for reforestation and as ornamental trees. Now widely planted as Christmas trees. Opengrown specimen trees become quite open and flat-topped resembling trees in a Chinese painting. Tree originally from Europe. Many strains and varieties have been developed for timber growing, Christmas trees and ornamentals: 'Fastigiata', Pyramidal Scotch pine. Columnar and narrow. 'Watereri'. Waterer Scotch

pine. Dense, slowgrowing form, almost as wide as it is high when young.

Pinus thunbergii. Japanese black pine. Zones 5-8. Needles 2 in a cluster, 3 to 5 inches long, stiff. Cones 2-3 inches long. Tree to 90 feet tall. Large, white, terminal buds help to identify the tree. One of the best evergreens for seashore planting. Fast-grow-ing. Crown becomes irregular and spreading as it approaches maturity.

P. aristata. *Bristlecone pine.*

P. strobus. *Eastern white pine.*

weeping willow have endeared it to many, it is hard to picture a lake or stream without a willow on the bank. "When there's water, there's willows." For an interesting explanation of the common name, weeping willow, see page 28.

Where choice is wide, willows are often frowned upon, as they have many drawbacks. The wood is brittle. It is impossible to garden under them because roots are invasive. They have many pests and are constantly dropping leaves. However, they do serve a useful purpose in many climates and their graceful, weeping habit is hard to match. Willows are good, quick-growing temporary trees, widely adapted to soil and climate, asking only for lots of moisture.

Salix alba tristis. Golden weeping willow (Deciduous).
NATIVE TO: Europe, northern Africa, Asia. ZONES: 3-9. HABIT: Fast growing to 80 feet with greater spread. Broad, open, round-topped, low branching.

Distinctly corky, yellow-brown to brown bark and polished yellow stems make this tree one of the most beautiful of the weeping types. Leaves are bright green to yellow-green, pale beneath. Tolerates floods and seashore conditions. Needs training as a shade tree.

Salix babylonica. Weeping willow (Deciduous).
NATIVE TO: China. BEST ADAPTED: ZONES 7-9, can be grown 5-6. HABIT: Fast to 30-59 feet with greater spread. Heavy, roundheaded with branchlets drooping to the ground.

More pronounced weeping form than *S.a. tristis*. Longer leaves are medium olive-green turning yellow in the fall. Branchlets are greenish to brown. May need training to develop single trunk. Needs room to develop. Makes a good screen. Interesting winter silhouette.

Salix matsudana. Hankow willow (Deciduous).
NATIVE TO: Northern Asia. ZONES: 5-9. HABIT: Fast-growing pyramidal tree to 35-45 feet.

Two selections are more common than the species. 'Tortuosa,' the corkscrew willow, is a novelty grown for its corkscrew branches and twisted leaves. More of an oddity than an effective landscape tree. On the other hand, 'Umbraculifera,' the globe

About street trees

We talked to many arborists involved in street tree programs and feel you'll learn more from their views than from a bare listing of street trees. We believe Frank Chan, arborist for the city of Sacramento, California, speaks for all of them:

"Major emphasis on tree selection should be based on adaptation of the tree to the environment. Because of this, street tree recommendations will vary from location to location, depending on prevailing environmental conditions. In addition to adaptation, tree size and use should be foremost in our minds. The kind of street, whether it is a residential, arterial, downtown, or mall street planting, makes a difference.

"A tree must fit the space where it is to grow. Overhead wires, underground utilities, traffic, and sign clearance must be considered. Damage to sidewalks, buildings, and other structures must be prevented or compensated for. Spacing between trees should provide for optimum growth as well as environmental and aesthetic enhancement.

"Trees should also be given adequate planting areas. Whenever possible, off-street planting in back of the sidewalk is desirable. Here, in the lawn or other landscaped area, adequate watering and aeration can be provided. Where there is much pavement and reflective surfaces of buildings, trees are limited by moisture deficiencies, poor aeration, and extreme temperatures. Tree selection in these areas should be based on trees that can withstand abuse, and by size. Although the greater the environmental impact, with larger trees, the greater will be the maintenance potential and cost. Street tree selection should also be based on longevity, or expected life span. The longer the tree provides service and beauty, the more invaluable or economical the tree is.

"A large tree modifies the environment more than a small tree, making it possible to save on energy to cool or heat buildings. We need to preserve our large trees as long as practical, however, we must also recognize when trees become liabilities. They should then be removed and replaced by the most promising or proven tree species of our time. We should use to our advantage trees that plant scientists have found to be resistant to pests and diseases. We should observe those trees that have performed well locally, and perpetuate them by asexual propagation.

"A basic requirement for a sound street tree program is the selection of adaptable trees to attain a diverse and well-balanced tree population. Street tree culture is a dynamic, evolutionary, and evolving process. It must be based on sound planning, management, and practices to assure that the community is getting the most for its tax dollars and that a healthy and aesthetically pleasing environment is attained. Because we have a wide variety of desirable trees, it makes sense to select more variety, in order to avoid high maintenance on a considerable portion of the plantings because of diseases or pests specific to any one group of trees.

"To attain a balanced population, it is helpful to establish various percentage levels for trees planted in relation to the total tree population. This prevents overplanting any one kind of tree and avoids any enormous impact if a specific devastating disease or pest strikes, such as Dutch elm disease, chestnut blight, and, lesser known, ceratocystis canker in plane trees. Percentage levels should be established by each community.

"The higher the tree population, the greater the need for variation. No tree should represent over 2-3% of the total population. Also, there is a need to use more tolerant species in the maximum percentage level. The lower the tree population, the greater the chance of using the most desirable species. Some species can be used at a rate as high as 4% to 5% of the total tree population without much chance of negative impact. The reason for this is you are using the most promising trees, and as the tree population grows, the percentage will be reduced if no further planting of that species takes place.

"Trees have a monetary value. However, no money value can be placed on them when, through the years, you have cared for and admired them. For this they have reciprocated by providing beauty and comfort. Indeed, a tree can be a long-time friend, and no money can replace this sentiment."

Cinnamomum camphora. Camphor tree.

Acer saccharum. Sugar maple.

Liquidambar. *Sweet gum.*

Melia azedarach. *'Umbraculifera.' Texas umbrella tree.*

Sapium sebiferum. *Chinese tallow tree.*

Magnolia grandiflora. *Southern magnolia.*

Lagerstroemia indica. *Crape myrtle.*

willow, is a valuable plant in the desert. Like the species, it stands more drought than most willows. Forms a roundheaded tree 35-40 feet high.

A third cultivar, popular in arid regions, is 'Navajo,' a wide-spreading tree to 60-70 feet. Like 'Umbraculifera,' it is widely adapted.

Sapium sebiferum. Chinese tallow tree (Deciduous).

NATIVE TO: China. ZONES: 8-9. HABIT: Fast-growing to 35 feet with equal spread. Round-headed to conical in form.

Dense foliage, but with an airy feeling, provides a light shade throughout the summer. Leaves are aspenlike in appearance and turn bronze to bright red after a sharp frost. Pruning in the early stages will confine it to a single trunk.

A good lawn or street tree or use it as a shade tree in patio or on terrace. It also makes a good screen.

Tolerates moist soils but prefers acid conditions. Ample water will encourage fast growth. The Chinese tallow tree is a good pest- and disease-free substitute for the poplar.

Sassafras albidum. Sassafras (Deciduous).

NATIVE TO: Eastern United States. ZONES: 5-9. HABIT: Moderate growth rate to 30-50 feet. Irregular habit.

A tree common to eastern hedgerows and woodlands. It really deserves more attention — it seems to be all but forgotten by nurseries selecting superior forms of other eastern hardwoods.

Interesting foliage and excellent yellow to red fall color. Several shapes of the bright green leaves may be found on the same branch. They vary from two lobes, to a one-lobe mitten shape, to no lobes at all.

Flowers on female trees are followed by interesting fruit; dark blue berries with bright red stalks. Attractive up close.

Native to acid soils. Commonly bothered by Japanese beetles (see page 85 for information on control). Somewhat difficult to transplant, which accounts for the fact that it is not too available. Transplants best in smaller sizes. Can be effectively used in naturalized areas, woodland borders, parks, and other large areas. An 'old-time elixir', sassafras tea, can be made from the roots.

Populus — Poplar

Few trees hardy in temperate zones grow as rapidly as poplars. An unrooted cutting, spring-planted in an area of rich soil and abundant moisture, can reach 12 or more feet in height by the following autumn. Although such fantastic growth slows down as the tree grows older, it is still unique among hardy trees. This rapid growth rate, coupled with tolerance of a wide variety of soil types and the production of wood with definite industrial value, has led to considerable interest in poplars for reforestation.

Trees with the remarkable growth rates of the best hybrid poplars have caught the fancy of home gardeners and shade tree commissions. While these new hybrids have definite value for their growth on poor soil sites, for soil reclamation, and for shelter belts or screening, they are merely faster growing

poplars, subject to the same traditional drawbacks for street tree and garden use.

In some very arid areas of the West, locally native poplars are among the few trees which will survive and grow large enough to provide shade. Of these adapted species, male trees that do not produce clouds of cotton-like seed such as the cottonless cottonwood, 'Siouxland', are much to be preferred over ordinary seedlings. Another important use for poplars, particularly the narrow-growing varieties, is for quick-growing screening to hide unsightly areas and buildings or to make windbreaks. Narrow-growing conifers like arborvitae make denser and more permanent screens, but the better poplars grow immeasurably faster, and some are quite long-lived. Being deciduous, they conceal less in the winter, but they are twiggy enough to provide some visual

barrier. When there is room enough, the ideal solution to a screening problem is to plant a row of the very rapid-growing but short-lived Lombardy poplars besides a row of arborvitae, spruce, or narrow junipers. By the time the poplars begin to decline, the evergreens are tall enough to do the job. The following species and varieties of poplars are useful for various purposes in the larger home landscape, parks, and along highways.

Populus alba. White poplar.

This tall and wide-spreading species is very hardy and its foliage is among the prettiest of all poplars. The leaves resemble small maple leaves, dark green above and silvery white underneath, especially attractive on a breezy day. It grows exceptionally well at the seashore, being highly resistant to salt spray and even temporary immersion of the root

P. nigra 'Italica.' Lombardy poplars.

area. Its great fault is the persistent sprouting of shoots from the wide-spreading root system. But at the seashore in poor, sandy soils where few trees will grow at all, it has a real place.

There is a narrow-growing, columnar variety called the Bolleana poplar (*P. a. 'Pyramidalis'*) which has the same fine foliage, but is well suited for screening purposes. Fortunately, it does not sprout from the roots like the wild type.

Populus angustifolia. Narrow-leafed cottonwood.

This very hardy and drought-resistant tree is one of the relatively limited choices for ornamental planting in dry

Above: P. tremuloides. *Quaking aspen.*
Right: *Fall color of the quaking aspen.*

Sciadopitys verticillata. Umbrella pine (Needled Evergreen).

NATIVE TO: China. ZONES: 6-8. HABIT: Slow growth to 80-100 feet. Usually much smaller (35-40 feet). Dense pyramidal form.

Often overlooked because of its slow growth rate, this tree is well worth the wait. We quote Frank Chan, Sacramento, California. "Umbrella pine has handsome, interesting foliage; useful both for landscape effect and flower arrangements. Glossy, dark green leaves, 3 to 5 inches long, grow in dense clusters radiating out from the center, resembling the ribs of an umbrella, hence the name.

"Although slow-growing, it is useful in all stages of growth. A good container tree when young; as it gets larger it can be used as a portable Christmas tree for many years, and, finally, it can be a valuable landscape tree.

"Plant in partial shade in hot areas. Prefers slightly acid, well-drained soil."

Sophora japonica. Japanese pagoda tree, Chinese scholar tree (Deciduous).

NATIVE TO: Japan, Korea. ZONES: 5-10. HABIT: Moderate growth rate to 20-30 feet; slow to 50-70 feet with comparable spread. Dense, upright form when young, becoming round and spreading with age.

Raymond Korbobo, Rutgers University has this to say:

"The sophoras start blooming when they are from 8 to 10 years of age. Then they are covered with large loose clusters of creamy-white, pea-shaped blossoms. The blooming period is at least six weeks. In good cool summers it can last two months, which is quite remarkable.

"The sophoras are extremely regular in their blooming habits. They all come into bloom almost on the same day no matter where they are growing in a given geographic area — on streets, in gardens, or in parks.

"The fall color of the compound leaf is a very nice, clear yellow. Sophora is ordinarily recommended where you want filtered shade. That is the coolest kind of shade, compared to the solid shade of a heavily-foliaged Norway maple, for example.

"There is hardly any tree, including the American elm, with more

P. nigra 'Italica.' Lombardy poplars.

areas of the West where supplemental irrigation is not available. It reaches 60 feet in rich soils where there is subsoil moisture present but is less tall in drier sites. Choose a male tree to avoid cotton masses. Other species, like the Fremont cottonwood *(Populus fremontii)* and the Texas cottonwood *(Populus wislitzeni)* are useful for hot and dry regions and the highly alkaline soils of the Southwest.

Populus canadensis. 'Eugenei' Carolina poplar.

This variety, and its many hybrids, are among the fastest growing of the hardy trees. It is being extensively planted for pulp, wood and lumber production because it reaches usable size in a very short time when grown in rich, moist soil. It is weak-wooded, constantly dropping small branches and sometimes dangerously long branches during wind storms. Its use should be confined to forestry planting.

Populus maximowiczii Japanese poplar.

This rapid-growing tree has large oval leaves quite unlike those of cottonwoods and aspens. It grows rapidly, ultimately reaching 80 feet in height, with pale bark and handsome, dark green foliage. It does not sprout or sucker from the roots and hence is often used for a quick-growing shade tree, as is its hybrid offspring NE-48 *(Populus maximowiczii x P. berolinensis).* Unfortunately it develops stem cankers at maturity in the East, and thus becomes unsightly just when it should look its best. Select a male form.

Populus nigra 'Italica.' Lombardy poplar.

This handsome columnar tree is one of the oldest known varieties of ornamental trees. It is unbeatable as a tall screen or accent tree in every respect but one — it is very susceptible to stem canker disease as it reaches maturity. There is great variation in disease incidence, the general rule being that Lombardy poplars grow better and more healthily the farther north they are planted. There are some places such as around Seattle, Washington, where they do exceptionally

P. alba. *White poplar.*

well. Elsewhere, the tree is still useful for "instant screening" with the knowledge that there may be disease losses after 15 to 20 years of vigorous growth.

There is a similar variety called Theves or Algerian poplar *(Populus nigra thevestina)* which is said to be much more canker resistant and also a broader grower than the Lombardy poplar. NE-10, a hybrid between *P. nigra* and *Populus trichocarpa,* is a narrow variety but not as slender as the Lombardy poplar. It is said to be much better in canker resistance, but this point still needs further testing.

Populus simonii 'Fastigiata'. Pyramidal simon poplar.

This beautiful, narrow tree is a variety of one of the most hardy of all poplars, from the harsh climate of northern China. It has pretty, reddish branchlets bearing shiny, bright green leaves. It reaches approximately 45 feet in height at maturity and, while not as narrow as a Lombardy poplar, it is still much taller than broad and makes a fine, quick growing screening plant. In addition to its other good qualities, it is very resistant to canker disease, which guarantees a long life. It does not sucker from the roots.

P. fremontii. *Fremont cottonwood.*

graceful branching habits than an old *Sophora japonica.*

"Even the healthiest of sophoras will prune themselves. Small branches on the inside of the tree will naturally die off. In a year or so they drop and the parent branch heals over. This self-pruning process allows the wind to blow through these trees and consequently, they don't suffer from wind or ice-storm damage. Best used as lawn specimens, for shade on golf courses, as street trees or highway plantings, and any other place where the have enough room to develop.

"All of the good points of the species are retained in the cultivar 'Regent.' It is more round-headed and is disease free. Leaves are glossier,

and it comes into bloom at an earlier age (6 to 8 years.)"

Sorbus. Mountain ash.
The mountain ash is championed by William Flemer, III, Princeton, New Jersey:

"This is a group of colorful, small trees noted for their large clusters of showy berries but also for their flat heads of white flowers borne in late spring. They are native to the northern hemisphere in North America, Europe, and the Orient, with over a hundred species and varieties known. Some of the finest species occurring in the Orient, are little known and less planted in our streets and gardens, and are perhaps superior to any of the forms which are commonly grown."

Sorbus alnifolia. Korean mountain ash (Deciduous).

NATIVE TO: Central China, Korea, Japan. ZONES: 5-6. HABIT: Moderate growth to 25-35 feet. Dense oval form.

We continue to quote William Flemer, III:

"This is one of the best species with dense shiny leaves which are not compound like most of the species, but the leaves resemble certain crabapples. The flowers are pure white, abundantly produced in small clusters like hawthorn flowers, followed by masses of bright scarlet berries in the fall. The fall foliage assumes brilliant shades of scarlet and crimson. This variety remains scarce, despite its great merits, because the seed is very difficult to germinate."

Quercus — The Oaks

Oaks are among the most useful and important native trees of the United States. The word "oak" conjures up many familiar tree expressions, such as "Tall oaks from little acorns grow" . . . "Little strokes fell great oaks" . . . "Tough as an oak" . . . "Sturdy as an oak."

The American Forestry Association List of Big Trees includes some giants among the oaks, both in size and longevity. Oak furniture and flooring are synonymous with wood that is hard and long-lasting. Park land with a high percentage of oaks is highly desirable. Prospective new subdivisions, located where there are noticeable quantities of mixed native oaks, bring premium land prices. However, if the contractor does not protect the trees during all

phases of construction, their root systems will be injured by soil compaction and grade level change. Such trees gradually die.

Since most of the larger species are long-lived, they are preferred landscape trees where space permits. Were it not that some of them are rather difficult to transplant and require more growing space than other trees, they would be much more heavily planted.

Experts generally regard the pin oak, *Quercus palustris,* as the easiest to transplant. This fact, plus its very desirable form, glossy-fingered leaves and rather good tolerance to a wide variety of planting sites, has made it easily the most popular native oak in the eastern United States.

1. *Q. chrysolepis*
   Canyon live oak
2. *Q. douglasii*
   Blue oak
3. *Q. ellipsoidalis*
   Northern pin oak
4. *Q. lyrata*
   Overcup oak
5. *Q. macrocarpa*
   Bur oak
6. *Q. palustris*
   Pin oak
7. *Q. phellos*
   Willow oak
8. *Q. rubra*
   Northern red oak
9. *Q. vacciniifolia*
   Buckleberry oak
10. *Q. wislizenii*
    Interior live oak

½ life size

Most nurserymen and landscape architects specify large sizes with a soil ball for transplanting. When they have ideal conditions and all cultural factors under their control some experienced

landscapers will transplant pin oak and a few others, up to 2 inches in caliper, as bareroot. Their present success, however, is based on years of averaging previous bareroot transplanting results.

Q. alba. *White oak.*

Q. palustris. *Pin oak.*

Q. rubra. *Red oak.*

'Redbird' is even more showy than the wild species, erect-growing with fine dark green leaves, and an abundant fruiter.

Sorbus aucuparia. European mountain ash (Deciduous).

NATIVE TO: Europe and Asia. ZONES: 4-6. HABIT: Moderate growth to 25-30 feet. Narrow, upright form rounding with maturity.

William Flemer, III, says of this tree:

"This is the most commonly grown and most popular species and its enormous clusters of bright red berries are most showy when they color up in late summer and early fall. Its great enemies are borer insects, which are more serious the farther south it is planted. Having been cultivated for so long, it has given rise to many varieties, some with yellow berries, one with doubly cut leaves, and others with distinctive habits of growth."

Stewartia. Stewartia.

The stewartias contain some of the choicest small trees for garden use, but they are virtually unknown to the gardening public. These are trees with multiple endorsements by our authors and consultants.

Stewartia koreana. Korean stewartia (Deciduous).

NATIVE TO: Korea. BEST ADAPTED: Zones 6-9, can be grown 5. HABIT: Slow growing to 30-35 feet. Pyramidal form.

William Flemer, III, was among those who praised this tree. "The Korean stewartia is the hardiest of the various species and also has the showiest flowers. They are white with golden centers (like single camellias), 3 inches across, and open successively for a long period starting in early July. Interesting mottled bark and striking orange-red fall color. This is definitely a lovely and different tree."

Stewartia pseudocamellia. Japanese stewartia (Deciduous).

NATIVE TO: Japan. ZONES: 6-9. HABIT: Slow growth to 50-60 feet. Pyramidal.

Like *S. koreana,* an all-season performer. The bright green foliage is neat and attractive, turning shades of crimson and purple in fall. Large white flowers with gold centers are borne in abundance over a long period in mid-summer. The beautiful branch silhouette and red, flaking bark are especially attractive in winter.

Each genus of trees usually has one species that is outstanding for pronounced fall color. Among the oaks, this favored spot belongs to the scarlet oak *(Quercus coccinea).* When the scarlet oak is not available, the red oak *(Quercus rubra)* is a close second in fall color and has the added advantage of being easier to transplant and faster growing.

Because oaks can reach such an impressive size and age, they are usually thought of as slow-growing trees — not always true! On soil types to their liking, they are surprisingly fast-growing. At the Ohio Research and Development Center, Wooster, Ohio, one of the landscape plantings includes two thornless honey locust trees and two red oaks. They were all the same size at planting time and now, years later, both species are are of comparable size and trunk diameter. Generally the pin oak is the only oak considered to be a rapid grower among the common oaks.

The beauty of oaks is by no means limited to their changing leafy appearance during the growing season. The mature oak is impressive in winter with its pillarlike trunk and its sturdy, long, and twisting branches. A fine example is the burr oak, *Quercus macrocarpa.* Its younger twigs are irregularly covered with corklike ridges, sometimes extending one-half inch or so above the diameter of the twig. It is judged to withstand North Central Prairie conditions better than any other native oak species.

The size and shape of the acorns, and the way their "caps" are worn, are ways to tell one species of oak from another.

Oaks hybridize and, when found, such hybrids are frequently the equal of or better than their parents. Still, propagation of these superior trees continues to be a real challenge to the nurseryman.

Where space permits, a properly selected oak species is a top-rated candidate for shade and longevity. And certainly not to be overlooked is the enhancement of the property value.

Which oak you choose to plant depends largely on your location. In returned questionnaires from all over the country, we found that the most admired oaks were often local natives. Keeping in mind what has already been said about the growth rate of oaks, why not circumvent the transplanting problem and start a local oak from an acorn? Refer to what Dick Harris has to say about growing trees from seed in "Last Words" on page 112.

Check with your local nurseryman or other experts for recommendations as to the kind of oak best suited to your particular landscape. Many widely recommended species and varieties of oaks are listed in the encyclopedia.

Q. nigra. *Water oak.*

Q. rubra. *Red oak.*

Q. phellos. *Willow oak.*

Sassafras albidum. *Sassafras.*

Sassafras leaves.

Like other stewartias, it grows best in acid soils, protected from wind, and in partial shade.

Styrax japonicus Japanese Snow-bell, Japanese Snowdrop tree (Deciduous).

NATIVE TO: Japan and China. ZONES: 5-9. HABIT: Slow to moderate growth rate to about 15-20 feet. Horizontal branching, forms spreading flat-topped tree.

Observers from across the country rated this as one of the choicest small

Flowers of the pagoda tree.

garden trees. William Flemer, III, of Princeton Nursery, Princeton, New Jersey, has this to say. "This neat, very bushy little tree with its clean foliage and attractive zigzag habit of branching is especially nice to plant overhanging a patio because the pendant flowers, which look like white fuchsia blossoms, are most effective when viewed from below. They are borne in great abundance in early June so that the whole tree looks white during the long period when it is in bloom."

Tolerates shade, grows best in rich, well-drained soil. Will need training to control shrubbiness. Good tree to garden under on the lawn or patio.

Syringa amurensis japonica.
(S. reticulata). Japanese lilac tree (Deciduous).

NATIVE TO: Japan. BEST ADAPTED: Zones 5-8, can be grown 4. HABIT: Moderate growth to 20-35 feet with a

spread of about 15-25 feet. Open, upright, spreading branches with round outline.

A multiple-endorsement tree summed up by William Flemer, III, in "Trees that need a friend," on pages 80-84.

Taxodium distichum. Bald cypress (Deciduous). ZONES: 5-10.

We quote Bartow H. Bridges, Jr., Virginia Beach, Virginia:

"The bald cypress is native from Delaware to Florida and west to 'Old Man River.' It is tolerant of local weather, poor drainage, and has tiny leaves that don't need raking — that are, in fact, too small to rake. It is deciduous and, therefore, good as a shade tree that will let in the winter sun. It has a rather slender shape that allows it to fit where space is somewhat limited.

"Many people assume that because they see it in swamps, it has to have this setting to thrive but have you ever driven up Route 13 near Salisbury on the Eastern Shore of Maryland and wondered what the pyramidal trees are in the median strip? They are bald cypress, high and dry. And they are thriving.

"In aquatic situations, there are few woody plants that survive. The few that do, such as the bald cypress, multiply and are prominent because of their large numbers. Air is important to the root systems of most plants. The bald cyress solves the problem

Sophora japonica. *Japanese pagoda tree.*

Ulmus parvifolia. *Chinese elm.*

in submerged conditions by having the roots come up for air — the cypress knees we see projecting from the swamp water. In a higher setting, these knees don't form.

"Bald cypress, usually known simply as cypress in the South, is an important lumber tree and can grow to 150 feet. Fine branches and foliage give it a delicate appearance. The fruit is a round cone. It is one of the few deciduous conifers. Its relatives are the redwoods, dawn redwoods, cunninghamia, and cryptomerias, which adapt locally."

Thuja. Arborvitae.
A genus containing several valuable shrubs and two important trees.

Thuja occidentalis. American arborvitae, northern white cedar (Needled Evergreen).

NATIVE TO: Southeastern Canada, northeastern United States. BEST ADAPTED: Zones 3-8, can be grown 2-9. HABIT: Slow to moderate growth rate to 40-50 feet tall in 60 years at the Secrest Arboretum, Wooster, Ohio. Narrow pyramidal form.

Bright green to yellow-green foliage in flat sprays on branches with up-sweeping tips. Turns unattractive yellowish brown in cold winters.

Will tolerate wet soils, but subject to wind-throw in open wet areas. More stable on drier sites. Takes clipping well and makes an effective hedge or tall screen. Columnar forms, commonly sold as 'Fastigiata,' 'Columnaris,' or 'Pyramidalis,' are most useful hedge or screen trees. Other selections vary in height and foliage color.

Thuja plicata. Western red cedar, giant arborvitae, canoe cedar (Needled Evergreen).

NATIVE TO: Alaska to northern California and across to Montana. BEST ADAPTED: Zones 6-8, can be grown 5-9. HABIT: Slow growth to as high as 130-200 feet where native; usually much less in cultivation. Pyramidal.

An ever-present tree in the north-western United States. Bright to dark green, lacy foliage on slender drooping branches. Unlike *T. occidentalis,* it won't yellow in winter.

Tolerates wet soils but roots can pancake (see *Pseudotsuga).* Takes shearing. Valuable large hedge or screen tree. Looks great in large open areas where lower branches can sweep the ground. Excellent sky-line tree.

'Fastigiata' has an upright columnar form and is an especially effective tall screen.

Tilia. Linden.
This genus is evaluated on page 78.

Silver linden, *Tilia tomentosa,* has received multiple endorsement from our authors and consultants.

One of the most serious pests of lindens are Japanese beetles. Other pests include elm leaf beetle, aphids, and scale. Read about these pests on page 85.

Tsuga. Hemlock.
This is a large group of fine-textured, graceful trees that thrive only in deep, moist loam and tolerate light shade. They resent dry winds, drought, and prolonged heat. *Tsuga canadensis,*

Zelkova serrata. *Sawleaf zelkova.*

Styrax japonicus. *Japanese snowdrop tree.*

Seed of cucumber tree.

Carya illinoinensis. *Pecan.*

Magnolia acuminata. *Cucumber tree.*

the Canadian or eastern hemlock, is the most widely adapted.

Tsuga canadensis. Canadian or eastern hemlock (Needled evergreen). NATIVE TO: Northeastern North America. BEST ADAPTED: Zones 5-8, can be grown 4. HABIT: Moderate growth rate to 60-90 feet. Pyramidal.

William Flemer, III, Princeton, New Jersey, describes it:

"Graceful horizontal branches, drooping at the tips and bearing dense, flat, deep green sprays of short needles. Because of its small twigs and fine texture, it is extremely well-adapted to hard shearing and is easily trained into a thick hedge, which can be maintained at a very slowly increasing height for decades."

Young hemlocks look best in mass plantings. However, if you can wait, they do make outstanding specimens with age, especially in a lawn.

Another hemlock is *Tsuga caroliniana,* which has denser growth, but is not as hardy.

Ulmus. Elm.
This genus contains the much admired, but now disease-ridden (Dutch elm disease) American elm, the workhorse Siberian elm, and the widely accepted Dutch elm disease-resistant Chinese elm.

Ulmus americana. American elm (Deciduous). NATIVE TO: Eastern United States. ZONES: 3-9. HABIT: Fast growth rate to 100 feet. Vase-shaped, spreading head.

The future of this tree that has for so long graced the streets of American cities is in the hands of Dutch elm researchers. Individuals or cities wishing information on preventive measures should write to either the United States Department of Agriculture, Forest Service, or the Elm Research Iinstitute, Harrisville, New Hampshire 03450.

Ulmus parvifolia. Chinese elm, lacebark elm (Deciduous or evergreen depending on the winter cold). NATIVE TO: China. BEST ADAPTED: Zones 6-9, can be grown 5.

John Copeland, Tidewater, Virginia, shares his thoughts on *Ulmus parvifolia:*

"The lacebark elm is a fast-growing, medium-sized tree with an oval form. It has durable storm-resistant wood and small, clustered

Tilia — Linden

The fame of the fragrant lindens has long been known in Europe. Parts of the trees have been used for everything from salads to pianos. The leaves are edible, and although not as tasty as lettuce, they have brought families through periods of starvation and famine and have long been used to feed livestock. The fibers of the inner bark are used to make cord in Germany and Poland. Commonly called bast, the fibers give rise to the other common name, basswood, and were used to make mats, shoes, and even paper. Oil from the seed pods has been used as a substitute for olive oil. Perfume comes from the distilled flowers and honey, made from the nectar, is highly prized.

Today in the United States the lindens are known as versatile street and shade trees. They can stand adverse city conditions, heat and drought and a wide variety of soils (although they grow best in moist, fertile soils).

In late spring or early summer, the lindens bear clusters of very fragrant yellow flowers that bring the trees alive with the buzz of bees. Flowers are followed by small clusters of round fruit.

The most familiar linden to Americans is *Tilia cordata,* the littleleaf linden (zones 4-8). A finely textured tree with moderate growth rate, it has the typical linden, heart-shaped dark green leaf, only smaller (1¼ to 2½ inches long, as compared to 3-5 inches of most lindens). Its symmetrical habit has made it a very popular street, lawn or shade tree, and it can even be trimmed into an effective hedge.

The two most common selections of the littleleaf linden are 'Chancellor' and 'Greenspire.' 'Greenspire' grows to 30 to 40 feet with an upright oval head. 'Chancellor' is fastigiate in youth, eventually becoming a 35- to 40-foot pyramidal tree. The consistent form of these two selections makes them two of the finest choices for street planting. Another selection worth noting is 'June Bride,' which is slightly smaller than the others but bears 3 to 4 times the bloom of the species and has a glossier leaf.

'Rancho' is another upright oval form worthy of street planting. It reaches 35 feet and has attractive, small, glossy green foliage.

Tilia americana, the American linden, has the largest leaves of the group (4-6 inches long) and forms a dense head of dark green foliage 50 feet high; narrow-upright in form. Zones 4-8.

Another attractive member of the linden genus is the silver linden, *Tilia tomentosa* (zones 5-8). The dark green leaves have white to silver undersides that provide a pleasantly soft contrast in the slightest breeze and turn yellow in fall. Pyramidal when young, it eventually becomes oval-headed and grows to 40 to 50 feet. The silver linden is the favorite linden of many of our observers and deserves wider use.

Tilia euchlora, the Crimean linden, (zones 5-8) is a handsome hybrid with large clean, glossy, dark green leaves and especially fragrant flowers. It

T. tomentosa.

T. cordata. *Littleleaf linden.*

leaves that give it an open canopy. The leaves are dark green, turning pale yellow to purple in the fall. In Tidewater, the foliage is almost evergreen during mild winters. In late fall, subtle red clusters of fruit appear that add interest to the tree. The exfoliating bark, however, is this tree's best aesthetic feature. With age, the tree sheds the circular plates of its brown bark to reveal a pale yellow inner bark.

"Since the lacebark elm is a medium-sized, low-maintenance tree, one ideal use is in the urban and residential landscapes. It can be used as a dramatic specimen tree or in groups as a screen. The fast rate of growth that is characteristic of this species makes it worthy of planting in new residential areas for re-establishing a tree canopy. Furthermore, its scale fits most residential building heights."

Ulmus parvifolia is praised by Carl Whitcomb in "Trees that need a friend" on pages 80-84.

Ulmus pumila. Siberian elm (Deciduous).

NATIVE TO: China. ZONES: 5-9. HABIT: Fast-growing to 50-70 feet with an open, rounded crown.

Valuable tree in the harshest of climates, including extreme cold, drought, or heat. Tolerates poor soils. Often used in high-wind areas or as a shelter belt tree. Otherwise, weak branches and disease susceptibility rule it out. For a different look at this tree, see Richard Sutton in "Trees that need a friend" on pages 80-84.

Zelkova serrata. Sawleaf or Japanese zelkova (Deciduous).

NATIVE TO: Japan and Korea. ZONES: 5-9. HABIT: Moderate to fast growth rate to 50-60 feet, equally wide. Round-headed, eventually vase-shaped.

Heavily pushed as a substitute for a close relative, the American elm. Foliage similar to the elm, turns shades of yellow or red in fall, most commonly russet. With age, the gray bark takes on an attractive mottling.

A well-proportioned tree for the lawn or street; it is relatively pest free.

'Village Green' has added valuable uniformity to the species, as well as increased hardiness and faster growth. Like the species, it is quite irregular in youth and may need extra pruning.

has a broad oval crown with slightly pendulous branches. It grows to 25 to 40 feet. 'Redmond' is pyramidal with less glossy foliage.

Another hybrid worth mentioning is *Tilia europea,* the European linden (zones 4-8). Widely used as a street tree in Europe, it is not common in the United States. Pyramidal in youth, it eventually becomes a 40 to 50 foot roundheaded tree. 'Pallida,' the paleleaf European, maintains a pyramidal shape and has a larger leaf.

Evaluations of lindens at Secrest Arboretum

The following is a list of evaluators who, in the spring of 1977, rated trees: representatives from other Ohio arboretums, members of forestry or shade tree departments of several utility companies, Ohio Nurserymans Association, International Shade Tree Conference, Ohio State University department of horticulture, and Davey Tree Co. They scored the trees at the Shade Tree Evaluation Plot, Secrest Arboretum, Wooster, Ohio. Ratings were fed into a computer; the results included 7 lindens in the top 20 rated as excellent.

#5 *Tilia europea* 'Pallida'
#8 *Tilia cordata* 'Chancellor'
#10 *Tilia cordata* 'Greenspire'
#11 *Tilia tomentosa*
#13 *Tilia europea*
#14 *Tilia cordata* 'XP110'
#16 *Tilia cordata* 'Rancho'

A group performance not matched by any other genus. Scores have gotten consistently better over the years. As explained by curator John Ford, "All tilias are slow in becoming established. One should not expect too much growth the first two or three years after transplanting. After they establish their root systems, they grow well and soon become very attractive. Our biggest problem has been skeletonizing of the leaves by Japanese beetles. We have to spray weekly or every 10 days with Sevin while the beetles are in flight in midsummer. The beetles do the most damage to young trees." Lindens are also bothered by aphids in some areas.

T. euchlora. Crimean linden.

Flower of the Crimean linden

Stewartia.

Above: Chionanthus. Fringe tree.
Below: Cornus kousa. Kousa dogwood.

Trees that need a friend

Trees have a way of making friends. They may be trees that have been poor mouthed or, in certain situations, are weed trees. They may be trees the author is sure should be used more, or trees that need special care.

All trees change in the eye of the beholder. When anyone speaks for a tree that needs a friend, consider his location and point of view.

Lance Walheim, Los Altos, CA
Viewpoint: Researcher of trees, world-wide.

As one of the editors of this book, I can't help but notice that many of the trees that need a friend today were also listed in *TREES, Yearbook of Agriculture,* 1949, as trees that merit more use. Unless some positive action is taken, they will probably still need friends years from now.

These are all trees that have a great deal to contribute, but for the most part they are slow growers and, in our highly mobile society, most gardeners overlook them in favor of fast-growing trees that will give an immediate effect. Unselfishly, the friends of these trees may have to plant them for their grandchildren, or for that matter, someone else's grandchildren.

Besides planting on private property, why not call them to the attention of city arborists or park and recreation departments so they can be planted, observed and enjoyed in the years to come?

Bartow H. Bridges, Jr., Virginia Beach, VA
Self-employed landscape architect and horticultural consultant.
Viewpoint: Observer of tree performance in Virginia, North Carolina, and Maryland.

Amelanchier canadensis — Shadbush

One of the first native plants to show beauty and life each year is a small tree that pops out with pretty white flowers before the leaves appear. The timing of its blooming has an interesting correlation with, of all things, fish. Many generations of Tidewater (Va.) people have been interested in the spring shad run and even more interested in shad roe and baked shad. The tree is called shadbush because it blooms more or less at the same time the shad head upstream to spawn.

Like many native plants, the shadbush has several common

names, others being shadblow, downey serviceberry, sarviceberry and juneberry.

The flowers are white, about an inch in diameter, in clusters somewhat like delicate apple blossoms. Since they bloom before the plant leafs out, they are more effective against an evergreen background.

The shape of the plant is that of a small tree, slightly taller than wide, with a mature height of about 25 feet. The bark is smooth and light-gray and the branches and twigs are thin and graceful. Leaves are smaller versions of those of its relative, the apple, and the fruits are miniature apples which are edible, ripening in late spring. Since they are small and somewhat hidden by foliage, birds usually get to them before humans do.

Shadbush is native from Maine to Georgia, is usually found in light shade, and often in low places close to rivers — no doubt to see when the shad are running. Shadbush will tolerate a high water table but thrive better in rich, well-drained but moist soil.

L. C. Chadwick, Columbus, OH
Professor Emeritus, The Ohio State University, Columbus, Ohio.
Viewpoint: Observer of tree performance, world-wide. Dr. Chadwick lists the following trees (see encyclopedia for descriptions):

Acer campestre — Hedge maple

Aesculus carnea 'Briotii' Ruby-red horsechestnut

Alnus glutinosa — European alder

Betula nigra — River birch

Celtis laevigata — Sugar Hackberry

Eucommia ulmoides — Eucommia, hardy rubber tree

Fraxinus excelsior 'Hessei' — Hessei European ash

Ostrya virginiana — American hop hornbeam

Quercus shumardii — Shumard's red oak

Tilia tomentosa — Silver linden

William Collins, Circleville, OH
Staff Horticulturist, American Garden-Cole Nursery, Circleville, Ohio.
Viewpoint: Observer of tree performance throughout the North and Midwest United States.

Alnus glutinosa 'Aurea' — Golden European alder

Few trees have impressed me so much on first contact as has the golden European alder. Although observation is limited to two summers and one winter, I am willing to suggest we give this tree, already

well known in Europe, a test in landscape situations calling for its special attributes. Few yellow-leafed trees tolerate the wet soil or poorly drained sites on which poplars and willows grow — this alder does!

Growth rate of young trees is fast — a condition that appears to be necessary if the tree is to show its full color range in both brightness and intensity. The impressive foliage color range includes light greenish-yellow, creamy-yellow to lemon-yellow in the fall. Typical of most trees with or without colored foliage, the new twigs become shorter and less vigorous as they grow older. Consequently, the color becomes less pronounced, but this is easily overcome by severe pruning every two or three years, or as required.

Magnolia salicifolia — Anise magnolia
Here is a lovely, fragrant, early, white-flowered species that is pyramidal in form and not likely to get over 25 feet tall. Growth rate is about a foot per year.

Populus alba 'Richardii' — Richard's white poplar

In the North Central Prairie States, especially the colder, drier areas, the number of really good colored-foliaged trees is limited by lack of hardiness, so when one does exist that will brighten the summerscape, someone ought to do a little shouting about it!

Imagine a vigorous-growing branch with all of the leaves woolly white on the underside and most of them butter-yellow topside. With the wind blowing, the swaying branches give the tree a very distinctive effect. Richard's white poplar is a little less vigorous than the species *Populus alba,* but even so it can average up to two feet in height a year for the first 20 years. Many tree experts consider the species too coarse and perhaps, eventually, too big. Vigorous pruning early in the spring will curb the size somewhat and assure the continued color intensity in the new growth. However, when the mature tree has served its usefulness, there should be a good cord of firewood.

John Copeland, Norfolk, VA
Landscape Designer, Norfolk, Virginia.
Viewpoint: Observer of tree value and performance in Virginia.

Ulmus parvifolia — Lacebark elm
In this area, the crape myrtle and the American plane tree are best known for their dramatic exfoliating (or peeling) bark. The lacebark elm also

displays this bark characteristic and is an ideal insect- and disease-resistant elm for Tidewater, Va.

The lacebark elm is a fast-growing, medium-sized tree with an oval form. It has small, clustered leaves that give it an open canopy. The leaves are dark green, turning pale yellow to purple in the fall. In Tidewater, the foliage is almost evergreen during mild winters. In late fall, subtle red clusters of fruit appear that add interest to the tree. The exfoliating bark, however, is this tree's best aesthetic feature. With age, the tree sheds the circular plates of its brown bark to reveal a pale yellow inner bark.

Since the lacebark elm is a medium-sized, low-maintenance tree, one ideal use is in the urban and residential landscapes. It can be used as a dramatic specimen tree, or in groups as a screen. The fast rate of growth characteristic of this species makes it useful in new residential areas to re-establish a tree canopy. Furthermore, its scale fits most residential building heights.

Cornus kousa — Kousa dogwood

After the blooms of dogwood, cherries, crabapples, and other spring-flowering trees, have faded, *Cornus kousa* spreads its sheets of white bloom to prolong the spring show into May.

The flowers are very similar to those of our native dogwood. Each consists of a tight cluster of small true flowers surrounded by four bracts, which are green as they start to expand, but soon turn white. These bracts differ from those of our native dogwood by being slightly pointed at the apex, instead of notched. Also the flowers appear after the tree has leafed out, rather than on bare branches.

On the flowering dogwood each flower cluster develops a group of separate fruits or berries. On *Cornus kousa* the flowers in the cluster unite to form a pink mass about an inch across, which weighs down its stalk when fully developed and looks a bit like a raspberry.

The kousa dogwood grows to about 20 feet in height and can be as broad as it is high. It is more bushy than the native dogwood, with more slender branches and twigs. However, it can be pruned into a treelike appearance, if that is desired. The bark is interesting, as it peels in patches, so that the dark brown outer bark contrasts with tan inner bark. The winter flower buds are narrow and pointed.

Good autumn color is another plus shared with our native dogwood. However, *Cornus kousa* turns to its rich red later than the native dogwood and does not last as long if caught by frost.

William Flemer III, Princeton, NJ

President, Princeton Nurseries, Princeton, New Jersey.
Viewpoint: Lifetime of experience observing, breeding, and growing trees of North America.

The following list of trees is composed of species or cultivated varieties that have never attained the popularity they deserve. Some are new and greatly improved varieties that are still not well known in the rather conservative garden world. Others are species or older selections which are unusual and very decorative but have never benefitted from a good publicity program.

Acer palmatum — Japanese maple

Wherever Japanese maples can be grown, the red-leaf forms are the ones planted. There is no question that they are striking and graceful accents in the landscape, however, the wild green-leaf types are often even more beautiful, though in a more subtle vein. They are notable for the fantastic color changes which the leaves undergo during the growing season. Often coral or bright red when they first unfold, they become a restful green during the summer months, only to turn brilliant scarlet, crimson, or even canary-yellow before they finally drop in the fall. No other small tree combines such incredible color changes with such a delicate, lacy foliage texture. Twenty feet tall, very handsome at maturity, the wild forms of the Japanese maple merit a place in any landscape where they are hardy, either in full sun or as an underplanting beneath taller trees.

Amelanchier canadensis — Shadblow or serviceberry

This is one of our loveliest native small trees, with something to offer throughout the year. In the early spring it is covered with masses of fleecy white flowers. In the fall the foliage turns attractive shades of orange and red, and in the winter the pale gray bark is as pretty as that of any beech. Like so many trees with handsome bark, the stem display is greatly increased by growing the trees in clump or multi-stemmed form.

Syringa amurensis japonica (S. reticulata) — Japanese tree lilac

This lovely and hardy (Zone 3) little tree was popular in Victorian times, but is rarely planted today. It has many good qualities, including the large pyramidal heads of flowers borne in mid-June, clean, disease-free foliage, and interesting cherry-like bark. It is very drought-resistant and will thrive where dogwoods and other less tolerant trees soon die out. A new selection called 'Ivory Silk' from Canada has even larger and showier clusters of flowers than the best seed-grown strains and is well worth planting.

Bill Flemer also nominates for "Trees that need a friend" the following trees, which are described in the encyclopedia:

Aesculus pavia
Red buckeye

Chionanthus virginicus — Fringe tree

Cornus kousa — Japanese dogwood

Cladrastis lutea — American yellowwood

Crataegus oxyacantha (laevigata) 'Crimson Cloud' — Crimson cloud hawthorn

Halesia carolina — Carolina silverbell

Magnolia virginiana — Sweet bay magnolia

Oxydendrum arboreum — Sorrel tree or sourwood

Prunus subhirtella 'Autumnalis' — Autumn cherry

Sorbus alnifolia — Korean mountain ash

Stewartia koreana — Korean stewartia

Styrax japonicus — Japanese snowbell

John Ford, Wooster, OH

Curator, Secrest Arboretum, Wooster, Ohio. A forester and observer of trees at Wooster, Ohio, and throughout North America.

Picea omorika — Serbian spruce

To most people, Sarajevo is the place where World War 1 started, with the assassination of Archduke Ferdinand. To the forester and botanist, it is near the area where the last remaining natural stands of Serbian spruce are growing. There were a few scattered stands totaling some 200 acres growing on the limestone hills near the Drina River. This spruce had survived centuries of heavy grazing, fire, and cutting, but was on its way to extinction when discovered in 1875.

It is tough. I tried a new tree-spade machine in April, selecting a poor suppressed Serbian spruce as a subject. After planting and replanting it several times, the tree was dropped at the roadside. In October the spruce was still there lying on top of the ground, rootball and all. I planted the tree, and now, after seven growing seasons, it is one of the best trees on my home grounds. It is hardy and tough, even when growing in poor soil on exposed sites.

Serbian spruce is a striking tree with its dense drooping foliage and ascending branches. The tree has a narrow spindlelike form and is much more graceful than the commonly planted Norway spruce, having much smaller needles and cones. The underside of the needles is white, which imparts a silvery appearance to the foliage, especially when the wind is blowing. It is the most attractive of the spruces in appearance.

Betula nigra — River birch

The most beautiful of American trees — that's what Prince Maximilian thought of river birch when he toured North America over a hundred years ago.

River birch is quite different from our other native birches. It is the only birch found naturally in the Coastal Plain of the southern United States. It is the only typically southern birch. It can grow on very wet sites or on dry sites. It forms its seed in the late spring and the young seedlings of the current year are well established before other birches mature and drop their seed.

The name river birch fits its preference for growing on wet areas beside streams and rivers subject to frequent flooding.

The tree changes in appearance as it ages. On young trees the bark is reddish, resembling cherry bark. As the tree grows older, the bark begins to peel and tatter similar to the familiar white birches. The bark on river birch at this stage is reddish to brownish white. When the bark fully matures, it becomes scaly and dark chocolate in color. During the winter, when the leaves have dropped, all three types of bark can be seen on large trees; reddish cherrylike bark on small branches and twigs, peeling white bark on larger limbs, and scaly dark bark on the trunk.

A young river birch has a conical or pyramidal shape to the crown but as the tree matures the crown becomes more open and spreading. The tree usually has a short trunk, which often divides 15 or 20 feet above the ground. This habit of branching makes a desirable ornamental. Grown in the open, mature trees develop a well-rounded crown with somewhat drooping branches.

The tree needs room in which to develop as it can grow 65 to 70 feet tall in sixty years. It grows rapidly when young and can average a two-foot increase in height a year.

Chrysolarix amabilis (Pseudolarix kaempferi) — Golden larch

A tree seldom grown is the golden larch, although it has been known in the United States for over 125 years. It is well named as it greatly resembles larch and its foliage turns a gold color in the fall. Like the larch, it is deciduous, the cones, however, are borne upright along the upper sides of branches as on firs. Also, like the firs, the cones mature in the autumn, open, shatter, and fall to the ground usually before the snow flies.

Golden larch has striking golden yellow foliage in the fall. The bark on older trees becomes furrowed and is a reddish-brown. The tree requires plenty of room as its spread can almost equal its height. Golden larch grows into a broad pyramidal tree with open branches. Best growth is made in a sunny location on a well-drained, moderately moist site. It has been reported to grow to heights of from 120 to 130 feet. Seventy-year-old trees can be 90 feet tall.

The tree has been quite hardy at Wooster, Ohio, and has survived —24° F.

James A. Foret, Lafayette, Louisiana
Dean of the College of Agriculture, University of Southwestern Louisiana. Viewpoint: Trees of the southern United States.

Acer rubrum drummondii — Swamp maple. Mardi-gras maple

The common names of this tree are derived from its native habitat (swamplands of South Louisiana) and its season of color (about Mardi Gras time in New Orleans). This large maple (60-70′) flowers shortly after January first and seed development is noticeable by late January, with a great display of color in late winter in shades of pink, red, tan, and brown before leaves appear.

Although somewhat brittle, it is fast-growing, adapted to all soil types and will tolerate bog conditions. Hardy in zone 8, its northern range has not been determined.

Ilex vomitoria 'Pendula'
Folsom weeping yaupon
A most attractive, graceful form of our common yaupon. Its growth habit is unique in that it grows upright, then secondary growth forces the branches to bend downward. Female selections are spectacular in full fruit; however, male selections form more compact plants. Adapted to any soil type where other yaupons grow, this graceful plant deserves a place where large accent plants are desired since it will grow to 20′ in as many years.

Melia azedarach 'Umbraculifera' — Umbrella China Ball,
Texas umbrella tree
A very fast-growing small deciduous shade tree (15-20′) adapted to all soil types in Zone 9 and 10. An escapee from cultivation, Melia was planted around homes of the early settlers on the southwest Louisiana-southeast Texas prairies as a ready supply of firewood and shade. The trees were topped each fall and winter as needed to supplement the regular wood supply.

The large clusters of fragrant lavender flowers are attractive in early spring as are the lemon yellow fruit in the fall. It is best grown as a temporary shade tree. Adapted to all soil conditions. Melia can readily be removed after five to ten years' use.

Francis R. Gouin, Ph.D., College Park, MD
Associate Professor Ornamental Horticulture, University of Maryland. Viewpoint: Observer of tree performance from Maryland to Maine.

Halesia monticola — Mountain silverbell

A little-known tree with outstanding characteristics. With emphasis being placed on flowering trees and trees that require minimum maintenance, the mountain silverbell has those features and more. In the spring, it produces branch-loads of small, white, bell-shaped flowers on the underside of the branches. It does not have any serious insect or disease problems.

For a plus feature, it produces a light shade, enabling the gardener to grow healthy turf or a shade garden up to the trunk. For maximum appreciation, the tree should be planted near paths where pedestrians can enjoy both its flowers in spring and the light shade in summer. When grown by itself, the mountain silverbell has a pleasing pyramidal habit of growth, but, except in the spring, tends to lose its identity when growing with other trees.

Richard W. Harris, Davis, CA
Professor of Landscape Horticulture, University of California at Davis. Viewpoint: Teacher and researcher on care of landscape trees, primarily in California.

Trees in a Lawn
Trees really in need of a friend are young nursery trees recently planted in an established lawn. All but the most vigorous trees will grow slowly and be a disappointment if the grass is too close to the trunk. Grass near the trunk invites debarking by the lawn mower. Be a friend and keep the grass at least 15 inches from the trunks of young trees.

John E. Kissida and William Gould, College Park, MD
Professors of Landscape Architecture, University of Maryland. Viewpoint: Observers of tree performance in the northeastern and southern United States.

Carpinus caroliniana — American hornbeam
The American hornbeam, also known as blue beech and ironwood, names that describe some of the features of this small tree, is commonly found in the woods of the eastern United States where it is native to stream bottoms and moist fertile soils. It tolerates a fairly wide range of soil conditions as long as moisture is not the limiting factor. In low wet areas, adjacent to water features and drainage ways, this small tree, with its tough, rugged character has considerable merit (possibly as a smaller-scaled replacement for the weak-wooded weeping willow).

The hornbeam's very hard, durable wood gives it a vandal-proof quality that might be desirable. However, its slow growth rate and transplanting difficulties somewhat restrict its use and might be reasons for its limited use until now as an ornamental. It is rarely bothered by any disease or insect pests and requires minimal pruning.

The American hornbeam makes an excellent small tree for a small place. The often yellow-orange to reddish fall color and pendulous clusters of fruits provide much interest during the growing season, and its muscled trunk, smooth gray bark, and umbrellalike form give it special value in the winter months. The tree has extremely high value as an ornamental and even possibly as a street tree, and should be grown and used more.

Nyssa sylvatica — Black gum
This is an excellent ornamental native over the greater part of the eastern

United States. One of the most handsome of American trees, with very early, gorgeous autumn color — brilliant scarlet to orange —the black gum should be used much more than it is.

When young, it has a pyramidal habit similar to that of the pin oak, gaining a more rounded crown with age. The lustrous foliage is dense and dark green. The dark blue fruit, about the size of small cherries, somewhat limits the use of the tree to lawn areas, since they can be messy on sidewalks, patios, and paved parking areas. With no serious pests and a noncompeting root system, many plants, including grass, can be grown successfully under its canopy.

The black gum seems to tolerate most urban conditions, even wet, compacted soils, and its wood is tough and resistant to wind damage. Because of difficulty in seed germination and transplanting, it has been largely by-passed by the nursery industry, but with proper root pruning it can be handled quite readily.

Raymond Korbobo, Rutgers Univ., New Brunswick, N.J.
Landscape Design.
Viewpoint: Observer of trees of North America.

Oxydendrum arboreum — Sourwood

This is a tree that landscape people should use ten times more than they do now. It prefers an acid and well-drained soil. However, I have seen it growing on very rocky soils and even in shallow topsoil. It is a four-season tree. The branching habits can be fantastically picturesque in the winter time. The fresh, shiny foliage in spring is a picture of health. When the tree flowers in June, it reminds one of the curves on pagoda roofs in the Orient or a lady's graceful hand whose fingers can be turned upwards. These flower heads are extremely graceful. They are white and, the seeds that form after they drop, are almost as white as the flowers.
Raymond Korbobo also praises *Styrax japonicus* and *Sophora japonica*. See encyclopedia.

Dr. N. T. Mirov, University of California, Berkeley, CA

Dr. N. T. Mirov talks about old trees in *TREES, Yearbook of Agriculture,* 1949. "Old age comes to trees, as to all other living organisms. The span of life of a tree is specific. Gray birch is old at 40. The sugar maple lives longer, up to 500 years. Some oaks may live 1,500 years, junipers 2,000 years. Some of the giant sequoias are believed to be 4,000 years old. Old trees are like old people — the infirmities of age are upon them. They have difficulty with respiration (its rate in old plants is much lower than in young plants); the annual shoots are not so vigorous as they once were, and the weakening cambium activity is reflected in the formation of fewer and fewer wood cells. Hence, the annual rings become narrower. As the rate of growth of the tree decreases, dead branches appear in ever-increasing numbers. The recuperative capacity of an old tree is impaired, and its wounds do not heal over so easily as before. The leaves become smaller; their moisture content decreases; the tree finds it more and more difficult to provide water for its vital functions; the inflow of food to the growing points drops; and the growth hormones probably cannot be transported in large enough quantity to the places where they are needed.

"By taking good care of the tree, one can prolong its life. The tree should be well provided with water and light and be well nourished, or at least not deprived of nutritive substances. A healthy tree will resist attacks of insects and diseases; it will develop a large crown and a strong root system, and it will withstand the action of the wind.

"If a tree is treated as a living organism, with an understanding of its vital functions, it will be a constant source of profit and pleasure to men."

Dr. Henry P. Orr, Auburn, ALA
Professor of Ornamental Horticulture, Auburn University.
Viewpoint: Observer of trees throughout the southeastern United States.

Oxydendrum arboreum — Sourwood

I agree with many lovers of native plants that the sourwood is second only to the flowering dogwood in beauty throughout the year.

It is ideal where a relatively small, often multi-trunked, slow-growing tree is desired. The sourwood is a multi-faceted tree, with lily-of-the-valley flowering effect in early to mid summer, attractive seeds in summer and fall, early orange to scarlet leaf color, and in winter, a pleasing trunk. And if you are a honey fancier, the bees produce a delicious honey from the nectar of the flowers.

Richard K. Sutton, MLA, Lincoln, NB
Assistant Professor of Horticulture, Landscape Design Specialist.
University of Nebraska, Lincoln.
Viewpoint: Observer of tree performance in Nebraska.

Ulmus pumila — Siberian elm
Morus alba — White mulberry

It seems to me much of our urban landscape more closely exhibits the characteristics of a desert than those of a forest, including severe heat, extreme winds, and dryness. The urban scene is also dynamic; land uses and attending structures rapidly come and go. These two factors, severe environment and rapid change, require a "weed tree," or more euphemistically, a pioneer. Why fuss with planting climax trees in a non-climax environment just to remove them for street widening and urban renewal, as they reach maturity.

Two maligned trees, Siberian elm and white mulberry can provide a much larger tree, in a shorter time than many "desirable" species. With proper, semi-annual, corrective pruning, these two trees can be rid of their weak limbs. Removal of these two rapidly-maturing trees will never be untimely. They will have reached their maturity within the lifespan of our changing urban land use.

Dr. Carl E. Whitcomb, Stillwater, OK
Associate Professor of Horticulture, Oklahoma State University. Author of Know It and Grow It.
Viewpoint: Observer of tree performance in Oklahoma and Florida, and the United States east of the Rockies.

Ulmus parvifolia — Chinese elm

Probably the most erroneously condemned tree is the lacebark or true Chinese elm, *Ulmus parvifolia.* The confusion exists with the Siberian elm, *Ulmus pumila,* which is a tree of questionable merit.

Chinese elm is widely adapted in hardiness, Zone 5 and southward. A medium-sized tree , it is very tolerant to alkaline, poor, and compacted soil, heat and drought. Grows rapidly under good growing conditions. It is highly resistant to Dutch elm disease and the elm leaf beetle. The wood is strong, leaves are small and easily shredded by a rotary mower, and the bark is flaking and attractive. Seedlings are variable and potential exists for the selection of superior cultivars. The current "elm phobia" should be ignored in the case of this fine tree.

Tree insects and disease

That often used word — stress — is frequently the key to insect and disease problems in trees. Proper care will do much to reduce tree problems (see pages 87-110).

But often, even if we're able to reduce several stress factors, a tree will be affected by some insect or disease pests. The tree owner then has the option of calling the professional arborist or handling the problem himself. There are advantages in having the tree owner treat the problems himself; owners are better observers because they can walk through the garden each day. Early detection of problems and proper timing of sprays are valuable tools against tree pests.

The older and larger trees become, the more difficult they are to treat yourself. Ideally, that is the time to call a professional arborist.

The following are some common tree pests and control methods. Spraying is not always recommended treatment, but when it is, read the directions and follow them. This will benefit your tree, yourself and your neighbor.

Control measures will change. The best advice always is to read the label and follow directions.

Anthracnose. This disease frequently affects maple, ash, sycamore, oak, and linden trees, among others. It usually attacks leaves and produces small brown spots which may coalesce giving a scorched appearance to the entire leaf before it drops. Usually young leaves are attacked, particularly in a wet spring. "Witches' brooms" (groups of brushlike, weak stems) often develop because of the repeated cycle of defoliation followed by a second crop of leaves. The disease weakens trees and is particularly serious after several consecutive wet springs.

CONTROL. The fungicides Maneb and Zineb are often recommended to be applied when buds are first opening. Trees should also be well fertilized and growing vigorously.

Beetles. There are many leaf-eating beetles. Two of the most destructive are the elm leaf beetle and the Japanese beetle. Elm leaf beetles skeletonize leaves. Attacked elms can be completely defoliated, a devitalizing process that invites borers and then Dutch elm disease.

The Japanese beetle (presently not a problem in the West) is a one-half inch metallic green beetle with a coppery back. Many trees are severely damaged by them. They usually eat the entire leaf between the veins, skeletonizing it.

CONTROL: These beetles can be controlled with sprays of Sevin, applied when damage is first noticed and repeated as necessary. Read the label. Also read the label of Orthene for control of elm leaf beetle.

Borers. Any tree that is in a weakened — stressed — condition will attract borers. Drought, sun scald, frost cracks, poor soil, bark injury, and air pollution are some of the major causes of stress and, consequently, of borer attack. Damage caused includes structural weakening, death by girdling the cambium layer, and disease transmission (see Dutch elm disease). Holes in the bark indicating the presence of borers, may be very tiny or up to one inch in diameter; they may be round or oval.

CONTROL: First, do everything possible to reduce stress (see Care and Maintenance, p. 87-110). Only long residual types of insecticides, such as Lindane, are commonly used against borers. It must be on the bark either before egg-laying or before egg-hatching. Timing is very important. Read the label. Commercial tree wraps are helpful and available. See *Fraxinus* in the encyclopedia.

Cankers. This word describes dead and diseased areas that occur, usually on woody branches or trunks. A common symptom is die-back starting at branch tips. Virtually all plants can be attacked by canker-forming diseases.

CONTROL. Prune and burn dead and infected branches. Paint pruning wounds with a disinfectant. When trunks are seriously invaded, it is often impossible to save the tree.

Some cankers "bleed". Maples, elms, birch, and trees in low vigor are particularly susceptible.

Bleeding cankers are best controlled by restoring the tree's vigor by supplying proper water and fertilizer. Control insects and prune to thin in late winter when bleeding is reduced, clean the wound back to healthy bark so callus can form.

Caterpillars. Moths and butterflies are harmless creatures but their larva — tent caterpillars, bagworms, gypsy moths, and loopers, to name a few — are some of the most damaging leaf-chewing pests. At first they are small and feeding damage is light. When full-size, they are ravenous and can defoliate entire trees.

CONTROL. Contact insecticides such as Sevin and Diazinon are effective against these pests, as is the systemic Orthene. Read the label.

Drip. Insects that feed on trees by sucking their sap cause drip or honeydew. Abnormal numbers of ants, flies, and even honeybees are early symptoms of the presence of these insects. (The famous Black Forest Honey is made by honeybees from honeydew). In time, a black sooty mold will grow where the honeydew drips, often blackening the leaves of Norway maples and tulip poplars. Aphids, soft scales, and leaf hoppers are the insects responsible for drip.

CONTROL. In winter, a dormant oil spray will control overwintering eggs of many pests including drip causers. In summer, the systemic Orthene or contact insecticides such as Diazinon and Malathion are effective against these pests. Read the label.

Dutch elm disease (DED). This is one of the most common tree diseases. See *Ulmus* in the encyclopedia for description and control.

Fire blight. This is a bacterial disease that affects many plants of the rose family including crabapples, hawthorn, loquat, and mountain ash. See *Malus* in the encyclopedia for the description and control.

Powdery mildew. Powdery mildew is a fungus disease that causes a grayish, powdery coating to form over young shoots, leaves, and flower buds. It can deform or kill them. Powdery mildew thrives where air circulation is poor, and it grows best in shade. Many shade and flowering trees are attacked by this disease.

CONTROL. Use a fungicide labelled to control this disease.

Scale. These are small, sucking insects. The largest is less than $\frac{3}{8}$ of an inch in diameter. They are largely immobile except when in the "crawler" stage, which usually occurs in the spring after eggs hatch. There are many scales that damage trees. Left unchecked, scales can build up large populations that weaken and even kill trees.

CONTROL. A dormant oil spray in winter smothers scales or their overwintering eggs with a thin layer of oil. When applying dormant oil sprays, read the label carefully and follow directions literally. During the summer, watch for scale crawlers to appear, then spray with Orthene, Diazinon, or Malathion.

Scab. This is the most serious disease of apples and also occurs on crabapple, mountain-ash, and hawthorn. See *Malus* in the encyclopedia for details.

The major insect and disease problems are discussed throughout the encyclopedia section of this book (pages 30-75). For additional information, check with your county extension agent. He is the watch dog in this ever-changing world of tree problems.

LEAVES

1. Leaves produce food for the tree, and release water and oxygen into the atmosphere.

2. Chloroplasts are the chlorophyll bodies within cells in which photosynthesis takes place in order to manufacture carbohydrates (starches and sugars) for the tree. They give the leaf its green color.

3. Stomata are specialized "breathing" pores through which carbon dioxide enters and water and oxygen are released. They close when water is limited.

TWIGS

4. Buds occur at the ends of the shoots (terminal buds) and along the sides of the shoot (lateral buds). These buds contain the embryonic shoots, leaves, and flowers for the next growing season.

5. Lateral buds occur below the terminal bud at leaf axils. If the terminal bud is removed, a lateral bud or two will grow to take its place.

6. Each year's new growth is marked by bark of a slightly smoother texture and lighter color which will darken and get rougher with time.

7. Bud scale scars mark where previous years' terminal buds have been, and provide a means of measuring tree growth of many trees.

BRANCHES

8. Scaffold branches are the large limbs that give the tree its basic shape and structure.

9. Laterals are secondary branches, mainly horizontal, that create the outline of the tree.

TRUNK

10. The trunk is the main support of the tree to better expose leaves to the sun.

11. Bark is the "skin," an external protective layer.

12. Inner bark (phloem) is part of the circulatory system, carrying organic compounds where needed.

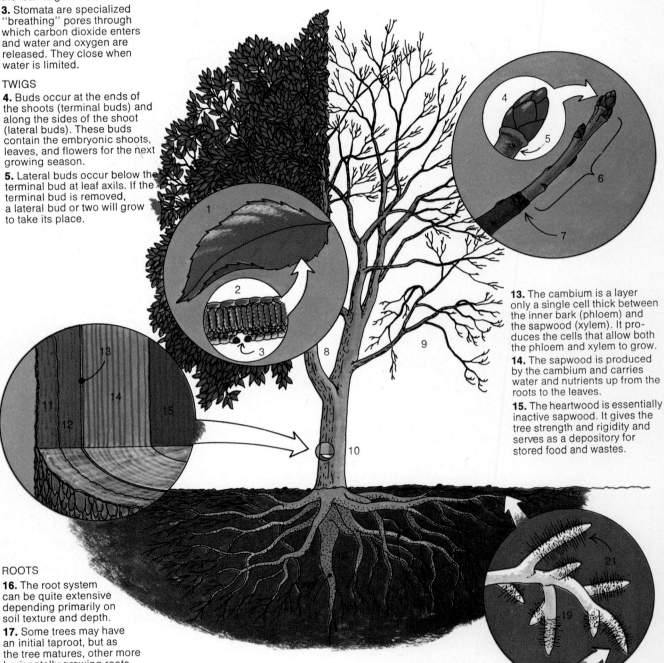

13. The cambium is a layer only a single cell thick between the inner bark (phloem) and the sapwood (xylem). It produces the cells that allow both the phloem and xylem to grow.

14. The sapwood is produced by the cambium and carries water and nutrients up from the roots to the leaves.

15. The heartwood is essentially inactive sapwood. It gives the tree strength and rigidity and serves as a depository for stored food and wastes.

ROOTS

16. The root system can be quite extensive depending primarily on soil texture and depth.

17. Some trees may have an initial taproot, but as the tree matures, other more horizontally growing roots predominate.

18. The lateral roots develop at base of the trunk and spread, forming an extensive network which serves to anchor the tree. They also provide storage for carbohydrates.

19. Feeder roots grow from the lateral roots and serve to transport water and nutrients absorbed by root hairs. They tend to be concentrated within the "dripline" (where the rain drips off the tree), but some may extend great distances.

20. Root caps produce a continuous supply of new cells that are sloughed off and serve to lubricate the advance of the growing root tip through the soil as it forages for water and nutrients.

21. The root hairs are microscopic appendages to the feeder roots; root hairs absorb water and nutrients the tree needs in order to live.

How a tree grows and how to care for it

Dr. Richard W. Harris, teacher and researcher on the care of landscape trees at the University of California, Davis, discusses the influence of growth and proper care on the performance of landscape trees.

Trees are so much a part of human life, both in themselves and their products, that we seldom consider how they grow — from street trees to orchards, from managed forests to trees grown just for beauty. Their seeds are so small and the final results so big, that the transition is hard to conceive.

To become large, a tree must have a way for branches to get longer. It must develop a structure strong enough to hold it upright against the elements. All this is accomplished through its plumbing system which transports water and nutrients from the soil to the aboveground parts.

Some trees are deciduous, shedding their leaves each fall, while leaves of evergreens persist longer, usually about three years. Evergreen trees drop their older leaves each year. In fact, evergreen trees usually drop leaves for a longer period than most deciduous trees.

At the tip of each shoot, in tissue no larger than a pin point, leaves, flowers, and the support and conductive elements have their beginnings. This region and that of stem elongation are within the top one to two inches of the stem. Tree growth in height takes place only in shoot tips or from buds that will develop into shoots.

Shoot growth of some trees lasts for only three to four weeks in spring; on others, it occurs in "flushes" during the growing season; on still others it occurs almost continuously when conditions are favorable. The growth of trees with a single flush is determined the year before by the number of shoot initials formed in each bud. On such trees, shoot

response to many cultural practices will not show up until the next year. Response to fertilization would be a good example of such a delayed action. Annual shoot growth is a good measure of tree vigor and is easily noted on trees that have just one flush of growth each year.

For shoots to grow upright, plants have developed the ability to grow away from the pull of gravity (geotropism). However, to hold ever-elongating shoots upright, trees and shrubs form woody cells and have the ability to increase their number. Growth in trunk caliper is by cell division and expansion from a thin cylinder of cambium cells. Inner cells conduct water and nutrients, and support stem tissues called xylem or, more commonly, wood. Outside the cambium, the phloem conducts organic substances from the leaves to other parts of the tree. This outer cylinder is the bark.

As with shoot elongation, the amount of cambium activity differs in different species and under different climatic conditions. Annual rings are evident in most woody plants because wood formed in the spring has larger cells than wood formed later in the year. Wet and dry years are clearly shown in the annual rain record of the xylem of many trees. The width of annual rings can be used as a measure of the vigor of a tree in individual years.

Trunk development

The development of a strong, upright trunk is desired in most trees for street, patio, and landscape use. Lateral branches encourage caliper growth of the trunk, but unless they

are shortened, the total height of the tree will be reduced. Horizontal laterals are slow growing. In contrast, upright shoots are more vigorous, likely to compete with the leader.

When an upright leader of a tree is bent from the vertical, the new xylem forms "reaction" wood which counteracts the lean. The new xylem cells on the lower side grow longer than the ones on the upper side. This is true not only for new growth at the shoot tip, but even on the trunk where several layers of xylem have already formed. The forces developed by reaction wood can become great, bending trunks a foot in diameter back towards the vertical.

Trees subjected to wind form reaction wood to help keep them upright. However, reaction wood (when dry) warps, twists, and splits, and is weaker than straight-grained wood. Because of this, trees are planted close together in reforestation areas. The wind effect is then minimized and there is less reaction wood.

Each branch within a tree has a particular angle of growth which it attempts to maintain by the formation of reaction wood. In most cases more wood is formed on the lower than the upper side of the branch. If a branch is forced from its angle of growth, whether up or down, reaction wood will attempt to return it to the original angle.

The formation of reaction wood does not always completely overcome changes of the trunk from the vertical, or of branches from their normal angle of growth. That's why it's possible to train young trees or branches to desired shapes, such as bonsai

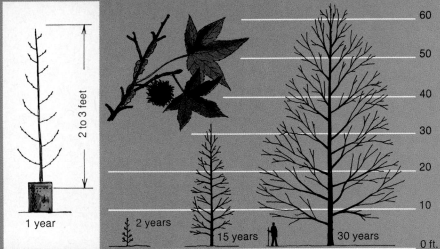

Sweet Gum (*Liquidambar styraciflua*) retains its conical shape throughout much of its long life as a result of apical control. It begins to spread very late in life. It's fast growing in subtropical climates like the southeast — 2 to 3 feet per year for the first twenty to thirty years. It's slower growing in the northern latitudes.

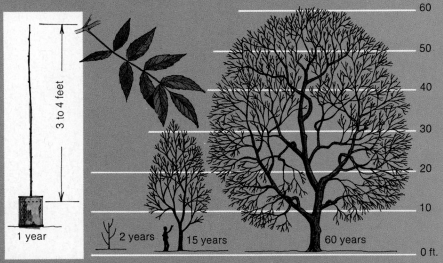

Ash (*Fraxinus*) grows as unbranched whips the first year because of strong apical dominance of the terminal which prevents the lateral buds from growing. The second year, vigorous lateral shoots may outgrow the terminal. Similarly, the following year the primary laterals may be outgrown by their laterals. This pattern of growth leads to a round-headed tree after several years.

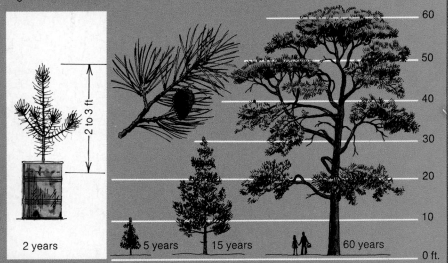

Pine (*Pinus*) similar to Liquidambar, has strong apical control in its early years which decreases as it becomes older. Some species become round-headed at maturity. Different species of pine grow at different rates. To learn how fast a particular pine will grow in your area, check with a nearby arboretum, ask at your local nursery or garden center, or call your Extension Agent.

or espalier. If a branch or trunk is held for a year or two so that it can't, of its own accord, correct the angle at which it is growing, the new wood that's formed makes it difficult for the branch or trunk to return to its original, or natural, position when the external force is removed.

Not only do wind and gravity influence tree growth, but light is a factor in determining the direction of shoot growth and tree form. Almost everyone is familiar with shoot tips growing towards the light, especially some house plants. The tips of tree shoots react similarly. In addition, light can influence the growth of the trunk many feet below the shoot tip. Tests have shown that young trees tied to a single stake will tend to bend away from the stake. You can observe this easily by untying a young staked tree; invariably it will fall away from the side of the stake to which it was tied. It would still bend away from the stake if the tree were held upside down. The new xylem cells formed on the shade side of the trunk are longer than those on the other side and the trunk "tries" to grow away from the stake. This is why it is not a good idea to tie a young tree to a single stake (see illustration, page 99). Light also plays a part in tree form when trees grow close to one another, particularly if the trees are different species or sizes. The branches growing towards a taller or more dominant tree will not grow as much as those on the more open side of the tree. In time such a tree will appear to be growing away from the other tree. This may not be noticed by most people until the more dominant tree is removed for some reason. To develop their characteristic form, trees should be given enough room.

Tree form

Trees come in all sizes and shapes. Their natural form is largely determined by the growing tip of the terminal shoot. By observing how the shoot tip of a young tree influences the buds below it, you should be able to decide the form or shape of the mature tree even though you had never seen the plant before.

The influence of a shoot tip on whether or not the buds below it will grow is called *apical dominance,* dominance or control of the tip. The dominance of some tips is so strong that no buds will grow on the shoot below during the year that the shoot is growing. That the shoot tip is responsible is easily shown by cutting off the shoot tip. Soon one to several buds below the cut will grow. Apple, honeylocust and ash are examples.

Some species have weak apical dominance so that a shoot grows from the axil of almost each new leaf soon after it is formed. Liquidambar and tulip tree are notable examples.

It would seem that trees with strong apical dominance would tend to be central-leader trees with one main trunk. Such is not the case; the next year the terminal bud is not able to control the buds that are formed the year before. Of the ones that grow, several may grow higher than the original terminal growing point. While these laterals are growing their terminals have strong dominance, but they in turn lose control the next season. As this keeps on for several years, branches are formed which in turn are outgrown by new branches, thus forming a round-headed tree.

And yet trees with weak apical dominance, in which laterals form on the developing shoots, keep the laterals that do develop from outgrowing the terminal or the branches below. This control continues for a number of years, sometimes for the life of the tree. These are the typical central-leader trees, best represented by the conifers.

Not all species fall neatly into one category or the other, but the above are their general tendencies. As they mature, or become less vigorous, their growing points become more dominant, which makes for a more round-headed-tree form. Many conifers, for example, become round headed as they mature.

Roots

The above-ground parts of trees depend upon roots for anchorage, water, mineral nutrients, and the production of certain organic materials. Tree seedlings may have either a tap or a fibrous root system. Most trees have fibrous root systems although many young trees initially have a tap root system.

If the tip of a tap root is pinched, lateral roots develop a fibrous system above the pinch. This will lead to a much branched root system resembling fibrous roots.

If there are no internal inhibitions, roots will grow wherever soil conditions of aeration, moisture, temperature, nutrition, and soil tilth are favorable.

A year in the life of a plum branch

1-YEAR-OLD SPUR

Fruit/flower scar
Leaf scars
Bud scale scar
Flower buds
Terminal leaf bud

TERMINAL BUD
Bud scales
Leaves

FLOWER BUD
Flower
Bud scales

Terminal shoot

Winter: Buds formed in spring and summer are dormant during the winter. Flower and leaf buds continue differentiating essential parts in preparation for spring. Winter cold must prevail long enough to satisfy the chilling requirement before buds will begin to swell — ready for growth when the weather warms.

Spring: The flower and leaf expansion, which causes the buds to swell and eventually break, is triggered by warm weather. The flowers are usually the first to show, a benefit for pollinating insects, and delight all who see them. Next come the leaves. In plums, the terminal buds are always leaf buds, so growth of shoots continues in more or less straight lines.

Summer: The leaves grow to reach full size, manufacturing the food the tree needs, to grow, ripen the fruit, and store for the next season. Some plum varieties produce flowers, but few or no fruit. The buds for next year's flowers and leaves are formed in the leaf axils in late spring and summer.

Fall: Shorter days, cooler nights, often less water initiate the seasonal shift toward dormancy. With shoot growth and fruit-ripening complete, sugars continue to expand trunk and branch girth, and increase root growth. They are also stored in the branches, roots, and trunk to stimulate growth the following spring. Day length and cool nights trigger color in leaves before they fall with the onset of cold weather. Root growth slows, but may continue as long as the soil is warm enough. The tree assumes its silhouette for winter.

How to buy a tree

Once you have decided to plant a tree, feel good about it; it's a good deed. You will be helping a tree establish itself in surroundings (sometimes hostile compared to its pampered life in the nursery) which will be its home for many years. Even though nursery conditions may have been nearly ideal for rapid growth, a young nursery tree may not be well adapted for good performance in the landscape. Keep this in mind as you go through the check list of things to look for in a tree at the nursery. Don't expect to find the perfect tree — you probably won't. But you can, with a little looking, find a good tree; one that will live up to your expectations once planted in the landscape.

After you've read this section, keep on reading through the entire Tree Care chapter. With a good understanding of tree care, selection becomes easier.

Not too big — not too small

Select a medium-sized tree. Many people think the biggest of the bunch will grow the best, but this is not necessarily true. Balance is more important than size. Look up as well as down. You want a tree of moderate size because the top and roots will more likely be in better balance.

Most field-grown, deciduous trees are undercut, dug, and handled with little or no soil on the roots; hence, the term bareroot. Trees are dug in late fall and stored so their roots are kept moist and tops are dormant.

Large, vigorous trees will have a large proportion of roots cut and left in the field when dug. With this low root-to-top ratio, more severe pruning is necessary to reduce the top to a size where the roots can supply it with sufficient water during the first warm days after the leaves begin to grow. If left unpruned, the end result may be a smaller tree of low vigor.

Most field-grown evergreen trees are dug with soil around the roots. The soil ball is wrapped in burlap. This method of handling is called "ball and burlap" (B&B). The bigger the tree the bigger the rootball. If different sizes of trees are dug with similar size root balls, the ones with larger tops may have poor vigor because of poor root-to-top ratio.

For greater uniformity, ease of handling, and increased mechanization, the last 20 years has seen a surge in container-grown trees. Skill and careful planning are needed in nurseries to ensure container-tree vigor. In a group of trees in containers of the same size, a medium-sized tree will provide the best chance of satisfactory performance.

To sum up, then, whether you're buying a bareroot, balled-and-burlapped, or a container-grown tree, avoid the smallest and the largest of a group. For whatever reason, the smallest's less than average growth is likely to continue. The largest ones may have their vigor checked by a low root-to-top ratio.

Root quality

Root quality at the time of planting cannot be overstressed because certain root defects can doom a tree to death or poor growth. The top of a young tree is not necessarily a good indicator of the quality of the root system.

A well-formed root system is symmetrically branched with the main roots growing down and out to provide trunk support. Container-grown and balled-and-burlapped plants should have fibrous roots sufficiently developed so the rootball will retain its shape and hold together when removed from the container or the ball is moved. The main roots should be free of kinks and circles.

Kinked and circling roots, if not corrected, can cause weak root support, with the result that a tree cannot stand upright without support. Also, girdling of the main roots restricts movement of water, nutrients and food. Trees so afflicted grow poorly and may die.

To check for kinked or circling roots, brush away soil on top of the rootball or stick your finger in the top two to three inches near the trunk. You can usually see or feel them in the top of the rootball.

Straight, tapered trunk

Ideally, the tree you select should have a straight, tapered trunk that can stand by itself. It should bend evenly in the wind as a fishing pole would. Half the leaf area should be along the lower two thirds of the trunk, with branches along its entire length.

The unstaked tree is a better buy than the staked tree. Read staking section before you buy (page 98).

An easy way to check for adequate trunk development is to untie the tree from its stake and bend the top to one side. It should bend evenly along the trunk and return to within 20 to 30 degrees of vertical. If it doesn't, try to find a stronger tree. If you can't, realize that you must then provide special care for your tree to develop properly in the landscape.

Before you select a tree, check to see if it has been headed: trees in leaf will have several branches close together growing from below the cut; look for pruning scars on trees out of leaf. Depending on its landscape use, it may need corrective pruning later.

The bark should be free of injury from staking or improper handling.

Sunburn may be common on plants exposed to the afternoon sun or that have trunks with few or no leaves. Split, flattened, or dull-colored bark are indicators. Sunburned trunks are extremely slow to heal and are subject to borer infestation.

Foliage

If the tree is in leaf, foliage is a good indicator of tree condition. Leaves should be dark green and evenly colored according to the species. Scorched edges or unusual yellowing are signs of problems.

Intermediate care

Proper care of the tree after purchasing is as important as proper selection and planting. It should be kept moist and cool (especially true with a bareroot tree) so buds won't grow before the tree is planted. It may be kept in cold storage, bundled with moist packing material around the roots. If necessary, the planting of a tree from cold storage can be delayed two to four weeks beyond the usual time because the buds will be delayed in opening.

Bareroot plants can also be "heeled in" for a short period near the planting site, preferably in shade to prevent moisture loss and to keep buds dormant. Cover the roots with either moist sawdust or soil worked in around the roots to avoid air pockets. If heeled-in in the open, set the plants in a trench so that their tops can be leaned toward the southwest.

Most containers are made of dark-colored materials. If left exposed to the sun, soil temperatures near the side of the container can get high enough to kill the roots. Protect from sun as shown in the illustration on the opposite page.

Bareroot

For a better selection buy and plant bareroot trees as early as you can after danger of soil freezing has passed. Plan to plant within 2 days of purchase.

1. Look for several good-sized roots going in different directions at different levels from the main root (sometimes trees grown close together have roots on one plane).

SIDE VIEW
This —   Not this

TOP VIEW
This —   Not this

2. Don't buy the biggest tree in a group. Medium-sized ones are better. They all have similar root systems so larger trees have less root area for the amount of foliage.

This —   Not this

3. Try for a tree whose leader has not been pruned. If the leader has been headed, look for a tree with branches well spaced vertically.

This —   Not this

4. If you can't plant right away, gently pack roots in moist peat moss or sawdust and store in the shade. Keep roots as cool as possible without freezing. As long as roots are moist there's no need to water.

Roots in damp peat moss or sawdust

Prewrapped bareroot trees must be checked occasionally to be sure wrapping is moist.

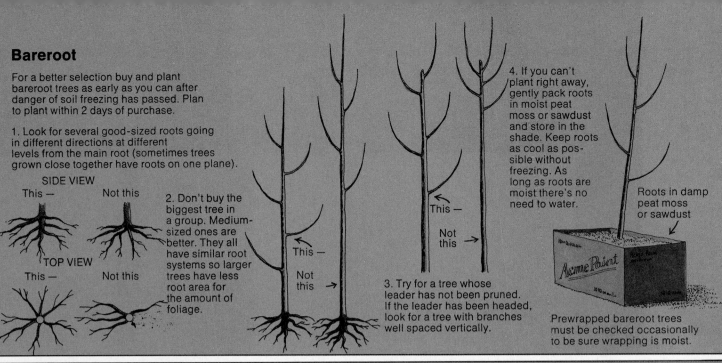

Ball and burlap

Balled-and-burlapped trees can be bought and planted at any time of year, though spring is preferred. Choose medium-sized trees — they have a better root system in proportion to the top.

Select this one

1. Untie top of burlap and look carefully at the rootball. You want a firm, solid ball of soil. Don't choose one that's cracked or broken.

2. Also look for circling roots. If they circle the trunk at the soil surface, select another tree.

3. After you select the tree carry the rootball gently from the bottom — don't use the trunk as a handle.

4. Keep B & B tree from falling over by tying or leaning it against a fence or wall.

5. Until planting, keep your tree in the shade and keep the rootball moist by watering slowly from the top. Also wet the foliage occasionally.

Container

Trees in containers may be planted at any time of year where ground does not freeze. Buy medium-sized trees rather than the largest for a better root/top ratio.

1. Look for circling roots at the soil surface; these may girdle the trunk and provide inadequate support.

2. Untie tree from stake. If it bends over at the soil level, roots may be bad; probably large roots circling or kinked below soil level.

3. Lift tree slowly by grasping at base. If the tree moves up before the can and soil do, roots are not well developed or are circling.

4. If, when untied from the stake, the tree bends down as shown below, it has a weak trunk. Try to find another tree which can stand more upright and has lower laterals.

5. If the tree will not be planted right away, keep the soil moist and mist the leaves occasionally. Keep cans in the shade or shade the containers as shown here . . .

Put several cans together so they shade each other,

shade with a board or foil,

or a pile of peat moss or soil.

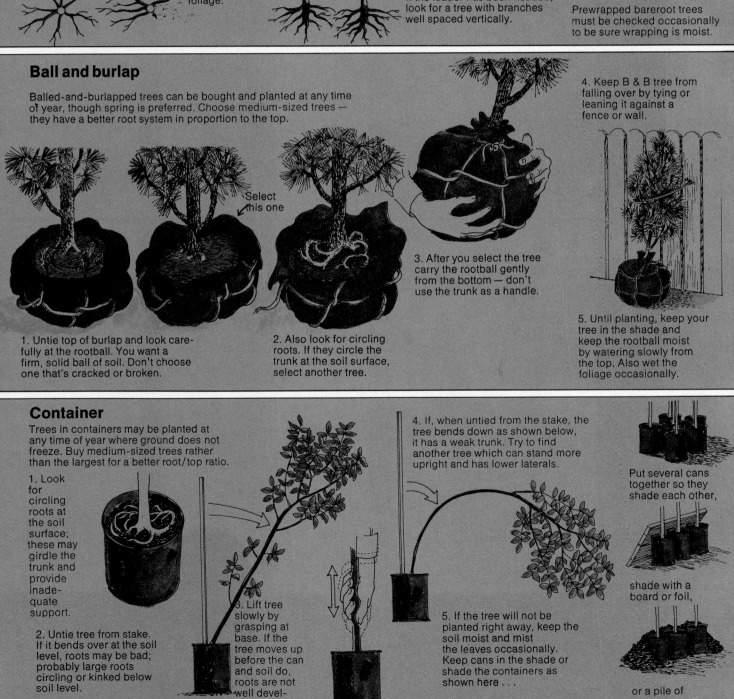

Soil texture

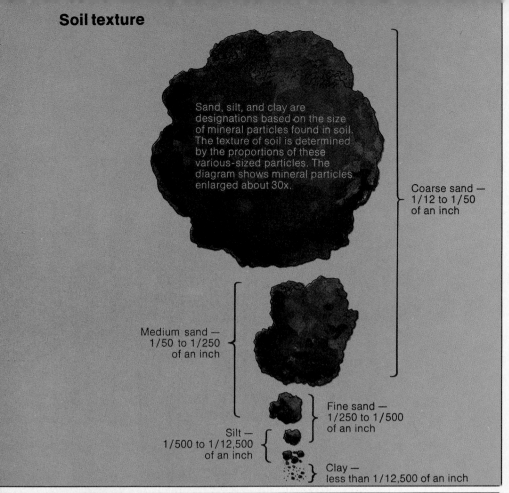

Sand, silt, and clay are designations based on the size of mineral particles found in soil. The texture of soil is determined by the proportions of these various-sized particles. The diagram shows mineral particles enlarged about 30x.

Coarse sand — 1/12 to 1/50 of an inch

Medium sand — 1/50 to 1/250 of an inch

Fine sand — 1/250 to 1/500 of an inch

Silt — 1/500 to 1/12,500 of an inch

Clay — less than 1/12,500 of an inch

Soil structure

COMPACTED SOIL: The particles are packed close together with little space left for air or water.

CRUMBLY SOIL: Decomposition of organic matter helps aggregate dry particles into porous crumbs.

SATURATED SOIL: If about half the water from rain or irrigation does not drain through the soil, plants may drown.

MOIST SOIL: A film of water between soil particles, and air in all but the small pores, means soil is well drained.

Planting hole

Slightly above grade

WIDTH: Dig the hole twice the rootball diameter or large enough to accommodate bareroots.
DEPTH: In clay soil, dig 1 to 2 inches less than the depth of the rootball or original soil line
In sandy soil or loam, the original soil level should be at or slightly higher than the garden soil.
BE SURE bottom soil has settled, sides are straight up and down, roughened-up for easy root penetration, and the bottom is flat or slightly raised in the center (see text).

Site preparation

A hole is really a transition zone in which the roots of a tree adjust from the planting mix of the nursery to the soil in your garden.

How large that transition zone needs to be depends upon the soil situation. A little exploration with a shovel, your fingers, or possibly a soil auger, will help you determine what you need to do to ready the soil for planting. Important things to note are:

1. Soil texture — size of soil particles — is your soil sandy, on the clay side, or a mixture of sizes (see illustration) — a loam?
2. Soil structure — arrangement of particles — is your soil of good tilth, compacted, or somewhere in between?
3. Soil depth. Is your soil deep enough to anchor a tree and to drain well enough not to restrict root growth and function?

Texture and structure

Most soils need little or no amending to provide a suitable rooting medium that holds moisture while allowing proper aeration. They are a mixture of soil particle sizes of acceptable structure — a loam soil. Such soils crumble easily when a shovelful is dumped beside the planting hole or is manipulated between your fingers. Just crumble it and use as is for backfilling.

Soils which are either quite sandy or clayey will be improved by adding organic matter (peat, compost, nitrified bark or well-decomposed sawdust) to the backfill at a rate of two parts soil to one part organic matter. Sandy soils usually are well drained and have good aeration, but do not retain much water. Organic matter will increase somewhat the moisture-holding capacity of sandy soil.

At the other extreme, clay soils hold a lot of water but may be poorly drained and aerated. Organic matter will help improve drainage and aeration of clay soils by separating some of the particles to provide paths for water and air.

There's an easy way to find out what kind of soil you have. Pick up a handful and squeeze. A ball of clay will remain in a tight, ridged lump. Loam will hold its shape, but will crumble if you poke it. Sandy soil will begin to fall apart as you open your hand.

To know how well your soil drains, dig a hole and fill it with water. Let it drain, and refill. After the second filling, the water should drain at about a quarter of an inch per hour. If it drains much faster, the soil is sandy and well drained. If it drains much slower, there are several possibilities: clay soil, compacted soil, or a compacted layer below the surface.

Compaction

Soil around new homes, former paths or drives, or old farmland may be severely compacted. If your soil is near its original grade, only the top six to ten inches will be compacted. If fill soil has been brought in, the compacted zone will be that much deeper. In these situations, the planting hole should be large enough in diameter and deep enough to get through the compacted soil. Surface soil or soil from below the compacted layer, mixed with a little organic matter, should be used for backfill.

Shallow soils

Shallow soils may restrict growth and provide inadequate anchorage of the tree. Such soil may be underlain with rock or hardpan. Hardpan is a layer of fine clay particles which have accumulated some distance below the soil surface to form sedimentary rock. In shallow soils water may collect on the impervious layer, threatening plants with drowning.

There are two alternatives for living with shallow soil; you can either go over it or through it.

To go over it, it's possible to build raised beds or mounds which provide depth for root development in a soil with more amiable moisture conditions. Raised beds have the added advantage of making the tree a focal point in the landscape. Unless your garden soil is quite unacceptable, use it in the raised planter. Very sandy or clayey soil can be amended with organic matter. Loosen the original soil surface before filling the planter.

If the soil is completely unworkable, and some soils are, large containers can be the answer. A container allows you to select a lightweight, well-drained soil.

It may be possible to go under hardpan. To do so, break through the impervious layer with a pick, post-hole digger, or a well-auger. Use only surface soil, or surface soil mixed with organic matter for backfill. Allow it to settle and plant as usual.

When it is not possible to go through the impervious layer, use a tile drain to remove excess water (see illustration).

Drainage

When shallow soil is underlaid by a layer of impervious soil or hardpan, excess water cannot drain away. Here are some solutions.

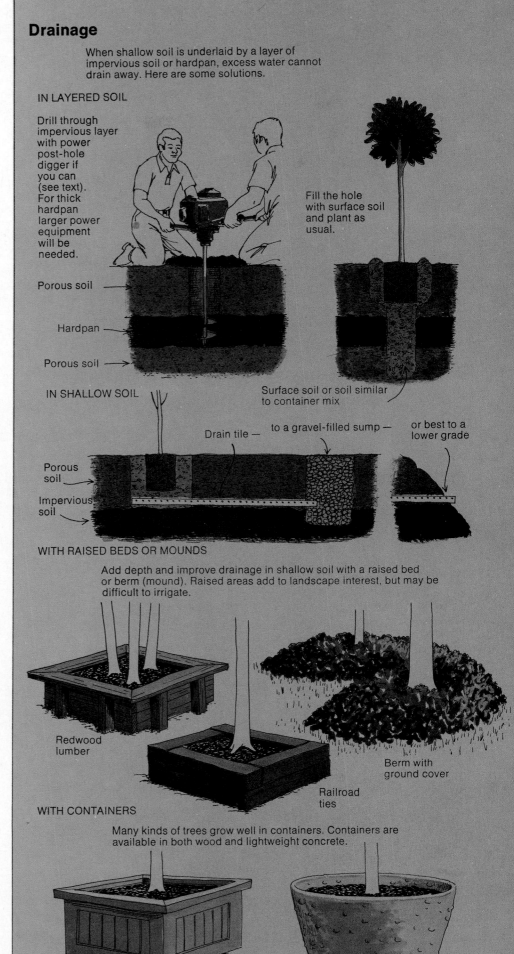

IN LAYERED SOIL

Drill through impervious layer with power post-hole digger if you can (see text). For thick hardpan larger power equipment will be needed.

Porous soil

Hardpan

Porous soil

Fill the hole with surface soil and plant as usual.

Surface soil or soil similar to container mix

IN SHALLOW SOIL

Drain tile — to a gravel-filled sump — or best to a lower grade

Porous soil

Impervious soil

WITH RAISED BEDS OR MOUNDS

Add depth and improve drainage in shallow soil with a raised bed or berm (mound). Raised areas add to landscape interest, but may be difficult to irrigate.

Redwood lumber

Railroad ties

Berm with ground cover

WITH CONTAINERS

Many kinds of trees grow well in containers. Containers are available in both wood and lightweight concrete.

Orientation

Although not necessarily critical to the survival of a tree, how you set it in the ground may make a difference.

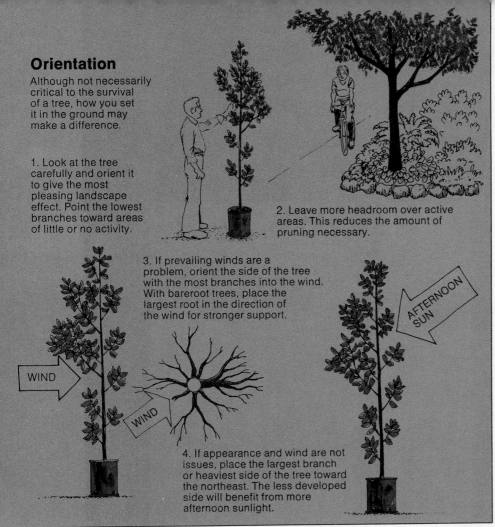

1. Look at the tree carefully and orient it to give the most pleasing landscape effect. Point the lowest branches toward areas of little or no activity.

2. Leave more headroom over active areas. This reduces the amount of pruning necessary.

3. If prevailing winds are a problem, orient the side of the tree with the most branches into the wind. With bareroot trees, place the largest root in the direction of the wind for stronger support.

4. If appearance and wind are not issues, place the largest branch or heaviest side of the tree toward the northeast. The less developed side will benefit from more afternoon sunlight.

WIND

WIND

AFTERNOON SUN

Planting B and B

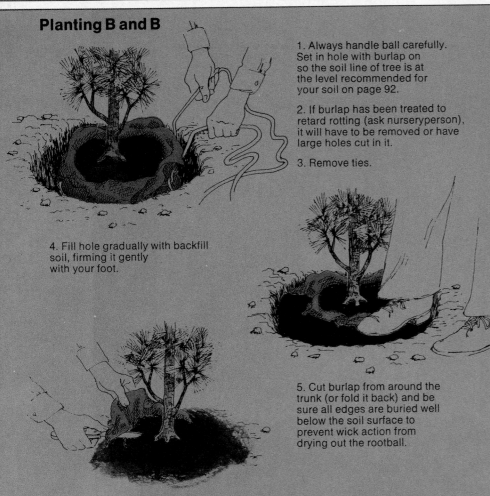

1. Always handle ball carefully. Set in hole with burlap on so the soil line of tree is at the level recommended for your soil on page 92.

2. If burlap has been treated to retard rotting (ask nurseryperson), it will have to be removed or have large holes cut in it.

3. Remove ties.

4. Fill hole gradually with backfill soil, firming it gently with your foot.

5. Cut burlap from around the trunk (or fold it back) and be sure all edges are buried well below the soil surface to prevent wick action from drying out the rootball.

Planting

Although not necessarily critical to the survival of a tree, a number of factors should be considered in setting a tree in the hole. Prior to planting, check the illustrations on this page.

Another consideration is sunburn. Place the scion (the bud or graft) of grafted trees toward the afternoon sun to reduce the possibility of sunburn just above the bud union. Low foliage may shade this area or, if exposed, the trunk may be painted with white latex paint or wrapped with a commercial tree wrap.

Before planting, cut back any injured, diseased, twisted or dead roots on bareroot trees to healthy tissue. The bottom of the hole should be firm and level for container-grown trees. A slight rise in the center makes spreading of the roots of bareroot trees easier. Spread the roots in the bottom of the hole to provide good anchorage and to prevent circling.

For container-grown trees, cut, and remove some of the roots that are matted at the bottom or circling around the outside of the rootball. In freeing the roots at the periphery of the rootball, break away some of the soil to provide better contact between the rootball and the fill soil. Straightening the periphery roots so they extend two or more inches into the fill soil will double the soil volume available to the plant. In addition, the roots will be in the fill soil and able to grow in it more easily than if they had to grow out of an undisturbed rootball. Removing one-fourth to one-half the roots in the outer inch of the rootball should not set back any but the most sensitive plants. If anything, most plants will be stimulated.

With balled-and-burlapped trees, fold back the burlap at least two inches below the soil level. Leaving it exposed creates a wicklike action that will dry out the soil faster than normally. Carefully slice the burlap on the sides and bottom of the rootball to allow for easy root penetration.

Burlap generally rots away within a year; however, some burlap may be treated with a preservative for nursery keeping, in which case the burlap should be removed before planting. Ask your nurseryman. If it is treated, gently rock the rootball to one side, pushing the burlap as far under it as possible. Then rock it back and the burlap should be free. With smaller rootballs, just lifting the plant carefully away from the burlap may be easier.

Backfill the hole with the original soil unless it is undesirable. Add organic matter to heavy, extremely light, or compacted soils. See Texture and structure, page 92, for instructions on mixing backfill.

Don't place fertilizer in the planting hole or mix it with the backfill soil. This can result in plant injury. Most trees will grow well the first season without additional fertilizer.

If staking is necessary, plant the stake with the tree.

Set the roots or rootball on a firm base with the center slightly higher than the edge of the hole. This will help in spreading the roots, and to a certain extent, in draining water away from the base of the roots. Work the soil in around the roots so they are not compressed into a tight mass, but are spreading and supported by soil underneath. After filling in each three to four inches of soil, firm the soil around the roots or rootball with your foot, taking special care not to tear, bruise, or debark the roots. The original ground level in the nursery or of the rootball should be one or two inches above the finished ground level for clay or loam soils, and about even with the surrounding soil if extremely sandy. You can plant bare-root trees one to two inches deeper in sandy soil. A dark-to-light color change below the bud union, if any, on the trunk indicates the original soil level in the nursery.

Basins

Make the watering basin for trees at least 30 inches in diameter. Twice the size of the rootball is a good rule of thumb. A ridge four or five inches high — with soil dug from the planting hole — makes it possible to wet the soil thoroughly.

Fill the basin with water to further settle the soil and to provide roots with water. This can be done effectively by using a three- or four-foot pipe on a hose. Force the pipe, with water running, through the soil around the roots or rootball. This will improve the contact between fill soil and roots.

For several weeks after planting, the rootball will need more frequent watering than the surrounding soil, which has few roots.

To make certain the ball receives adequate water, build a dike inside the first, slightly smaller than the rootball itself. The inner circle will concentrate the water where needed. Water the inner circle thoroughly every one to three days for the first

Bareroot planting

Soil line

Broken

Twisted

Discolored

1. Before planting trim off any broken or twisted roots or discolored tips. Determine the location of the original soil line — look for soil or a change of color on the trunk.

2. Set the tree in the hole so the soil line is above the surrounding soil as shown on page 92. Spread roots evenly. Keep them radiating out from the root crown — not bent or circled.

3. Work backfill soil between and around the roots.

4. Firm soil gently with a tamp or your foot as you fill the hole, making certain roots and soil are in firm contact.

5. Eliminate air pockets, settle soil, and bring soil into firm contact with the roots by running water slowly over root area. Check soil level and build basin as shown on page 97.

Planting from cans (and other containers)

1. Move the tree by holding the can or lifting carefully by the trunk near the soil level.

2. Cut the container and lift the tree gently so as not to break the rootball.

Tap tapered containers gently on the sides to loosen soil; then pull the tree out carefully.

3. Cut or pull away any circled or matted roots so they radiate out from the rootball. Shorten roots to the width of the planting hole so they will not be bent when planted.

Cut or straighten roots that circle and remove all matted roots.

4. Set the tree carefully into the hole. Be sure the soil line of the tree is at the level recommended for your kind of soil on page 92.

5. Add and firm backfill soil gradually (see text) so you get good root contact.

few weeks to be sure the tree has adequate moisture. Irrigation frequency will depend on the amount of leaves the tree has and the weather. After the roots penetrate the transition zone — a month to six weeks after planting — remove the inner dike. In the meantime, the outer zone will need less water (the amount varying with your soil type), but should be kept moist.

In areas of high rainfall, temporarily knock down the dikes to avoid accumulating water at the base of the tree. If you don't, crown rot can result and kill the tree.

If the tree settles so that the original soil line is below the soil surface, you can raise a bareroot tree slightly higher than desired and then allow it to settle back into the soil to provide better soil contact with the roots. With container or balled-and-burlapped trees, use a shovel under the rootball, as shown in the illustration, to raise the plant.

You should keep correction of the soil level to a minimum, since the more the plant is raised, the closer the roots are drawn together. This weakens anchorage and reduces the volume of soil in contact with the roots.

After the soil has drained, you can create the final contour of the basin — with the base of the plant slightly higher than the bottom of the basin. Then water won't collect around the trunk. Unless some soil has fallen or been taken from the top of the rootball, do not add soil to the top of the rootball to obtain the final basin contour. This is especially important if the backfill soil is heavier than that of the rootball because the rootball may wet with difficulty or not at all.

Competition from turf

When trees are planted in a lawn area, keep the turf well away from the trunk of the tree during the first two to three years. The growth of young trees can be retarded by grass growing close to their trunks, even if additional water and fertilizer are applied. An area of 30 inches in diameter of bare soil around the tree will also prevent damage to young trees from lawn mowers. Mechanical damage to the trunks of young trees can severely dwarf them.

Use herbicides with caution in tree basins. They can injure the bark of young trees. Follow the manufacturer's directions closely.

See page 101 for mulching instructions.

Pruning

There is always some root loss in the process of transplanting. Damaged or discolored roots are cut off, circling roots are pulled out and cut, and both upset the root-top ratio. To bring the top growth back into balance with the root system, some pruning is necessary.

Even if no roots were lost during planting, the top might have such a large leaf area that frequent watering would be needed to prevent wilting. The top does not have to be reduced in actual size. Thinning out branches that are close together, crossing one another, or broken, removes considerable leaf area without affecting overall plant size. One fourth of the leaf area can be removed from most trees with little visual change in the plant except improvement.

Bareroot trees will probably need more pruning after planting than container or balled-and-burlapped trees because of the way they're dug. Check the pruning section (page 102) for proper methods of thinning.

It's possible that some pruning has been done at the nursery. If so, little more need be done. Check for pruning scars, or ask your nurseryman.

When good trees go bad

If the soil is ideal, the whole planting process is one of common sense. Many a tree is grown without the attention we have outlined. But things go wrong (and, in most cases, the nurseryman is blamed for lack of growth). You should check these points before blaming the nursery.

Has the tree settled? Check the planting depth. Many a tree has died from crown rot because soil was not allowed to settle before planting.

Has the tree dried out? Until roots can spread into surrounding soil, container or balled-and-burlapped trees should be watered more often than if they were in their respective packaging. Remember, a transpiring tree uses water faster from its rootball than moisture evaporates from open ground. Surrounding soil can be wet and not indicate that the rootball of a newly planted tree has dried out.

Check planting depth

After watering to settle the soil, check to be certain the original soil line is where recommended for your soil (see page 92). If it's too low —

BAREROOT: Grasp the trunk near the soil and lift an inch or so higher than the proper level and let it settle back.

B & B or CONTAINERS: Carefully place a shovel beneath the rootball and pry up while lifting on the trunk. Raise it an inch or two above the proper level and let it settle back.

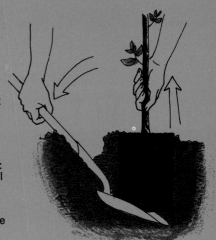

Water it again, if necessary, to resettle the soil.

Basins

Build a shallow basin so water soaks down into the rootball with a minimum of run-off.

With all of the tree's roots still in the rootball, it will dry faster than surrounding soil. To improve rooting conditions and save water, build a double basin system. Use the rootball-width basin for primary watering until some roots have grown into the surrounding soil — 6 weeks or so.

In rainy weather temporarily cut the basin berm so excessive water will drain away.

Pruning

Since there will always be some root loss in transplanting, part of the top growth of a tree should be pruned out to compensate, so that roots and top are better in proportion.

1. Use a thinning-out type of pruning so as not to reduce overall size or modify natural form of the tree (see pages 102-103).

2. If some pruning was done at the nursery (look for pruning scars, ask the nurseryman) you won't need to remove much. The purpose is to create a balance between the top growth and the root system so that the roots can supply enough water and nutrients to the branches.

Staking

A young tree exposed to wind and weather concentrates its energy on growing strong enough to remain upright. It develops a sturdy trunk, tapered to bend without breaking, and a strong root system to hold it in place. Unfortunately, there are some common practices which prevent the young tree from growing as strong as it should. In order to make maximum use of space in nurseries, trees are often too close together; the side branches which could nourish the trunk and strengthen it are shaded out or trimmed off. The tree is then staked. These practices encourage height growth at the expense of trunk development. By the time you get the tree, it often can't stand without a stake.

Ideally, look for a sturdy tree with some side branches that will strengthen the trunk. If none are available in the species of tree you want, you can stake it until it is sufficiently established to stand on its own.

Sometimes thinning alone will be sufficient to reduce the weight and wind-resistance of the top, or tilting the rootball slightly will be enough to help the tree stand independently. Try these methods before getting out the staking materials — you may save yourself a lot of time and have a stronger tree, too.

Mechanical damage can have a severe dwarfing effect; even a sturdy young tree needs protective stakes to prevent damage from lawn mowers and other garden activities. Three stakes, just tall enough to be seen

easily, should be placed at the outer edge of the rootball, at least six inches from the trunk.

The trunks of many trees will hold their tops upright as long as the roots are firmly anchored. Anchor stakes can be used to hold the roots where planted until they become established enough to hold the tree.

Anchor stakes can be the same as the ones used to protect the trunk. Loop or figure-eight ties between the stakes and the trunk will hold the roots and still allow the top to flex in the wind.

Support staking should be thought of as a temporary measure, to be used only until the tree is established.

Make support stakes just high enough to hold the tree upright under calm conditions; the tree should

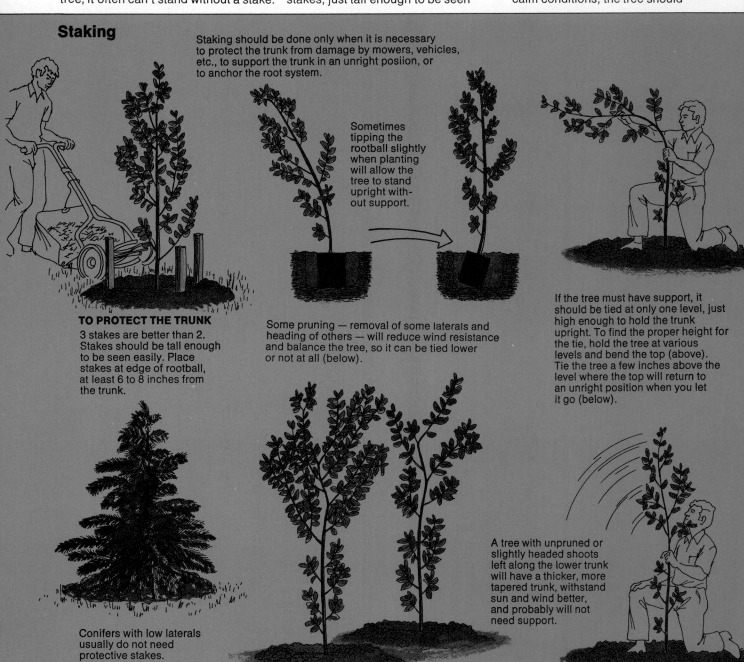

Staking

Staking should be done only when it is necessary to protect the trunk from damage by mowers, vehicles, etc., to support the trunk in an unright posiion, or to anchor the root system.

Sometimes tipping the rootball slightly when planting will allow the tree to stand upright without support.

TO PROTECT THE TRUNK
3 stakes are better than 2. Stakes should be tall enough to be seen easily. Place stakes at edge of rootball, at least 6 to 8 inches from the trunk.

Some pruning — removal of some laterals and heading of others — will reduce wind resistance and balance the tree, so it can be tied lower or not at all (below).

If the tree must have support, it should be tied at only one level, just high enough to hold the trunk upright. To find the proper height for the tie, hold the tree at various levels and bend the top (above). Tie the tree a few inches above the level where the top will return to an unright position when you let it go (below).

Conifers with low laterals usually do not need protective stakes.

A tree with unpruned or slightly headed shoots left along the lower trunk will have a thicker, more tapered trunk, withstand sun and wind better, and probably will not need support.

return to a vertical position after bending in the wind (see illustration).

Support stakes are usually required through the first season. Check deciduous trees to see if they can stand alone at the beginning of the dormant season (the end of autumn), but don't remove the ties until growth begins in spring. Leave the ties on in the interim to protect the tree from being broken by winter storms.

The tree should be firmly established by the end of the second season. If it isn't, there are some possibilities that need investigation. The top may need to be thinned to reduce weight and wind-resistance. Some pinching of lower branches may be in order to encourage additional side growth to nourish and strengthen the trunk. The root system may be

weakened by circling or kinked roots. If that appears to be the case, the tree must be dug up. Even though circling roots might be straightened and the tree replanted, starting with a new tree would be better.

A tree with a spindly trunk and not much trunk taper sometimes needs extra support along most of the lower trunk. A thin, flexible auxiliary stake of spring-steel wire tied to the trunk will provide the extra strength needed. Spring-steel wire is available in different diameters with various degrees of flexibility. Make it just long enough to permit the trunk to return to an upright position after being bent. It should stop at least two feet short of the terminal bud of the leader. Tie the auxiliary stake to the trunk with polyethylene tape at six- to ten-inch

intervals. Support stakes are usually needed for another year after auxiliary stakes are removed.

Make a stake

Either wood (2″ x 2″) or metal (T-iron) will do for protective anchor or support stakes. Treat wood with nontoxic preservative (copper sulfate base not pentachlorophenol) to keep it from rotting. Metal stakes need a flange or plate just below the ground for extra stability.

Ties can be almost any soft, flexible material. Green or black quarter-inch polyethylene tape is probably the least obtrusive. *Don't* use thin materials like fishing line, twine, or worst of all, wire. They will cut deep into the bark with friction, seriously damaging the tree. If you use wire to guy a tree, loop

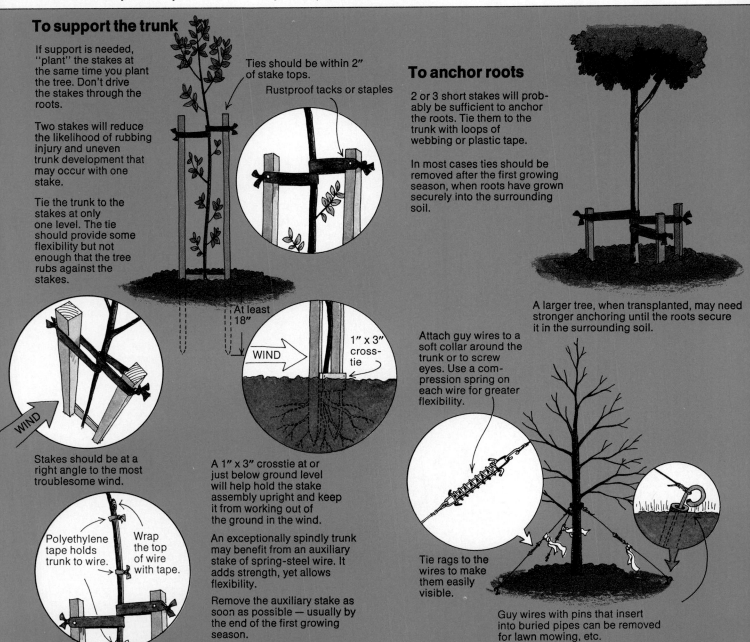

To support the trunk

If support is needed, "plant" the stakes at the same time you plant the tree. Don't drive the stakes through the roots.

Two stakes will reduce the likelihood of rubbing injury and uneven trunk development that may occur with one stake.

Tie the trunk to the stakes at only one level. The tie should provide some flexibility but not enough that the tree rubs against the stakes.

Ties should be within 2″ of stake tops.

Rustproof tacks or staples

Stakes should be at a right angle to the most troublesome wind.

WIND

At least 18″

WIND

1″ x 3″ crosstie

A 1″ x 3″ crosstie at or just below ground level will help hold the stake assembly upright and keep it from working out of the ground in the wind.

An exceptionally spindly trunk may benefit from an auxiliary stake of spring-steel wire. It adds strength, yet allows flexibility.

Remove the auxiliary stake as soon as possible — usually by the end of the first growing season.

Polyethylene tape holds trunk to wire.

Wrap the top of wire with tape.

To anchor roots

2 or 3 short stakes will probably be sufficient to anchor the roots. Tie them to the trunk with loops of webbing or plastic tape.

In most cases ties should be removed after the first growing season, when roots have grown securely into the surrounding soil.

A larger tree, when transplanted, may need stronger anchoring until the roots secure it in the surrounding soil.

Attach guy wires to a soft collar around the trunk or to screw eyes. Use a compression spring on each wire for greater flexibility.

Tie rags to the wires to make them easily visible.

Guy wires with pins that insert into buried pipes can be removed for lawn mowing, etc.

Drip line

The drip line is an imaginary line beneath the outermost ends of a tree's branches from which rain water would supposedly drip.

Shallow roots

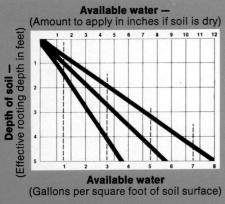

Drip line

Most feeder roots are found in the top three feet, where the soil is most fertile and best aerated. Roots may extend well beyond the drip line of the tree. The tap roots of most trees do not persist as trees mature; most root systems become more spreading as they age.

Available water —
(Amount to apply in inches if soil is dry)

Depth of soil —
(Effective rooting depth in feet)

Available water
(Gallons per square foot of soil surface)

Rate of water penetration in soils of different textures.

---

the wire through a soft collar, such as old garden hose, to prevent girdling, see illustration.

Watering and feeding

Trees are able to stand upright because their roots are firmly anchored in soil. The soil holds water and nutrients essential for tree growth.

The importance of soil texture, structure, and depth was presented in the section on digging the planting hole (see page 92). These same properties are also extremely important to trees throughout their lives.

Clay particles have the ability to become grouped together in aggregates so that each aggregate acts as a single, larger-sized particle. This aggregation is referred to as structure. Well-aggregated soils have the desirable properties of sand, such as good water movement and aeration, as well as the high water-and-nutrient-holding capacities of clay. Soils which are primarily sand or silt (intermediate in size) aggregate poorly, so their properties depend essentially on their texture.

Water requirements

All plants require water to grow. They get water from the soil and lose most of it through their leaves by evaporation (transpiration). Water to insure plant growth comes from either rain or irrigation. The amount of water available to a plant depends on the depth and spread of the roots. Most roots are within three feet of the surface. When there is sufficient water, most of it is supplied from the top three to four feet of soil. In dry periods, deep-rooted plants can draw water from lower levels.

During dry periods, or in areas where irrigation is a necessity, you must observe your trees to determine when they need water. Signs of water stress are wilting, a change in leaf color (from shiny to dull; from dark green to gray green), and premature leaf fall.

There are a number of ways to water efficiently: basins, furrows, sprinklers, soakers, or drip systems (see illustration). The most important goals are to eliminate run-off, to confine water inside the drip line of branches, and apply uniformly. The purpose is to make as much as possible of the water applied available to the tree.

Don't forget that watering a newly planted tree has its own rules. See Planting, page 94.

Fertilization

Nitrogen is the only element to which most trees respond. Young trees grow more rapidly following nitrogen fertilization, more quickly reaching landscape size. However, mature trees may need little or no fertilization as long as they have good leaf color and grow reasonably well. In fact, increased vigor may needlessly increase the size of trees and the density of the leaves. Leaves on the inside of such trees, or plants under them, grow poorly because of heavy shade.

As a starter, apply nitrogen at a rate of two to four pounds per thousand square feet. If you are not using a straight nitrogen fertilizer (ammonium nitrate, ammonium sulfate, calcium nitrate, or urea) a so-called "complete" fertilizer (containing nitrogen, phosphorus and potassium) is fine. Read directions and adjust pounds used according to the percentage of nitrogen in the particular fertilizer. If it's 20 percent, as in 20-4-4, use five times the recommendation.

Another way to figure how much to apply is to measure the diameter of the tree trunk. For each inch, use .1 to .2 pounds of actual nitrogen, or in other words, 1 to 2 pounds of a 10% nitrogen fertilizer such as 10-8-7.

Because nitrogen is transient, apply the necessary amount at two intervals. One-half in spring and the other half in summer is a good program.

Keep the fertilizer at least six inches away from the trunk to avoid injury. After the first year apply nitrogen fertilizer to an area having a radius of one and a quarter times that of the tree canopy. After application, sprinkle-irrigate the area to wash the fertilizer into the soil. This begins conversion of the less soluble forms of nitrogen, and avoids burning the grass if the tree is planted in a lawn.

Let the trees be your guide as to the amount to apply. If growth is excessive on young trees, put on less per area next time, or skip a year. If shoot growth is shorter than you want and leaf color pale, double the rate. As trees mature, fertilize only if growth or leaf color is not up to expectation.

In most soils you will not need to be concerned about the acidity-alkalinity of the soil. Most trees grow satisfactorily over a wide range of soil reaction. Well-drained soils in high-rainfall areas usually are acid, while poorly drained soils and those in areas of low rainfall are neutral or alkaline. In many alkaline soils, a number of trees may be low in iron as evidenced by their pale yellow leaves with fine, darker green veins. These symptoms are most obvious on the first growth during spring.

An acid-forming nitrogen fertilizer, such as ammonium sulfate, will help make the soil more acid. If symptoms are severe, soil sulfur can be worked into the surface soil at about 10 to 20 pounds per 1000 square feet. More expensive iron chelates are quicker acting and more certain, although the correction may only last one or two seasons. Apply chelates as directed on the label. In areas having alkaline soil, you may want to avoid species most likely to show iron deficiency. (Check the individual tree descriptions for special micro-nutrient needs.)

If a tree isn't responding to nitrogen, check with your nurseryman or County Extension Agent, showing or describing the symptoms.

Mulching

A mulch is any material that is put on the soil to cover and protect it. Straw, leaves, wood chips, gravel, and plastic all make effective mulches.

Mulches do many marvelous things. They reduce moisture loss, improve soil structure (black plastic and rocks excepted), reduce soil erosion, reduce soil compaction, keep weeds down, moderate soil temperatures, and provide a clean, firm surface for walking on during rainy weather.

Most mulches are organic and are the by-product of industry, agriculture, or your own gardening. Some organic mulches are wood shavings, wood chips, twigs, bark, sawdust, leaves, grass, straw, peat moss, rice hulls, corn cobs, cocoa hulls, and pomace. Inorganic mulches include plastic, gravel, crushed brick, rock.

Prepare the area for mulching by bringing to uniform grade and removing the weeds. Apply mulches three to five inches thick. Keep the mulch six inches away from the tree trunks.

Placing medium-sized gravel, coarse sand, or cinders between the trunk and the mulch will keep both mulch and hungry rodents away from the trunk.

A single sheet of black plastic eliminates the need for further weed control, but should have holes cut in it for water penetration to tree roots. It can be covered with an organic mulch or crushed rock to improve its appearance.

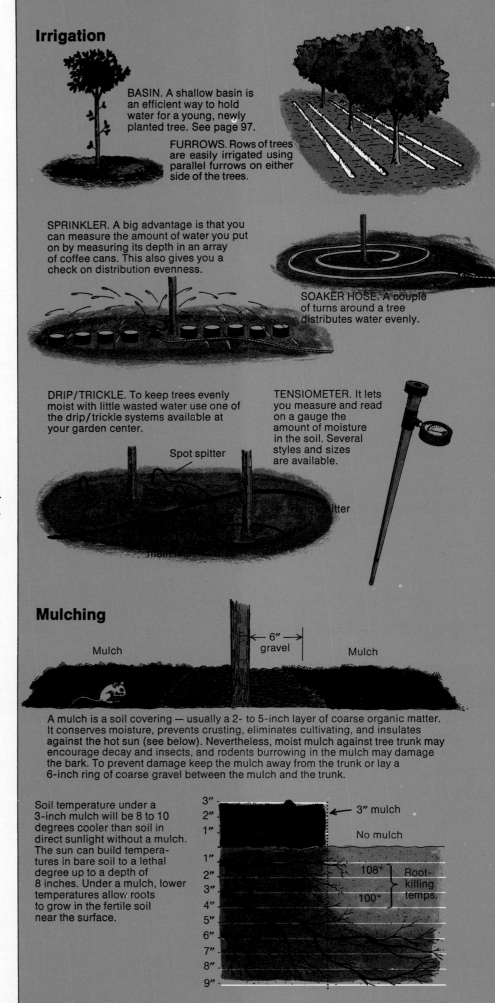

Irrigation

BASIN. A shallow basin is an efficient way to hold water for a young, newly planted tree. See page 97.

FURROWS. Rows of trees are easily irrigated using parallel furrows on either side of the trees.

SPRINKLER. A big advantage is that you can measure the amount of water you put on by measuring its depth in an array of coffee cans. This also gives you a check on distribution evenness.

SOAKER HOSE. A couple of turns around a tree distributes water evenly.

DRIP/TRICKLE. To keep trees evenly moist with little wasted water use one of the drip/trickle systems available at your garden center.

Spot spitter

TENSIOMETER. It lets you measure and read on a gauge the amount of moisture in the soil. Several styles and sizes are available.

Mulching

Mulch   6" gravel   Mulch

A mulch is a soil covering — usually a 2- to 5-inch layer of coarse organic matter. It conserves moisture, prevents crusting, eliminates cultivating, and insulates against the hot sun (see below). Nevertheless, moist mulch against tree trunk may encourage decay and insects, and rodents burrowing in the mulch may damage the bark. To prevent damage keep the mulch away from the trunk or lay a 6-inch ring of coarse gravel between the mulch and the trunk.

Soil temperature under a 3-inch mulch will be 8 to 10 degrees cooler than soil in direct sunlight without a mulch. The sun can build temperatures in bare soil to a lethal degree up to a depth of 8 inches. Under a mulch, lower temperatures allow roots to grow in the fertile soil near the surface.

3"
2" → 3" mulch
1"
No mulch
1"
2" 108° Root-
3" killing
4" 100° temps.
5"
6"
7"
8"
9"

Pruning

Trees grow in many and varied forms. Some develop spreading crowns. Others have central leaders with tall straight trunks. Intermediate forms can be found between these extremes. The natural characteristics of different kinds of trees should be emphasized through landscape use and maintenance practices. Pruning can do much to enhance tree health and appearance.

Pruning is useful for a number of reasons. Pruning at planting compensates for root loss of bareroot plants and improves water balance of container-grown trees. Strong branch structure and handsome form can be encouraged. Removing dead wood, crossed branches, and letting light into the interior of the tree will improve its health and appearance. Pruning is particularly useful in controlling tree size. On mature trees, pruning helps to maintain balance between vegetative growth and flowering. Stagnated trees may be brought back to life by severe pruning.

Responses to pruning

Pruning is the removal of any portion of a plant. Removing large amounts of healthy growth affects a tree in two seemingly opposite ways. The most obvious response is invigoration. Harder to determine and often overlooked is the dwarfing effect of pruning.

Removing leafy shoots and buds that would become leaves allows the roots, which are not immediately affected, to supply the remaining parts of the tree with relatively more water and nutrients than before. Shoots are stimulated into growing more rapidly and later into the season. Leaves become larger and darker green just as if the tree had been fertilized.

Even though leaves will be larger and shoots longer, the total amount of leaf area and new growth will be less on a pruned tree. There will be fewer leaves working for a shorter time so that less total growth will be made and less food stored.

The amount of invigoration and of dwarfing depends on the severity of the pruning. Removing dead, weak, and heavily shaded branches has little influence on growth, while pruning off healthy branches, well exposed to light, can have a significant effect.

Severe pruning can affect differently not only two different trees, but

Heading and thinning

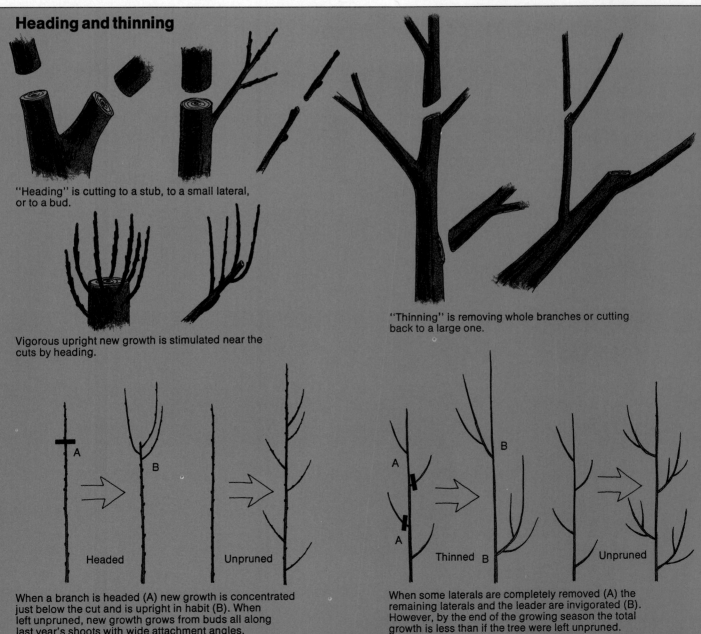

"Heading" is cutting to a stub, to a small lateral, or to a bud.

Vigorous upright new growth is stimulated near the cuts by heading.

"Thinning" is removing whole branches or cutting back to a large one.

Headed   Unpruned

Thinned B   Unpruned

When a branch is headed (A) new growth is concentrated just below the cut and is upright in habit (B). When left unpruned, new growth grows from buds all along last year's shoots with wide attachment angles.

When some laterals are completely removed (A) the remaining laterals and the leader are invigorated (B). However, by the end of the growing season the total growth is less than if the tree were left unpruned.

also various parts of the same tree. If you wish to subdue a branch within a tree, prune it more severely to reduce its total growth relative to other branches you wish to encourage. Conversely, to encourage a branch to grow more, prune it lightly or not at all. At the same time, prune other branches more severely, particularly those that might shade or compete with the branch you are trying to encourage. This is the principal way to influence trees to grow the way you want them to grow.

For every generalization there are always one or more exceptions. For this one there are two. Mature plants expected to set a heavy flower and fruit load may not be dwarfed by pruning. Pruning stimulates the remaining shoots, while the number of flowers and fruits on them remains the same. The other exception is the response to pruning by a stagnated young plant. For some unexplained reason, some young trees that are doing poorly, but show no symptoms other than lack of vigor, will respond with renewed vitality to extremely severe pruning. This usually is a kill-or-cure procedure.

The type of pruning determines the tree's response

"Heading" or "heading back" means cutting back to a stub, a lateral bud, or a small lateral branch. New growth comes from one or more buds near the cut; the lower buds don't ordinarily grow. The new shoots are usually vigorous, upright, and dense. The new branches and foliage may form a canopy so thick that lower leaves and plants growing under the tree are shaded out.

When large branches of mature trees are headed, it's called "stubbing."

"Thinning" or "thinning-out" is the removal of a branch at its origin or cutting back to another lateral branch. The new growth follows the tree's natural branching pattern and tends to be more evenly distributed throughout the crown. As the term suggests, it leaves the canopy less dense; more open. With more light penetrating through the leaves, interior foliage and plants under the tree will grow better. A thinned tree will also be less subject to wind damage.

For in-depth directions for pruning specific fruit trees for fruit production, see Ortho's *All About Growing Fruits and Berries*.

Spring-flowering trees

Plants flowering in the spring from buds on 1 year old wood, especially the flowering fruit trees, should be pruned at or near the end of the bloom period. If you prune in fall or winter you will remove buds that would flower the next spring.

Summer-flowering trees

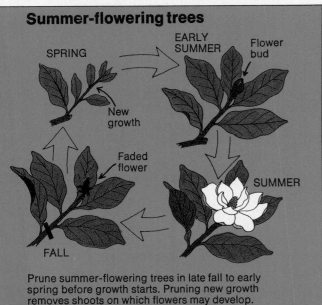

Prune summer-flowering trees in late fall to early spring before growth starts. Pruning new growth removes shoots on which flowers may develop.

Conifers

To make pines more compact and control size, cut off some of each "candle" in late spring to lessen distance between whorls.

Reduce open spaces in spruce by trimming half of terminal shoots in the spring when new needles are forming.

To keep branches short, pinch terminal buds.

Shorten long branches to an inner lateral.

If a top lateral doesn't replace a lost leader, train one with a support brace.

Remove the less desirable of two leaders as soon as you notice them.

The basics

Cutting at an angle or with blade moving up takes less effort.

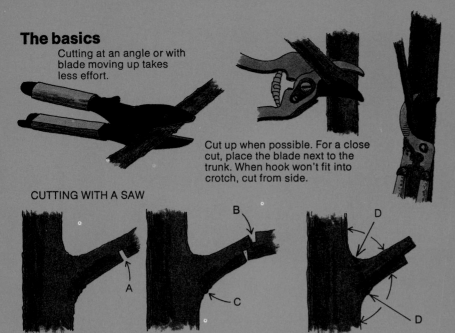

Cut up when possible. For a close cut, place the blade next to the trunk. When hook won't fit into crotch, cut from side.

CUTTING WITH A SAW

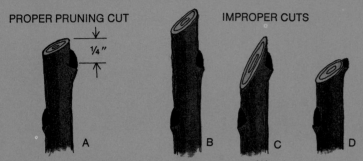

For heavy branches make first cut halfway through (A). Make a second cut (B) out from first cut and the limb will fall away without tearing the bark. Make third cut (C) at shoulder rings, or if the rings aren't visible, cut on a line (D) bisecting the top and bottom angles of attachment.

PROPER PRUNING CUT   IMPROPER CUTS

¼"

A   B   C   D

When possible, cut back to a side bud. A proper cut (A) is at an angle about ¼" above the bud. Improper cuts are: (B) too far from bud, (C) too sharp an angle, and (D) too close to the bud.

BRANCH ATTACHMENT STRENGTH

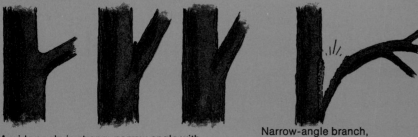

A wide angle is strong; narrow angle with bark ridge, fairly strong; narrow angle with bark imbedded in the wood is weak.

Narrow-angle branch, although weak, may not break until the branch is quite large.

Shoot removed

Most broadleaved plants have more than one bud at a node. But, unless growth is quite vigorous, usually not more than one develops. The first bud that grows may have a sharp angle of attachment (left). A wider angle is usually formed from the second bud if the shoot from the first bud is removed (right side). Modesto ash is an example.

Conifers do not need to be pruned as much as broadleaved trees. They are pruned primarily to remove dead wood, to control size and shape (see illustration), or to reduce wind resistance. Most conifers do not have latent buds on wood without foliage; if cut back to a stub, no new growth follows. Exceptions are yew, arborvitae, hemlock, sequoia, some junipers, and some pines.

Conifers typically have a central leader with branches radiating either at random or in vertical whorls around the trunk. Random-branching conifers — arborvitae, sequoia, and yew, for example — can be sheared or tip-pinched to control size and shape. Whorl-branching species — fir, pine, and spruce, for example — will form closer whorls if new growth is headed back to a bud.

When conifers get within a foot of the size you want, cut the new growth back to one inch; the tree will hold to size, but become more dense.

Columnar conifers can be trained by cutting upright branches back to short, spreading laterals or, in larger specimens, heading widely spreading branches just inside the desired foliage line of the column.

See illustration to replace lost leaders on conifers.

The pruning process

Pruning shears are for cutting small limbs up to an inch or so in diameter. Shears come in a variety of sizes and styles, see pages 110, 111.

It's easier to make a close cut if the shears are placed so that the blade cuts upward. Cutting upward also reduces the danger of the bark tearing as the limb falls. Small limbs, including suckers and water sprouts, should be cut as closely as possible to the trunk or branch. This diminishes the chances of new ones sprouting from latent buds left at the base. (Suckers are vigorous sprouts that grow from below the graft union or the ground; watersprouts are similar, but arise higher on the trunk or in the tree.)

Large limbs must be cut with a saw. The best way is to make three cuts, as in the illustration (top left second row).

Protection

Research has found that painting pruning wounds is of doubtful value. Upon exposure to the sun, most protective coatings crack to form openings which can entrap moisture, thereby compounding the problem.

Structural strength

Certain branch characteristics contribute to the structural strength of the trunk and the major limbs (scaffolds). Branches attached at a wide angle to the tree (45 to 90 degrees) are stronger than those attached at narrower angles. A wide angle allows strong connective wood to form in the crotches, on the sides, and on the lower portion of the branch.

Some narrow-angle branches (less than 45 degrees) are stronger than others. This occurs when the wood of the trunk and the branch are joined in the crotch, creating a rough ridge of bark (see illustration). Branches so attached are stronger than those with attachments having narrow angles with the trunk and branch surfaces forming a sharp "V." In these the bark becomes imbedded and new wood on top or inside of the crotch is not strongly attached to the trunk. These latter branches may not be a problem until the tree is older, then the branches may break. Such losses not only deform the tree, but are dangerous. In training a young tree, do not select a narrow-angle branch to be a main scaffold branch.

In addition to angle of attachment, relative branch size is also important in the strength of branch attachments. Branches should be smaller than the trunk or branch they're growing on. Wherever two branches fork, the supporting branch should be larger than the other.

If the branch is too large in relation to the trunk, remove some of its leaves so it will grow more slowly. If the branch has laterals, thin them. If it has no laterals, head it back. Either of these methods will slow its growth until the supporting branch is larger.

Branches get stronger as they get older, if the original angle of growth is good. New shoots from older wood, whether off the trunk or another branch, are held only by a thin layer of new wood, and are susceptible to breaking easily. They need to develop slowly to reduce the likelihood of breakage.

Training a young tree

It's important to decide how you want a tree to function in the landscape before you prune. Are you framing an attractive view or screening out the supermarket? Do you want low branches so children can climb the tree, or a high canopy to shade the house? Mature trees can be pruned to suit a particular landscape use, but it is preferable to start with a young

Branch strength

Laterals that grow from a branch or trunk for several years are deeply attached and strong (left). New shoots forced on older limbs are attached only by a thin layer of new wood (right) and can break off easily. These will become stronger as the tree grows.

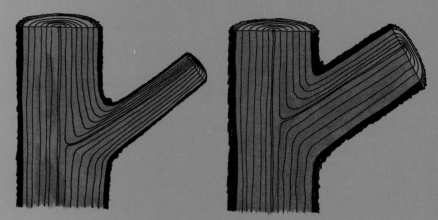

When a lateral is smaller than the branch or trunk from which it grows (left) it is relatively stronger than one that is the same size or larger (right).

Branch position

Branches retain their position on the trunk as the tree grows, but as they get larger they get a little closer to the ground.

The height of the lower branches should depend on the use of the ground area beneath the tree.

A tree with evenly spaced, well-developed laterals needs little or no pruning unless some limbs are too low.

Well-spaced branches (left) are less likely to split out than those close together.

When one limb is directly over another, each interferes with the proper development of the other. Remove one of them.

Good radial and vertical spacing of branches.

When thinning a young tree, leave more scaffolds than eventually will be needed. As the tree grows you can select those that will be the most desirable permanent branches.

A nonbranching leader can be pinched during the growing season to induce the development of laterals. 2 pinches, as shown, can produce branches at the height desired. Leaves have been left off the drawing for clarity.

tree. Two things determine how a tree should be pruned to the shape you want — the landscape use, and the growth habit of the tree. Weak branch attachments may need correcting, and the natural tree form may be accentuated into a living sculpture.

Trees should be pruned only enough to direct their growth effectively and to correct any structural weaknesses. Branches selected for permanent scaffolds (the large branches that give the tree its shape) should have wide angles of attachment.

The height of the first permanent branch will depend on the function of the tree in the landscape. The position of a branch on the trunk remains the same throughout the life of the tree. But as a branch increases in diameter, the distance to the ground actually becomes less.

Vertical branch spacing is important

The spacing of vertical branches can determine both structural strength and the shape of the tree. Unpruned trees of many species often have the more vigorous branches naturally well spaced; little or no pruning is needed. The distance between branches should be greater on a tree that will mature into a large specimen. Major scaffold branches should be spaced at least eight inches apart and preferably 18 to 24 inches. Scaffolds too close together will have fewer laterals, resulting in long thin branches with little structural strength.

Radial branch distribution should have five to seven scaffolds along the trunk. This can be accomplished in one or two rotations around the trunk, like an ascending spiral. A perfect spiral is not necessary for the tree to be well shaped, and the branches healthy and strong. The purpose is to prevent one branch from growing directly over another to the detriment of both — the upper one suffers from the extra competition for water and nutrients, and the lower one gets shaded out. Remove the less desirable branch of the two.

Direct growth during the growing season

Pruning during the growing season can often be done with just a little judicious pinching. Pinch the leader to force more laterals, or pinch back laterals that threaten to dominate the leader. Pinch back, or off, shoots that are too low, too close together, or in competition with branches you want to encourage. Pinching as little as one or two inches is effective in checking growth so that selected limbs will develop properly. There will be little or no setback to the tree if this pinching is done before the shoots are five inches long. It also reduces the necessity of removing large branches later. Growth will be channeled where you want it.

On a young tree, more shoots should be left than will ultimately be selected as permanent branches. After the second growing season, you will have a better selection from more developed branches.

If your tree is a species that doesn't branch on current growth, you can induce branching by pinching the leader at the height at which you want the first branch. On a vigorous tree, by pinching the new shoots, you can obtain as many as three well-spaced branches in one season, instead of ending up with a tall, unbranched whip.

Small, temporary branches along the trunk help strengthen and protect it. Odd as it may seem, trees can get sunburned. To avoid this, keep some temporary branches along the trunk, particularly on the south side, to shade it. More importantly, shoots along the trunk will increase the diameter and taper for increased strength and flexibility. Temporary branches should be about four to twelve inches apart, and should be kept short by pinching. This is one place where you want weak growth. Choose the less vigorous shoots along the trunk for temporary branches.

As the young tree develops a sturdy trunk and permanent branches that shade the trunk, the temporary branches can be reduced and eventually eliminated. You can begin reducing their number after two or three years when the trunk is two to three inches in diameter for small trees, or five to six inches for trees that will get larger. Remove them over a period of two to three years, each time pruning out the largest ones.

Sometimes the tree you buy will have been headed at the nursery. Such trees will have several branches close together coming from below the cut. For many landscape uses, these branches will be too low. Try to find a tree with well-spaced branches. Otherwise, when you plant the tree, prune it as shown in the illustration.

Upright branches are usually more vigorous than horizontal branches.

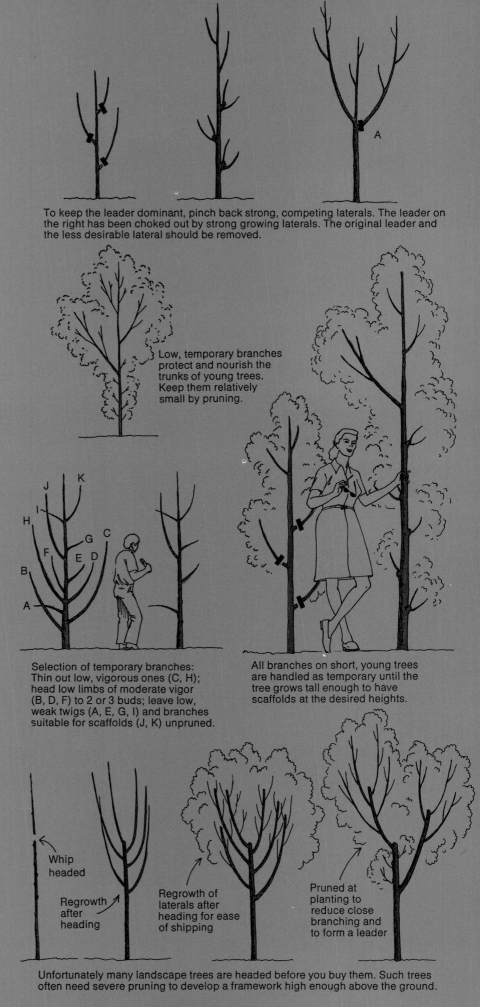

To keep the leader dominant, pinch back strong, competing laterals. The leader on the right has been choked out by strong growing laterals. The original leader and the less desirable lateral should be removed.

Low, temporary branches protect and nourish the trunks of young trees. Keep them relatively small by pruning.

Selection of temporary branches: Thin out low, vigorous ones (C, H); head low limbs of moderate vigor (B, D, F) to 2 or 3 buds; leave low, weak twigs (A, E, G, I) and branches suitable for scaffolds (J, K) unpruned.

All branches on short, young trees are handled as temporary until the tree grows tall enough to have scaffolds at the desired heights.

Whip headed

Regrowth after heading

Regrowth of laterals after heading for ease of shipping

Pruned at planting to reduce close branching and to form a leader

Unfortunately many landscape trees are headed before you buy them. Such trees often need severe pruning to develop a framework high enough above the ground.

A vigorous upright branch may compete with the leader and deform the tree. Remove it.

To encourage a limb to grow more upright, prune it back to a more upright branch, to an upward-growing bud, or at the top of a bend.

To help a tree deformed by wind to be more symmetrical, head wind-curved branch (A) to a windward bud; cut leader back to an uprifght lateral (B); and thin or head downwind branches (C, D).

When a leader has lost its dominance, prune it back to a newly selected leader.

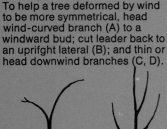

A weak young tree may be revitalized by heading the trunk close to the ground (about 6″) or the graft union. Select a new leader from the strongest of the new shoots.

Thin a tuft of short laterals near the terminal to encourage the remaining shoots.

Pruning shrubs into trees

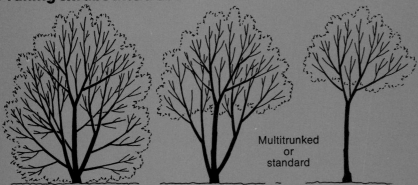

Multitrunked or standard

Many shrubs can be pruned into small trees to show off structure, open them for vistas to let the garden show through, or allow for an underplanting. This is the way to make a large shrub into a tree — to develop a young shrub into a tree follow the pruning directions for a tree.

If an upright branch is in a good position for a permanent branch, it will grow well and hold its own in competition with other branches. If the upright branch threatens the leader, select a more horizontal branch or reduce the size of the upright one. This is mainly a concern with a young tree — as a tree matures, the leader often loses control and the tree becomes more spreading.

Prevailing winds can deform trees. Most of the growth may be on the downwind side. Depending on wind conditions and the kind of tree, the main leader may or may not be bent. Many trees can stand upright under strong prevailing winds while others are easily modified by wind.

In certain situations, you may like the picturesque form sculptured by the wind. If not, thin out the top of the tree by removing moderate-sized, branches. The tree will offer less wind resistance. (See illustration.)

Sometimes a leader loses its control and is overtaken by one or more upright laterals. If the leader cannot be saved without severe pruning, choose the lateral in the best position and thin the leader back to it. Other laterals may need to be pruned to be sure the new leader will dominate.

Because pruning forces new growth, it is sometimes used as a "last ditch" effort to revitalize a weak-growing, stagnated tree. Before deciding on this method, make sure there's no other problem that needs correction — poorly drained soil, insect infestation, disease, girdled roots. All of these conditions weaken a tree and will not be improved by pruning. If nothing else seems to be wrong, take a deep breath and cut the tree to within six to twelve inches of the ground (or graft union). When new growth breaks from latent buds, choose the strongest upright shoot to be the new leader and cut back the other shoots.

Knowledge of plant responses to pruning can be used to accentuate the natural form of trees or even to modify them into almost any form desired. Guying, staking, tying, and twisting can be employed along with pruning to direct tree growth where you want. Trees can be thinned to better display interesting bark patterns and picturesque branching, as well as to let sunlight dapple the interior of the trees and the landscape below.

A number of pruning specialties are illustrated on page 109. Some are quite useful. The protection of borderline trees or fruit trees against warm walls is well known to gardeners who are weather-wise. See chapter on climates.

Pruning mature trees

The scaffold limbs and the main structure of a tree have usually been selected by the third or fourth year depending on the kind of tree and its growing conditions. If the scaffolds are well placed, the tree may need little or no pruning for several years.

Mature trees may need to be pruned for several reasons.

Tree health and appearance can be improved by removing limbs that are dead, weak, diseased, or insect-infested. Remove broken, low, and crossing limbs for appearance and safety.

The structural features of a tree may be emphasized by moderate thinning to open the tree to view. What had been just another tree is transformed into a picturesque feature.

To open up a medium-to-large-sized tree (40-60 feet), moderate-sized (1-2 inches in diameter) thinning cuts of limbs are effective. Somewhat smaller cuts for smaller trees are appropriate. These should be made around the tops and sides of the tree. Remove branches that are close to others. In some larger trees, cuts may remove limbs up to six inches in diameter. However, such larger cuts indicate the tree has not been properly pruned in the past or that its use in the landscape has changed.

Pruning large trees in the home landscape is put off as long as possible because the need is not easily recognized; you are not sure who should do the job, nor of the cost to have it done. Even if you know what to do, the trees are usually so large that you have neither the equipment nor the experience to prune safely.

You need to use care in selecting an arborist to prune your trees. Work of skilled arborists is not easily recognized by most people unless they see the pruning being done. It is mainly the severe stubbing that is seen and believed to be "the way to prune." In some cases, such heavy heading may be the only alternative, but, as shown in the illustrations, trees can be reduced in size and poor structure improved by proper thinning, including drop crotching. Be sure you know what the arborist is going to do before you let him go ahead. Your local nursery or garden center may be able to recommend a responsible arborist.

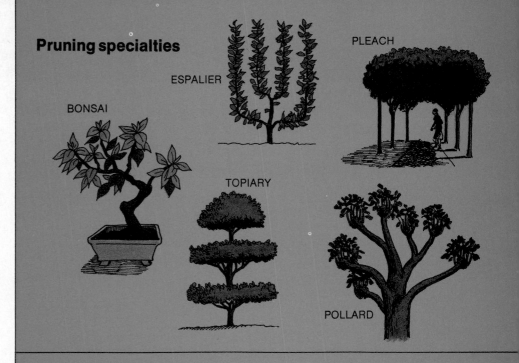

Pruning specialties

BONSAI

ESPALIER

PLEACH

TOPIARY

POLLARD

Pruning mature trees

Thinning opens up a mature tree while retaining its natural form and appearance (center). You can hold or reduce the height as desired. A headed tree (right) will force many weakly attached, vigorous upright shoots, destroying the tree's natural form.

When you wish to remove one (or more) of a group of trees which has become crowded, prune the expendable tree back more severely each year for several years until ready to remove. This will allow proper development of the remaining trees while retaining the value of the temporary tree.

Last Words

A book on trees is never complete. We devote these last two pages to some afterthoughts.

Winter chilling — rest

Although all trees will die if it gets cold enough, many trees native to temperate regions require a certain amount of winter cold in order to start growth satisfactorily in the spring. This is particularly true of fruit trees for successful flowering and fruiting. A number of fruit-growing areas experience winters that are not cold enough for profitable production of some kinds of fruit.

As the days of summer begin to shorten, the buds of many temperate-zone trees and shrubs begin to enter a condition called "rest" and will not grow even though conditions are favorable. This is an excellent device that keeps a tree from beginning to grow during warm spells in winter, only to be damaged by fatally low temperatures that may follow.

However, rest can be a problem if trees are grown in areas where the winters are not cold enough for the rest to be overcome or satisfied. When this happens, trees are slow to leaf out and bloom is delayed. Leaf buds are more seriously affected than flower buds. (This gave rise to the name "delayed foliation" for the problem before the cause was known.) In extreme cases, so few buds grow that branches are sunburned and the tree is weakened because of lack of carbohydrates. Since flower buds are less affected, a tree may bloom and set fruit and this further weakens the tree.

To rest, buds must be exposed to low temperatures, usually below 45° F. for 4 to 8 weeks. As might be expected, different species and different varieties or selections within a species differ as to temperature effective in overcoming rest, as well as in the length of cold they need.

Roots of some woody plants do have a period of rest that is dependent on the tops. However, roots of most species seem to grow whenever food reserves and soil conditions are favorable. Roots of most trees will grow at temperatures lower than will the shoots. For example, roots of silver maple will start growth at 40° F. but leaf buds do not expand until the temperature is at least 50° F. for 20 days. This is an important reason for fall planting in areas where the ground does not freeze. Roots can grow in soil that remains warm while the air begins to cool.

Be your own Johnny Appleseed

Planting seeds to get the trees you want may be the easiest and cheapest way if you have a large bare area to plant and are in no rush for quick effect. Even in areas with only ten inches of annual rainfall and a long rainless growing season, trees and shrubs will become established with little additional care. However, trees grow faster when there's more rain and weeds are not a problem.

If you want to give seeds a try, keep these things in mind. Select *species* you know will do well in your area. Check with your local nurseryman or horticulturist to find out if any special treatment is needed to overcome possible seed dormancy. If your soil does not freeze during winter, plant in fall when rains have wet the soil, otherwise wait until the soil thaws in the spring. Dig a small hole about four inches deep, put in about a quarter teaspoon of a nitrogen fertilizer, cover it with three inches of soil, place the seeds, and cover them with fine soil about three times their diameter. Three large seeds are

Tree pruning tools

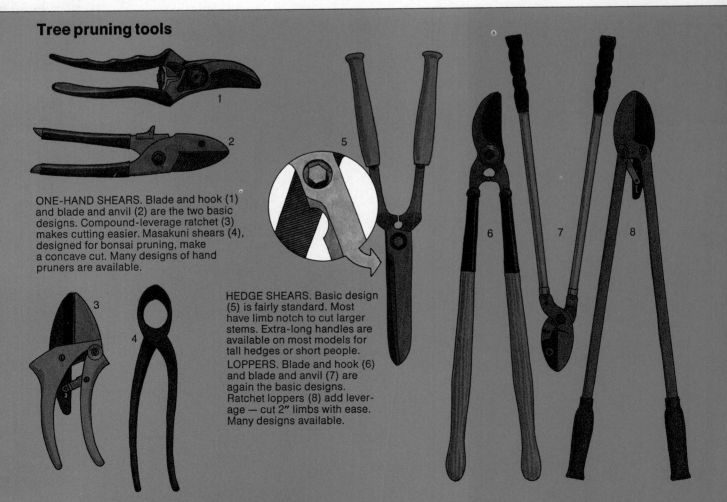

ONE-HAND SHEARS. Blade and hook (1) and blade and anvil (2) are the two basic designs. Compound-leverage ratchet (3) makes cutting easier. Masakuni shears (4), designed for bonsai pruning, make a concave cut. Many designs of hand pruners are available.

HEDGE SHEARS. Basic design (5) is fairly standard. Most have limb notch to cut larger stems. Extra-long handles are available on most models for tall hedges or short people.
LOPPERS. Blade and hook (6) and blade and anvil (7) are again the basic designs. Ratchet loppers (8) add leverage — cut 2" limbs with ease. Many designs available.

usually enough, but increase the number if seeds are fine.

If more than one plant grows in a hole, pinch back all but the most vigorous one to give it the best chance to grow well. Leave others until you are sure the selected one is established. If deer or rabbits are a problem, surround each seedling hole with a one-foot diameter, three-foot-high cylinder of woven wire fencing held in place with two stakes.

Given good soil, 15 inches of winter rain and no summer irrigation, several species in central California grew more than six feet in two growing seasons.

Help

For answers to general or specific questions, your County University Extension Agent or local nurseryman is the best bet. Here we list some other valuable sources.

If you are interested in trees, the planting of trees, and the care of trees, join the International Society of Arboriculture.

International Society of
Arboriculture
P.O. Box 71
5 Lincoln Square
Urbana, IL 61861

Tree roots in sewers are a perennial problem throughout the United States. Roots are unable to enter intact sewer lines, but as they increase in diameter they can break sewer lines and then enter. Once a root enters a sewer, it finds favorable conditions of aeration, moisture, and nutrients. What follows? Quick clogging of the sewer. If this is your problem, write to this address for their booklet:

Airrigation Engineering
Company, Inc.
P.O. Box H
Carmel Valley, California 93924.

To learn all about growing trees from seed, use the excellent *Seeds of Woody Plants in the United States.* It's the standard reference book on the subject and available from:

Superintendent of Documents,
U.S. Government Printing Office
Washington, D.C. 20402

It's price is $13.60.

Importance of seed source location

Seedling trees may vary greatly in certain characteristics particularly if the seeds are from different climatic areas. In fact, seed source may be the main reason for the common observation that some plants grow

poorly when propagated and raised in a climate different from the one in which they are to be planted.

An example: The natural range of the flowering dogwood *(Cornus florida)* extends from the northern parts of the United States to Central America. Trees grown from seeds from the southern range will not be as hardy as trees from the northern range.

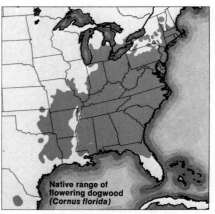

Native range of flowering dogwood *(Cornus florida)*

Here are two tree seed sources:
Carter's Seeds
P.O. Box 4006
Sylmar, CA 91342
Clyde Robin Seed Co., Inc.
P.O. Box 2855
Castro Valley, CA 94546

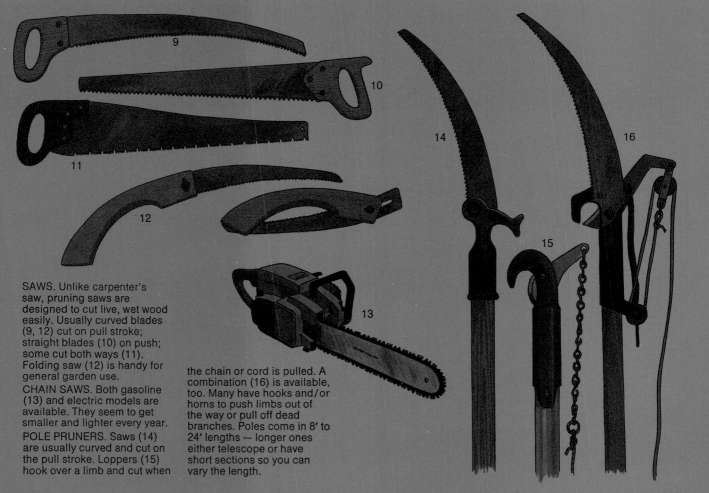

SAWS. Unlike carpenter's saw, pruning saws are designed to cut live, wet wood easily. Usually curved blades (9, 12) cut on pull stroke; straight blades (10) on push; some cut both ways (11). Folding saw (12) is handy for general garden use.
CHAIN SAWS. Both gasoline (13) and electric models are available. They seem to get smaller and lighter every year.
POLE PRUNERS. Saws (14) are usually curved and cut on the pull stroke. Loppers (15) hook over a limb and cut when the chain or cord is pulled. A combination (16) is available, too. Many have hooks and/or horns to push limbs out of the way or pull off dead branches. Poles come in 8′ to 24′ lengths — longer ones either telescope or have short sections so you can vary the length.

Index